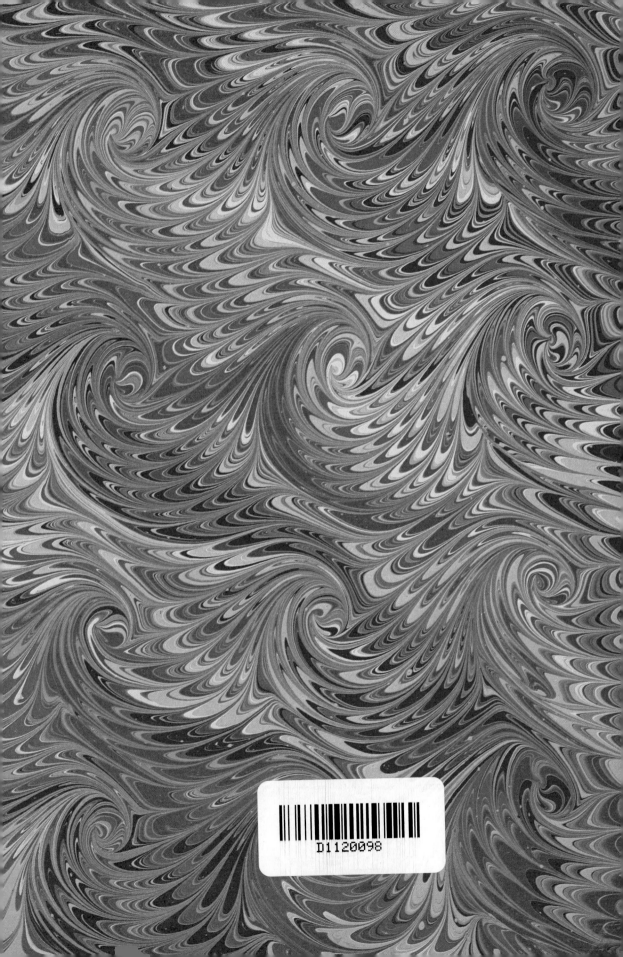

D1120098

THE MIDDLE AGES

the
MIDDLE AGES

NATIONAL GEOGRAPHIC SOCIETY

A VOLUME IN THE STORY OF MAN LIBRARY
PREPARED BY
NATIONAL GEOGRAPHIC BOOK SERVICE

PUBLISHED BY THE NATIONAL GEOGRAPHIC SOCIETY
MELVIN M. PAYNE, CHAIRMAN OF THE BOARD
ROBERT E. DOYLE, PRESIDENT
MELVILLE BELL GROSVENOR, *Editor-in-Chief*
GILBERT M. GROSVENOR, *Editor*

Foreword by
MELVILLE BELL GROSVENOR
Editor-in-Chief of the National Geographic Society

Editorial consultant
KENNETH M. SETTON
*Professor of History, The Institute for Advanced Study,
Princeton; former Henry Charles Lea Professor
and Director of Libraries, University of Pennsylvania;
author of* Christian Attitude Towards the Emperor in
the Fourth Century, Catalan Domination of Athens,
1311-1388; Europe and the Levant in the Middle
Ages and the Renaissance, Athens in the Middle Ages,
Los Catalanes en Grecia, The Papacy and the Levant,
1204-1571; *editor-in-chief of* A History of the Crusades

Special Essays by Dr. Setton and

T. S. R. BOASE
*Former President of Magdalen College, Oxford;
author of* Castles and Churches of the Crusading
Kingdom, St. Francis of Assisi; *editor of*
The Oxford History of English Art

URBAN T. HOLMES
*Former Professor of Romance Languages, University of
North Carolina; author of* Daily Living in the
Twelfth Century, A History of the French Language;
editor of Critical Bibliography of French
Literature (Medieval Period)

*Chartres Cathedral, enduring symbol of medieval faith,
bathes in the glow of a French sunset; Jonathan S. Blair
Overleaf: A gay court celebrates the first of May
below Riom's towers in the Auvergne; 15th-century miniature
from the* Très Riches Heures du Duc de Berry,
*Musée Condé, Chantilly; Giraudon
Page 1: Jewels adorn 1,000-year-old crown of the Holy
Roman Emperor; Kunsthistorisches Museum, Vienna.*

PAUL MURRAY KENDALL

Former Professor of English, Ohio University; author of
Louis XI, Richard the Third, The Yorkist Age,
Warwick the Kingmaker, The Art of Biography

NORMAN P. ZACOUR

Professor of History, University of Toronto;
author of An Introduction to Medieval Institutions,
Talleyrand: the Cardinal of Périgord, 1301-1364;
Petrarch's Book Without a Name

Chapters by

MICHAEL KUH, EDWARDS PARK; *and*
TOM ALLEN, HOWARD LA FAY, *and* FRANC SHOR
of the National Geographic staff

Photographs by

JAMES P. BLAIR, BRUCE DALE,
WALTER MEAYERS EDWARDS, GEORGE F. MOBLEY,
ALBERT MOLDVAY *of the National*
Geographic staff; JONATHAN S. BLAIR,
MICHAEL KUH, TED SPIEGEL, *and others*

Paintings by

ANDRE DURENCEAU, BIRNEY LETTICK,
TOM LOVELL, ROBERT W. NICHOLSON,
and others

427 Illustrations,
401 in full color, 11 maps

This book was prepared
under the guidance of
MELVILLE BELL GROSVENOR
and FRANC SHOR
by the following staff:

MERLE SEVERY
Editor

SEYMOUR L. FISHBEIN
Associate Editor

JOHN J. PUTMAN
Project Editor

CHARLES O. HYMAN
Art Director

ANNE DIRKES KOBOR
Illustrations Editor

THOMAS B. ALLEN,
ROSS BENNETT,
EDWARDS PARK,
DAVID F. ROBINSON
Editor-Writers

WERNER L. WEBER
Production Manager

WILLIAM W. SMITH
Engraving and Printing

ELIZABETH L. DONLEY,
JACQUELINE GESCHICKTER, *Editorial Research*
MARIANNE HURLBURT, *Picture Research*
EDWARD MARTIN WILSON, *Design*
WILHELM R. SAAKE, *Production*
CAROL M. McNAMARA,
BARBARA G. STEWART,
ALVIN L. TICE, *Assistants*
ANDREW POGGENPOHL, *Art*
JOHN D. GARST,
BOBBY G. CROCKETT, *Maps*
WERNER JANNEY, *Style*
DOROTHY M. CORSON,
ANNE K. McCAIN, *Index*
W. E. ROSCHER,
JACQUES OSTIER, *European Representatives*

FOREWORD

GREAT CURVES of the Seine beckoned me on through the hedgerowed fields of Normandy, veiled with apple blossoms, towered with stone churches, pastured with sturdy cows and powerful Percheron horses. The soft fragrance of May greeted me as I drove inland from the French coast on my quest for the springtime of our civilization.

Then suddenly, as I rounded a bend near Les Andelys, I spied Château Gaillard, grim walls rising atop sheer rock where the river narrowed. Richard the Lionheart's castle! It was a wonder in its day. It still is.

Street names in the village—Rue Richard Coeur-de-Lion and Rue Philippe Auguste—evoked challenges hurled by those royal rivals:

"If its walls were made of solid iron," sneered France's King Philip, *"yet would I take them."*

"By the throat of God!" roared England's King Richard. *"If its walls were made of butter, yet would I hold them."*

I climbed those very ramparts, stood where Richard had stood, and recalled his feats of arms in France and against the chivalrous Saladin in Palestine. In my youth my pulse had quickened to the tales of heroes like Robin Hood, Ivanhoe, Roland, the knights of King Arthur's Round Table, Richard the Lionheart, Joan of Arc— a lass in knight's armor. The very names ring with chivalry.

I recalled them all when I began to plan a book on the Age of Chivalry with Merle Severy and his brilliant Book Service team. Here was our opportunity to bring to life a resplendent pageant of adventure and romance, valiant knights and fair ladies, tourneys, codes of chivalry, heroic quests undertaken for sacred vows.

"Chivalry?" said Mr. Severy. "Basically it has to do with the horse. Oats as well as oaths."

I blinked. Then—of course! "Chivalry" comes from *chevalerie,* which derives from *cheval,* French for horse.

"The knight performed his great deeds on horseback. Without his horse he was lost. Remember Richard III's cry in Shakespeare: 'My kingdom for a horse!'"

"Those Percherons you saw were no accident," Mr. Severy continued. "Europe's scrawny horses had to be bred up to size and strength to carry all that armor, which got heavier after the crossbow was introduced.

"But without stirrups, a knight would topple at the first heavy blow. Stirrups didn't come in from the East until the eighth century. Before that, you clung on as best you could. The shock attack of medieval knights was a military revolution. The stirrup welded horse, armored rider, and lance into a weapon of great impact."

"So...no stirrups, no knight," I mused. "But a war horse and armor must have cost a pretty penny."

"Right. Worth about 20 oxen—the plow teams of ten or more peasant families. Add to that the cost of a remount and equipping a squire and you have a small fortune. This meant the heavy-armed cavalryman, the knight, was an aristocrat."

Herald on horseback proclaims a medieval joust in the Tuscan city of Arezzo; Jonathan S. Blair

A vision from the Age of Chivalry, San Marino raises its battlements over Italy's Adriatic coastland. Crossbowmen's bolts

"So you have to develop a feudal system to support such knights," I offered. "A lord grants lands to retainers in return for military service. Knight and manor go together. Thus we should explore the organization of the manor—"

"And the concept of fealty from Germanic tribes—" "And Christianity, which gave knightly ideals." Ideas flowed fast now as voice after voice chimed in.

The Crusades! We'd follow Crusaders' footsteps to the Holy Land, and pilgrims to shrines such as Santiago de Compostela in Spain. We'd show the vigor of Islam and Moslem gifts to Europe: arts and sciences, scholarship as well as spices.

"And Arabian steeds," Mr. Severy suggested.

We'd show how the resurgence of trade sparked the growth of towns, the rise of guilds, banking, the jury system, the parleying that led to parliaments, and the learning that gave us the universities of Bologna, Paris, Oxford, Heidelberg. We'd see Hanseatic merchants building empires of trade from London to Lübeck to Novgorod. At canal-laced Bruges we'd witness pageantry and tournaments.

Such jousts served to channel warlike passions into courtly display. Linked with them was the chivalric ideal of romantic love. This put woman on a pedestal, where she was worshiped from afar by knights who broke lances in her honor. As armor grew heavier the knight's role as warrior grew lighter. The noble

8

caused plates to replace mail, thus creating the knight in shining armor. James P. Blair, National Geographic photographer

gendarme (man-at-arms) had scorned as infants the peasants who fought on foot. When this infantry came of age and could hole his breastplate with a musket ball, the knight paraded his gleaming armor more for prestige than protection, and reserved most of his gallantry for the court. Our chevalier had become a courtier, sometimes cavalier in his treatment of lesser mortals, but ever chivalrous and courteous to the damsels he courted. . . .

We called on Dr. Kenneth M. Setton of The Institute for Advanced Study at Princeton to head a distinguished panel of authors. They and our photographers and editors traveled the length and breadth of the medieval world. At long last the labors of creating *The Age of Chivalry* were over. We paused to leaf through the final proofs, feeling the glow that comes from achieving what we had envisioned. We examined the 16-page foldout—the complete Bayeux Tapestry, with William the Conqueror's mounts splashing ashore, his knights riding to victory over the dismounted Saxons at Hastings on a day in 1066 that history can never forget.

I asked Mr. Severy why he was grinning.

"As you see," he replied, "basically it all has to do with the horse."

The horse—and heroes, and handsome ladies, and more than ten hundred years of thrilling history.

Melville Bell Grosvenor

CONTENTS

FOREWORD 7

DAWN OF THE MIDDLE AGES 13

THE WORLD OF CHARLEMAGNE 43
In the Wake of the Vikings 66

TRACING WILLIAM THE CONQUEROR 92
Epic Tale in Tapestry 101

THE WORLD OF BERNARD OF CLAIRVAUX 131
The Call of the Cloister 141
Building the Great Cathedrals 158
Pilgrimage to Compostela 172

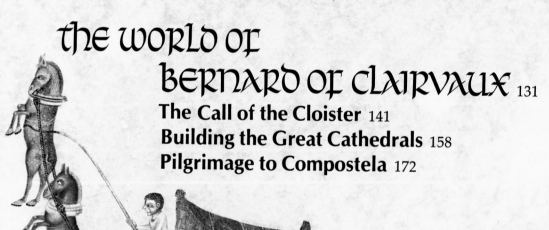

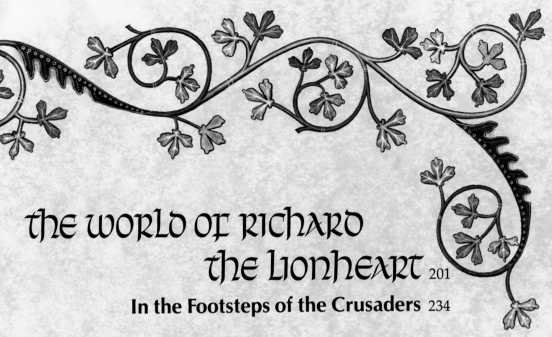

THE WORLD OF RICHARD THE LIONHEART 201

In the Footsteps of the Crusaders 234

QUESTING LIFE OF THE SCHOLAR 272

Voices from the Middle Ages 285

THE WORLD OF JACQUES COEUR 299

Miracle of St. Joan 320

Golden Realm of Merchant Princes 330

INDEX 370   **SPECIAL FEATURES:** Life on the manor 52   Rule of St. Benedict 138
Arms and armor 212   Legend of King Arthur 230   Surgeons, humors, and panaceas 292
Advent of the clock 314   Time chart 372   Medieval games 374
Acknowledgments and reference guide 377

MAPS: Barbarian invasions 18   Charlemagne's empire 45   Viking voyages 76   Norman Conquest 99
William the Conqueror's castles 127   Pilgrim paths to Compostela 174   The Lionheart's world 208
Crusader routes 238   Mediterranean commerce 300   Mission of St. Joan 324   Hansa trade arteries 336

Below: To the rhythm of the seasons, peasants reap and cart wheat and bend their backs to the ox-drawn plow.
Illuminations from the 14th-century Luttrell Psalter in the British Museum, London

By Kenneth M. Setton

ÐAWN OF THE MIÐÐLE AGES

NE NOVEMBER DAY in the year of grace 324, a majestic figure, spear in hand, paced a hillside above the Bosporus, marking the bounds of a new city. Behind him receded the sparse buildings of the ancient Greek city of Byzantium. His retinue watched nervously. Would he never come to a halt? Finally an attendant went up to him and asked:

"How far will you go, Sire?"

"Until He who leads me stops."

Thus tradition records the divine guidance given Constantine the Great when he founded Constantinople, eastern capital of the Roman Empire. Unlike Rome, where paganism still ran strong, the new capital immediately embraced Christianity. Only a dozen years before, Constantine had legalized the religion, ending nearly three centuries of intermittent persecution. Symbol of the dawning Christian age, his "New Rome" became one of history's most fabled cities.

Few travelers to Constantinople fail to fall under its sway. I shall always remember a beautiful afternoon in May when I stood on a height west of the city and looked down upon the gently winding Golden Horn—like the corridor of history itself as it made its leisurely way into the Bosporus. Centuries passed in a glorious panorama before my eyes.

For years I had lectured on Byzantine history, often speaking glibly of this crossroads where three continents met in the historic swirl from which so much of medieval civilization emerged. Maybe

Colossal Constantine, first Christian emperor, gazes into eternity from
Rome's Palazzo dei Conservatori; Merle Severy, National Geographic staff

13

Constantine *had* received divine guidance, I now thought as my eyes sought the outlines of the imperial city that had bridged those centuries—the fourth to the fifteenth—we call the Middle Ages, the link between antiquity and the beginning of our modern age.

Memory, performing its aesthetic function, cleared away the dark alleys and melon-strewn streets I had traversed that morning. Before my eyes rose the golden Byzantium that had awed pilgrims and Crusaders, who "never thought that there could be in all the world so rich a city: they marked the high walls and strong towers . . . the rich palaces and mighty churches . . . the height and length of that city which above all others was supreme."

I thought of the even more distant past, when Constantine's city, founded in the richer and more populous East, represented the future, while Rome and the West gradually sank under pressures from barbarians without and from political, social, and economic decay within. The Western

FOUNDING A NEW ROME,
Constantine sets the empire's center where Europe and Asia meet. Here the Bosporus links the Black and Mediterranean seas. Rome ceased to be the pivot 38 years earlier, when Diocletian made Nicomedia in Asia Minor his capital in the East, Milan in the West.

Destined to stand 1,100 years— bulwark of Christendom against onslaughts from the East, a center of commerce, classical learning, and Christianity—Constantinople will be a beacon shining through Europe's darkest hours.

Breached by the Turks in 1453, the city's walls (right) attest the grandeur of its Byzantine Empire. The name enshrines Byzantium, ancient Greek colony on the site.

scenes seem darkling in contrast to the gold-and-azure brilliance of Byzantium and the surging vigor of Islam. But these transitional centuries bore seeds of the glory, splendor, and achievements of the Age of Chivalry to come.

LATE ROMAN SOCIETY, the prelude to the Middle Ages, was compounded of immense wealth and degrading poverty, asceticism and debauchery, gross ignorance in high places and a nostalgic love of antiquarian culture.

The Roman noble still rode in a great carriage or ornate litter attended by a horde of hangers-on, and gave elaborate banquets. We find him reading Terence or Menander, overseeing his vineyards and olive groves, watching a mosaic floor being laid or a fresco painted. Excluded from a military career by the suspicious imperial government, a member of the senatorial class took more pride in the ceremonial offices of consul and praetor than in the responsible posts of provincial prefect or governor.

The city populace still thrived on free "bread and circuses," drank and brawled in taverns, roared at lascivious pantomimes, and lived from one chariot race to the next. Salvian, a fifth-century priest of Marseilles, tells us that "the Roman world was laughing when it died."

It had been dying for a long time.

In the maelstrom of the third century, when one military commander after another overthrew the government and was murdered in turn, debasement of the coinage encouraged a staggering inflation and reversion to a "natural

economy." More often than not the government collected the land tax in foodstuffs, materials, and services, and paid its soldiers and civil servants in kind.

In the fourth century Diocletian and Constantine reformed the coinage, but in an attempt to stabilize society they resorted to an overly simple solution. They decreed that all workers be fixed in their jobs for life. Sons of bakers and teamsters had to become bakers and teamsters.

Municipal beauty and comfort succumbed to the hard requirements of defense. Walled against invaders, some towns would survive as centers of ecclesiastical and royal administration. Few remained economic centers. Trade tended to pass into the hands of Levantines, who could move into an area and out again without having to share its misfortunes.

The aristocrat, repelled by the crowding and stench of the shrunken walled town, retired to his country estate, where he raised what he needed. His isolation from the city foreshadowed the rural life of feudal society.

Small free farmers, ruined by debt, plague, brigandage, the usurpations of powerful neighbors and the government's exactions, placed themselves in the hands of larger landowners, who maintained private armies of toughs. Tenant farmers called *coloni* and slaves worked by the thousand on vast estates. Legally free, the coloni were bound to the estate, and their children after them. An edict of Constantine states that "tenant farmers who meditate flight are to be put in chains and reduced to . . . servitude."

On into the Middle Ages peasants would till the soil on manors without hope of surcease. Manorialism, despite its defects as an economic system, would feed Europe.

As peasants toiled, lords of the manor protected them. These landlords, subject to greater lords, became military "vassals of their lieges." We shall see this develop into feudalism. Whatever its deficiencies as a political system, feudalism would help supply such law and order as existed.

But in the Roman twilight there were fear and starvation. Emperor Valentinian III describes the winter of 450-51:

"The most terrible famine has raged through all Italy . . . men have been forced to sell their children to escape the danger of impending death. . . . For there is nothing to which despair of his own life does not drive a man. . . . His only concern is to live in any way he can. But I think that it

INTO THE GOLDEN HORN, *fished by an Istanbul fleet, flowed furs of Scythia; spices, silks, gems from the Indies; slaves, gold, incense from Africa; grain from Egypt; embroidery, glass, metalwork from the Levant's teeming cities. "The winds themselves conspired to bring merchandise to enrich her citizens," exulted a Constantinople courtier.*

JOAN RAHN

16

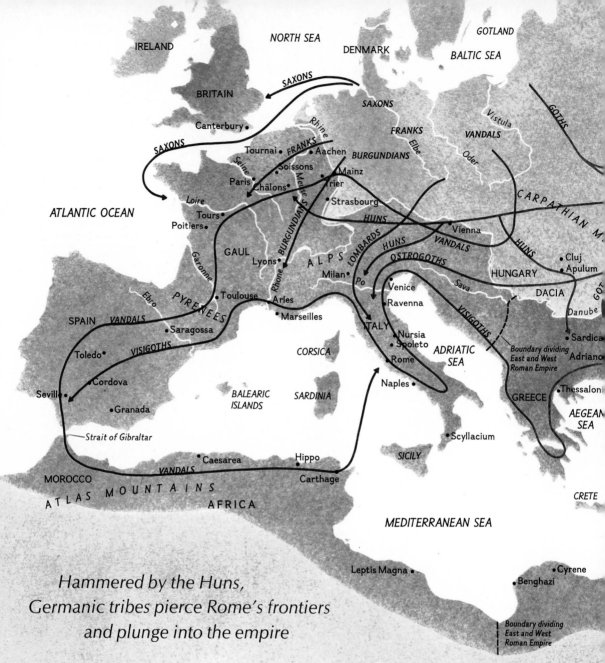

Hammered by the Huns,
Germanic tribes pierce Rome's frontiers
and plunge into the empire

is wrong that freedom should perish.... To whom is it not preferable to die a free man rather than to bear the yoke of slavery?"

But to the oppressed Roman provincial it mattered little who his master was.

WE ARE OFTEN told that the "fall of Rome" spelled the end of antiquity. But Rome did not fall; it declined gradually. For generations Germanic peoples had pressed on the northern frontiers. While Rome was strong, these barbarians were repelled. The Germanic invasions did not cause the decline of Rome. The invasions were successful because Roman power had already decayed.

From their original Baltic homeland the Germanic peoples began to move southeast toward the banks of the Vistula and the Carpathian Mountains near the end of the Bronze Age (500 B.C.). From Julius Caesar and from Tacitus (whose *Germania* dates from A.D. 98) we learn that the early Germans tilled the soil and

kept cattle, swine, horses, poultry, and bees. They populated their forests and groves with warrior gods such as Woden and Thunor (Thor), and lived under customary law which they regarded as sacred and eternal. Wives and children sometimes accompanied warriors to the battlefield to urge them on to great deeds.

An enterprising chieftain surrounded himself with tent "companions" (*comites*) who ate at his table, followed him into battle, and shared the plunder. For a member of such a following, or *comitatus*, to survive the chieftain in battle spelled lifelong disgrace. This relationship foreshadows the personal element in the fealty which later a vassal swore to his feudal lord.

Roman merchants who traded for furs, amber, and slaves in the northland may have stirred the Germans' thoughts of moving south. These peoples did not set out to destroy the empire; they wanted to share its riches.

By the mid-third century, Dacia (modern Rumania) stood like a no man's land between the Danube and the

LIKE A WEAKENING DAM, *Rome's once mighty legions on the Danube and Rhine strain to hold back Visigoths, Vandals, and other tribes fleeing before the nomadic Huns from Asia's steppes. Sons of Scandinavia, these Germanic tribes bred fierce warriors (above) to whom, wrote Tacitus, laziness was "acquiring by the sweat of your brow that which might be procured by the shedding of blood." Europe ran red as, in the fourth and early fifth centuries, the dam burst.*

ATTILA THE HUN, *encamped on a plain in Hungary, banquets in barbaric splendor. A Byzantine envoy whispers of the haughty overlord of Europe, who takes only meat and wine from austere woodenware of the steppes while retainers hoist silver service looted from Roman villas. The envoy's companion, white-maned Priscus, notes it all; later he will record this feast of 449. Similar ones welcomed emissaries from as far as Denmark and Persia.*

Attila's hand rests on his favorite son Ernas. Behind on a dais, a canopy shelters the royal bed. Priscus relates that two warriors came up to celebrate in song Attila's victories. Some "were pleased with the verses, others reminded of wars were excited in their souls, while yet others, whose bodies were feeble with age . . . shed tears."

From this stockaded village bowlegged bowmen, "glued to their horses," rode to conquest. Instead of flocks, Huns herded men, who slaved in the fields to feed their nomadic masters.

MOUNTED WARRIOR OF C. 700 FROM HORNHAUSEN, GERMANY; LANDESMUSEUM HALLE; FOTO MARBURG
OVERLEAF: PAINTING FOR NATIONAL GEOGRAPHIC BY BIRNEY LETTICK

19

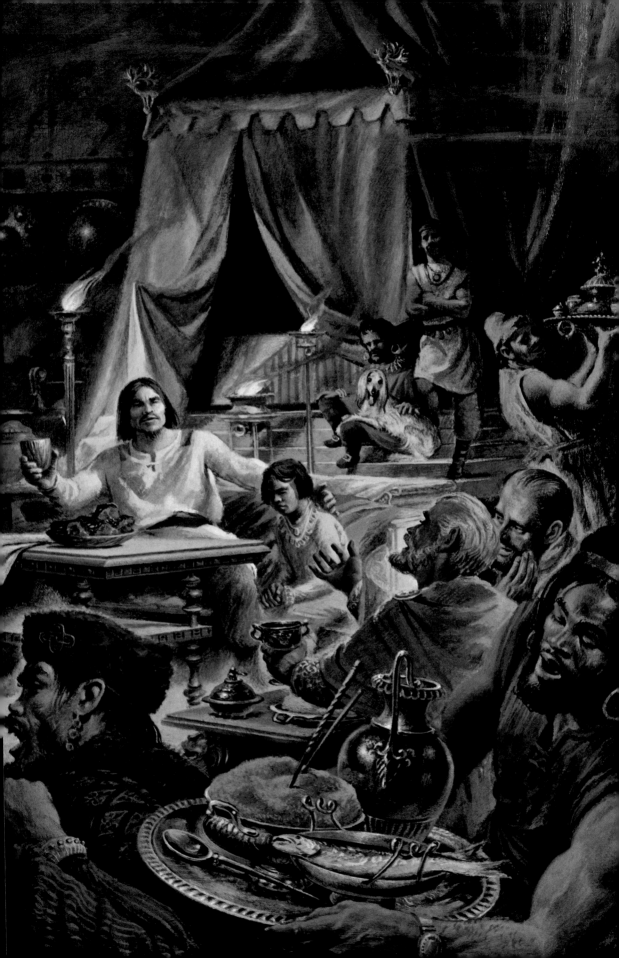

LIKE SHEEP *prodded by Rumanian shepherds (above), the Visigoths streamed south before that wolfish people of prey, the Huns. They crossed the Danube (right), mighty moat of empire, in 376. Emperor Valens gave permission to take up farmlands as* foederati, *confederates charged with keeping other tribes out. But exactions of officials drove them to revolt. At Adrianople in 378 they crushed a Roman army and slew Valens.*

Emperor Theodosius took them into his service. But a generation later, under Alaric, the Visigoths ravaged Greece, then turned west. Rome stripped the Rhine of troops to protect Italy. On the last day of 406, Vandals and other tribes driven westward by Huns, swarmed across the frozen river. The Rhine barrier ceased to exist and "Gaul smoked to heaven in one continuous pyre." The Franks extended their power in the north, the Burgundians in eastern Gaul.

22

ceaselessly probing Goths. To protect the province, Rome enlisted mercenaries from conquered tribes. "The introduction of barbarians into the Roman armies," wrote Edward Gibbon in his *Decline and Fall of the Roman Empire*, "became every day more universal, more necessary, and more fatal."

About the year 274 Emperor Aurelian pulled his legions back to the Danube, abandoning Dacia. A century later Asiatic nomads poured in from the steppes. Clad in skins, leggings, small round hats, and armed with short bows, they all but lived on their fleet, wiry horses. This hard-riding cavalry scattered the Goths like chaff and ranged from the Caspian almost to the Rhine, from the Alps to the Baltic.

They were Huns, a name that still conjures up images of savagery. "Truly the very faces of their infants have a gruesomeness all their own," we are told. The Huns had no written language and, said Romans, knew nothing of their past. But in the year 395 they made history by launching a two-pronged foray into the Eastern empire. One army galloped across the frozen Danube; the other stormed through Caucasus passes into Asia Minor. "They filled the whole earth with slaughter and panic," wrote St. Jerome. "By their speed they outstripped rumor, and they took pity neither upon religion nor rank nor age nor wailing childhood."

Melting back into the north before a hastily assembled imperial army, the Huns continued to raid the Roman frontiers and occasionally even served the emperors as mercenaries. Mostly they conquered other barbarian peoples.

Their short-lived empire reached its zenith under Attila, "the Scourge of God." In 443 he ravaged the Eastern empire and exacted an annual tribute of 2,100 pounds of gold. Four years later, greedy for more, Attila again invaded. "More than a hundred cities were captured," a witness tells us. "Constantinople almost came

into danger and most men fled from it. . . . The dead could not be numbered."
Next Attila turned west and slashed into Gaul. Checked near Châlons, he returned
the following year and devastated Italy as far as the Po. A threatening Roman
army, an outbreak of plague among the Hunnic horde, and the appeals of Pope
Leo I caused Attila to spare Rome and withdraw beyond the Alps. Soon after,
Attila added to his wives a bride named Ildico. On his wedding night he drank
heavily before retiring. When he did not appear the next morning, servants broke

SACK OF ROME, *city of Caesars inviolate for 800 years, shook the ancient world. Citizens cower amid monuments of bygone grandeur in the Forum as Alaric's Visigoths revel in three days of pillage in August 410. Flames spurt from the Tabularium, or Public Record Office, on Capitoline Hill. Temple of Jupiter Capitolinus (upper left) looks down on the Temple of Saturn and the Triumphal Arch of Tiberius with its bronze horses. Arch of Septimius Severus stands at right.*

Thrice the Visigoths invaded Italy. Stilicho, an able Roman general of Vandal blood, fended off the first two incursions. But he was executed by the distrustful Emperor Honorius, who holed up in his capital, Ravenna, and made no effort to forestall Alaric's capture of a Rome too weakened by famine to defend itself.

Rome recovered, but the West continued to sink. The Vandals, who had overrun Spain, carved out a North African kingdom, and closed the western Mediterranean with their sea raids, crossed over from Carthage. In 455 they seized Rome and pillaged it for two weeks. Memory of the wanton destruction lingers in our word "vandalism."

Power of the Western emperors had long since passed into the hands of their barbarian generals. In 476 one of these, Odoacer, dismissed the boy emperor Romulus Augustulus, who retired to a villa at Naples. The deposition of this last puppet emperor in Italy has been described as "the fall of Rome"—a "fall" unnoticed at the time. The Roman Empire would endure another thousand years in the Byzantine East.

PAINTING FOR NATIONAL GEOGRAPHIC BY ANDRE DURENCEAU

in. They found Ildico weeping beside his body. Attila's horsemen cut off their hair and slashed their faces with swords, thus mourning "the greatest of all warriors . . . with no feminine lamentations . . . but with the blood of men."

When the Huns first thundered out of Asia, they had pushed the East Goths, or Ostrogoths, toward the Dniester and the West Goths, or Visigoths, south of the Danube. In exchange for haven, the Visigoths served as Roman "confederates." When the Visigoths sacked Rome, a thrill of horror went through the civilized

CAESAR AND CHRIST *made Rome the Eternal City. As the bones of pagan temples bleached in the Forum amid rapine and ruin, the faith that lighted the catacombs (opposite) brought a new dawn.*

Christianity had spread swiftly from Palestine along roads and sea lanes of a mighty empire at peace. It sank roots in cities where New Testament Greek was widely spoken, but took longer to penetrate country districts (pagi) where dwelled pagans (pagani) or heathens (dwellers on the heath). By the third century Rome held 30,000 converts. They entombed their saints and martyrs in catacomb niches and serenely awaited resurrection.

world. For the first time in eight centuries an enemy force had entered the city, and the myth of power that had masked a long decline lay shattered. "The city that took the whole world is itself taken," mourned St. Jerome.

*I*N ROMAN NORTH AFRICA, St. Augustine, Bishop of Hippo, felt the shock of the news—then the sting of accusation. Pagans blamed Christianity for having caused Rome's ancient gods to withhold their protection. For 13 years he labored on his *City of God*, an answer that would stir men's minds through the centuries.

Rome was punished for her sins, concluded Augustine. Rather than put away their lascivious gods, men emulated them: "The fire of their base passions burned more fiercely in their hearts than the flames that devoured the city's roofs." Rather than mourn the loss of this earthly city, men should turn their eyes to the heavenly city, "glorious beyond compare.... There, victory is truth, dignity is holiness, peace is happiness, life is eternity."

Augustine, whose *Confessions* reveal how he himself had reveled in the fleshpots of Carthage and Rome while a student and teacher, had embraced with equal fervor the city of God following his conversion by St. Ambrose, Bishop of Milan. Returning to Africa, he founded a monastery, and left its seclusion reluctantly when called to become bishop of Hippo (today Annaba, Algeria). There he flung himself into the fight against heresy and continued his flood of writings until his death 34 years later as the Vandals pounded at the gates.

St. Augustine stands astride the ancient and medieval worlds. "I desire to know God and the soul. Nothing more? Nothing whatever," he wrote. Yet he dedicated to that quest a mind honed by the classics and inspired by Plato's thought. Christianity needed—and wanted—to learn from Athens as well as from Jerusalem.

In its coming struggles with the Holy Roman Empire, the Church would see itself as embodying Augustine's heavenly city, superior to the earthly city—thus the State should be subject to the Church. Philosophers, mystics, Protestant reformers—all would derive sustenance from his thought. But most important to

27

men of his day, who saw their world crumbling about them, he gave hope in the future. He helped usher in an age of faith that would see the sunlight stream through the rose windows of Chartres and Notre Dame. As Ambrose had said, "Amid the agitations of the world the church remains unmoved; the waves cannot shake her. While around her everything is in a horrible chaos, she offers to all the shipwrecked a tranquil port where they will find safety."

Not that Christianity had had easy sailing. It had to overcome competition from oriental "mystery cults"—the worship of Cybele, "Great Mother of the Gods" from Asia Minor, the Egyptian Isis, the Syrian fertility goddess Astarte, the Persian god of light Mithras, and other popular cults which held out salvation to initiates through esoteric rites and mystical experiences. It faced government hostility stemming from Christian refusal to participate in emperor worship.

But the "blood of the martyrs was the seed of the church." Constantine's conversion brought official recognition in 313, and Theodosius's edicts in 391-2 made Christianity the sole legal religion. Now pagan rites were prohibited, the mystery cults suppressed. Pagans were even barred from civil and military service.

The growth of heretical sects within the Christian communities remained of vital concern, for these disputed the very doctrines upon which the faith was based and challenged the unity of ecclesiastical authority. By the end of the fourth century it seemed everyone had become his own theologian, as St. Gregory of Nyssa wrote in despair and amusement at the people of Constantinople, whose preoccupation with the Trinity equaled their addiction to chariot racing:

"The city is full of theologians. . . . If you inquire about the value of your money, some philosopher explains wherein the Son differs from the Father. If you ask the price of bread, your answer is the Father is greater than the Son. If you should want to know whether the bath is ready, you get the pronouncement that the Son was created out of nothing!"

A S EASTERNERS DEBATED every iota in every doctrine, westerners were building a powerful ecclesiastical organization. Its prestige enhanced by Rome's historic role as the imperial capital, the Roman see based its claim to authority on the early tradition that it was on the Tiber that St. Peter (and St. Paul) had founded the church: "Thou art Peter, and upon this rock [petra] I will build my church. . . . And I will give unto thee the keys of the kingdom of heaven: and whatsoever thou shalt bind on earth shall be bound in heaven" (Matthew 16: 18-19). The pope came to be regarded as the "heir of St. Peter."

In 445, Emperor Valentinian III confirmed the bishop of Rome's supremacy over the Western church. When Germanic nations established kingdoms on Roman soil and imperial power failed in the West, the papacy helped fill the void. Arbiter of justice, symbol of moral power, armed with the majesty of Rome and the dread sanctions of interdict (barring the people of an area from sacraments) and excommunication (casting an individual out of the Christian community), the papacy began its rise to medieval prominence. Ahead lay the task of Christianizing all Europe; spearheading this missionary effort were the monks.

Monasticism had its roots in Egypt, where ascetics inspired by St. Anthony lived in the desert as hermits or in religious communities. In Syria and Palestine some went to extremes of austerity: St. Simeon Stylites dwelt 37 years atop a

ISLAND OF PEACE *in a stormy age, the sixth-century monastery at Scyllacium on the sole of Italy's boot toils to preserve classics, Christian and pagan, as its aged founder Cassiodorus welcomes all guests "as though they were Christ." In the world outside, where he served long years as an official to Theodoric the Great, King of the Ostrogoths, at Ravenna, Byzantine armies fight to reconquer Italy for Justinian. Here monks fight "with pen and ink against the devil's illicit temptations," instituting a monastic tradition. Tonsures recall the shaven heads of slaves; the fringe symbolizes thorns that crowned the new Master.*

29

pillar. St. Basil of Caesarea, opposing such practices, prescribed a communal life in which monks prayed seven times a day, took their meals in common, and labored together in the fields. Stressing obedience, chastity, poverty, and study as well as hard work, his fourth-century precepts still govern Orthodox monasticism in the Greco-Slavic world, including famed Mount Athos. Their Western counterpart is the rule formulated by St. Benedict of Nursia, who founded his monastery on Monte Cassino, between Rome and Naples, about 529. By Carolingian times the Benedictine rule was almost universal in Latin Christendom.

IN THE EAST, the brilliant reign of Justinian and his empress Theodora illumined the mid-sixth century. The Byzantine, or later Roman, Empire knew no separation of church and state. The emperor possessed authority as the gift of God and appointed and deposed the church's patriarchs as he chose. The imperial palace, treasury, chancery, and stables were all "sacred." Sacred but not safe. The emperor's life was filled with danger.

Throughout the Middle Ages, Byzantium stood as a bulwark shielding Europe from hordes of eastern invaders whose advance was stopped by Byzantine military prowess and diplomatic shrewdness. Enemies were always at the gates—and within. Of some 100 emperors who ruled in Byzantium only a third died peacefully in their beds, still emperors. Justinian was one of these, but he almost lost his throne in a revolt of the "circus factions" in the fifth year of his reign.

Constantinople's people had been divided in their support of two chief circus factions, the Blues and the Greens, sports-fan clubs that developed into political parties. Sometimes 50,000 gathered for the chariot races in the Hippodrome, which served as a popular assembly like the old Athenian Agora and the Roman Forum. Ranged on opposing tiers by party, spectators shouted political opinions and grievances at their ruler in the imperial box. The Blues, representing religious orthodoxy and conservatism, had the blessing of the upper classes. The Greens, more radical, enlisted the mob's support.

"NIKA!" "CONQUER!" The rallying cry rings in alleys and boulevards of Byzantium as passions boil over in the Nika Revolt of 532. Fear gnaws at Justinian in the imperial palace (below). Courtiers bid him flee rival factions venting a common wrath at the ruler whose taxes crush them. History hinges on Empress Theodora's eloquent plea: "It is impossible for a man, once born, not to die. But . . . exile is intolerable. . . . If you wish to save yourself, Sire, it can easily be done. . . . For my own part, I hold to the old saying that the imperial purple makes the best burial sheet!" Justinian stirs, orders an attack—and 30,000 rioters perish in the Hippodrome where they once shouted themselves hoarse as charioteers (opposite) rounded the spina, backbone of the long oval racetrack. Blue Mosque and distant Hagia Sophia rise near the obelisk-studded site.

The Greens generally dwelt in the Zeugma, a trading quarter and dockyard area beyond the Golden Horn. They also crowded around the Bakers' Market on the Mesê, or Center Street, a boulevard flanked by arcades, shops, and stalls where the empire's medley of peoples jostled donkeys, camels, and porters bent under heavy loads.

The Blues frequented the fashionable Pittakia, "on the east side," near the imperial and patriarchal palaces with their spacious grounds and the government bureaus. Palaces and slums could also be found side by side. Marble-faced houses of the rich enclosed garden courtyards where fountains played; huddled houses of the humble projected their second stories over alleys. And everywhere rose the churches and monasteries of this "God-guarded city."

The Blues and Greens stood watch over sections of the city walls and formed a municipal militia. More than once they helped to repel barbarians. But, arrogant and unruly, they terrorized the streets. Rowdy youths of the Blue party, sporting weird haircuts "in the style of the Huns" and purple striped tunics with immense sleeves, delighted in attacks upon citizens. The Greens swelled their ranks with impoverished farmers and townsmen who, dispossessed by Justinian's tax collectors, poured into the capital.

The Nika Revolt began when the Blues and Greens joined in protesting the execution of two ruffians, one from each faction. Riots grew to a storm, and the mob set fire to the

EMPRESS THEODORA, *spirit of steel immortalized in radiant mosaic, adorns Ravenna's Church of San Vitale. Justinian (below) heads a religious procession of clergy, courtiers, and guards, its formality as stiff as the brocades that bespeak the Oriental luxury of the exalted monarch's court.*

Ravenna, capital of Byzantine Italy, symbolizes Justinian's dream of a united empire: Since there was no emperor in the West, Latin countries reverted to him. Further, his reconquest was a crusade to rescue Catholics from Vandal and Gothic overlords who were Arian heretics (named for Arius, a 4th-century priest who subordinated the Son to the Father).

Procopius chronicled the devastating progress of Byzantine general Belisarius, also extolled the emperor's vast building program. But in his Secret History *he penned a poisonous portrait of Theodora as a harlot raised to the purple, ruthless, vindictive, deadly in intrigue; Justinian as "a faithless friend . . . a treacherous enemy, insane for murder and plunder."*

6TH-CENTURY BYZANTINE MOSAICS IN THE CHURCH OF SAN VITALE, RAVENNA; SCALA

city. After a week, blackened ruins smoldered where palaces, hospices, public baths, and shrines had stood, including the Church of Holy Wisdom, Hagia Sophia.

Drowning the riot in blood, Justinian set about rebuilding Constantine's city to a state of magnificence that dazzled visitors for centuries. In five years he created a new Hagia Sophia, making it the largest church in Christendom.

Like countless visitors before me, I found it still a vision of splendor. Its dome indeed seemed to "float in the air," as the historian Procopius wrote, and "sunlight grew in it." How understandable that Justinian, comparing his work with the Temple at Jerusalem, could cry, "Solomon, I have surpassed you!"

VICTORY MARKED the progress of his armies abroad, as Justinian turned to the reconquest of Constantine's empire. His legions defeated the Vandals in North Africa, wrested the southeast coast of Spain from the Visigoths, conquered Sicily, destroyed the Ostrogothic kingdom in Italy. Stupendous achievements in their day, these conquests did not last long. And the return of Western provinces to imperial control brought Justinian, who ruled as an Eastern pontiff, into conflict with the pope in Rome, who not only reigned spiritually but also had increased his temporal domains. In time other forces also helped split the Christian church into Roman Catholic in the West and Orthodox in the East.

Justinian ruled through a vast centralized bureaucracy. He worked tirelessly to reform the administration, eliminating abuses, regulating salaries, creating state monopolies. He founded a Byzantine silk industry when, according to legend, two monks smuggled silkworm eggs out of China, where the secret of silk production was jealously guarded. In codifying all imperial laws back to Hadrian's reign, he placed later ages in his debt. Revived in the West five centuries later, his Code and Digest underpin much of modern law.

Although Latin was the official language of law courts and government, most people in the East continued to speak Greek. By the mid-seventh century, Latin had gone the way of the toga, cherished symbol of Roman dignity replaced by long robes or caftans of eastern origin designed and worn according to rank. Associating nudity with sin, Byzantines covered the body carefully; their robes influenced Western dress down to the 12th century, when the "Gothic" style came in. Byzantine court etiquette found its imitators as late as the Bourbons, Habsburgs, and Romanovs. Indeed, the pope's exacting ceremonial routine is still very like that of a Byzantine emperor a thousand years ago.

The passion for detail and precision which manifested itself in diplomatic protocol and law, in theology and the liturgy, in statecraft and military organization also reveals itself in the arts. Ivories, silver work, enamels, brocades, manuscript illustrations, frescoes, and mosaics demonstrate the Byzantine artist's capacity to deal patiently with detail. God's work was done with wondrous care, and it behooved man, cast in His image, to copy it with all possible exactitude.

FLOATING ON A RING OF LIGHT, *Hagia Sophia's golden dome seemed to Procopius as delicately poised as if suspended from heaven on golden chains. Justinian's masterwork, dedicated on Christmas day in 537, was the crowning glory of a metropolis embracing almost half a million Greek-speaking "Romans" (while Rome shrank to far fewer souls). When Sultan Mehmed the Conquerer seized Constantinople, "city of the world's desire," Hagia Sophia became a mosque. Today, four minarets still spiking the sky, it is a museum.*

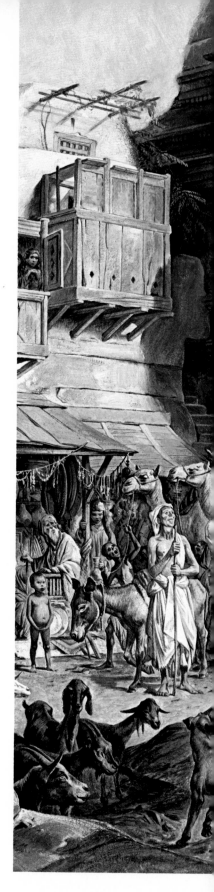

THE ERUPTION OF ISLAM burst upon the solemn liturgy of Byzantine life in the seventh century. For generations before the Prophet Mohammed, Arabs had entered the Byzantine Empire and the Persian kingdom as merchants and mercenaries. When Byzantium and Persia exhausted each other by long wars, the Arabs seized the historic opportunity. The new religion of Islam ("submission to the will of Allah") gave Arab tribes a cultural and social unity they had never known. Hunger, desire for plunder, love of combat, ambition spurred them to win an empire stretching from the Indus to the Pyrenees.

Syria, Palestine, Persia, Egypt were overrun in the decade 634-44 when Omar was second caliph. Armies of the Prophet swept westward through North Africa, conquered Spain, even pressed into France. Soon Christianity and Islam faced each other the length of the Mediterranean. In Spain the Christians would fight for generations against the "Moors," largely Berbers from Morocco, push them back into the kingdom of Granada, and finally expel them in the year of Columbus's first voyage to America.

In the 11th century the Seljuk Turks, already converts to Islam, invaded Mesopotamia and Asia Minor. Through them the First Crusaders were to cut a bloody swath.

Despite the hostilities, Italian city-states traded with the Moslems, whose Koran permitted commerce with unbelievers. Western merchants adopted many words of Arabic origin — *admiral, average, caliber, magazine, monsoon, tariff, traffic.* They drew on Moslem models when they developed their bill of exchange and joint-stock company.

For five centuries 37 caliphs of the Abbasid dynasty reigned in magnificence from Baghdad, notable among them the great Harun al-Rashid and his son al-Mamun. Al-Mamun was intrigued by the ingenuity of Leo the Mathematician, the mid-ninth century Byzantine courtier who devised telegraphic messages to warn of Moslem attack. Leo's messages could be flashed by hilltop beacons across

FLEET STEEDS AND SLASHING SCIMITARS *swiftly carved an empire when Saracens surged out of the furnace of Arabia. In 638 Jerusalem bowed to Caliph Omar. His general Amr ibn al-Asi, with only 4,000 horsemen, rode toward Byzantine Egypt. At Rafah a note from Omar overtook him. Guessing its message, he raced to El-Arish, inside Egypt's frontier, then opened it. Return if still in Palestine, it read; if in Egypt, proceed. Now his lieutenants cheer as he orders the advance that will add Egypt to Islam and melt a millennium of Hellenism there like snow in the Arabian sun. Though their empire embraced more than Rome ever held, the Arabs paradoxically strengthened Rome's popes by conquering rival bishoprics — Alexandria, Antioch, Carthage. Yet the Moslems forced no conversion; they preferred to tax infidels and remain a ruling elite.*

PAINTING FOR NATIONAL GEOGRAPHIC BY ANDRE DURENCEAU

Asia Minor to the imperial palace in Constantinople. Al-Mamun offered Emperor Theophilus eternal peace and 2,000 pounds of gold if he would allow Leo to reside a while in Baghdad. "But Theophilus replied that it was irrational to give away one's own advantages to others," relates a chronicle. "And so he withheld his assent."

Moslem scholars translated learned works into Arabic from Greek, Persian, Syriac, and Sanskrit. Moslem geographers, astronomers, and astrologers, alchemists, physicists, and naturalists enriched European culture. Our technical vocabulary contains evidence of their contributions in such words as *alkali, alembic, algebra, amalgam, zenith, nadir,* and *cipher.* Moslem mathematicians used the cipher, or zero, two centuries before it appeared in 12th-century Europe.

Exquisite Moslem metalwork and ceramics influenced Italian crafts; the enameled glass of Syria inspired Venetian glassworkers. Europeans imported Persian rugs and "Turkey carpets"; they prized Damascene steel and worked Cordovan leather. Mosul gave us our word "muslin," and Damascus, "damask." Spain copied the brown-and-yellow watered silks produced in Baghdad's Attabiyah quarter. Samuel Pepys's "false taby wastecoate" derives from Attabiyah, as does our term "tabby" cat.

Many were the ways medieval Europe would profit from the rich fusion of cultures in the Moslem world. But in the eighth century the armies of the Prophet posed a fearsome threat. If Byzantium had not stood firm in the East, if Charlemagne's grandfather, Charles Martel, had not hammered the invaders so resoundingly in the valley of the Loire, the pages that follow might have told a different story.

TWO GREAT FORCES *welded the wandering Arab tribes into a conquering juggernaut. One was hunger. It still gnaws Bedouin driving flocks over scorching sands in quest of forage for camel, sheep, or goat (below). The other was Islam, a new faith that needed neither priest nor sacrament, yet honored Christ and the Hebrew prophets, worshiped one God, and promised paradise hereafter. "Allah hath created the heavens and the earth," the Koran tells a believer (opposite) whose forebears quit the flinty wastes of* Arabia deserta *to rule under the palms of Damascus or by the fountains of Spain.*

FERVID PILGRIMS *circle seven times round the Kaaba (cube) in Mecca's Haram Mosque in joyful praise of their hajj, or pilgrimage, to the holiest shrine in Islam. Five times a day, the world's 513 million Moslems turn toward Mecca to pray. And as the Age of Chivalry slowly took shape in strife-torn lands of Europe, Moslems of a thousand years ago turned toward their neighbors in the north to war, to trade, and to share fruits of the many cultures united under their sway.*

THOMAS J. ABERCROMBIE, NATIONAL GEOGRAPHIC STAFF (ALSO OVERLEAF)

39

By Norman P. Zacour

the world of charlemagne

HE CROWD STIRS as a tall figure enters St. Peter's Basilica on this Christmas day in the Year of Our Lord 800. Frank and Roman, Greek and Lombard, Frisian and Saxon all crane to see this man who has summoned them to Rome.

His fellow Franks, in linen breeches and coats of fur, remark his strange dress: a Roman toga and cloak drape his "rather prominent belly." He kneels at the great altar, his eyes—"very large and animated"—on the golden diadem before him. Thick-necked, long-nosed, he towers over men even on his knees.

Now the pope places the diadem on the fair hair of this 58-year-old king who seeks all Christendom for his realm. The wooden-roofed basilica resounds with thrice-shouted acclamation: "Long life and victory to Charles Augustus, crowned by God to be the great and peaceful emperor of the Romans!"

A grateful pope falls to his knees to kiss the hem of the first Roman emperor in the West for more than 300 years. The man who entered St. Peter's as king of the Franks strides forth to rule what will become the Holy Roman Empire. History will dub him Charles the Great, his name living on in epics and romance as Charlemagne.

He had journeyed from Germany to Rome only a month before to pacify the riot-torn city and save the pope, Leo III. In the five years since his election Leo had struggled against Roman foes who charged him with immorality. They even ambushed a papal procession and took Leo captive. Escaping, he fled to Charlemagne's court.

For nearly half a century the tireless monarch in Frankish cloak rode to rule his far-flung realm.
Ninth-century bronze equestrian in the Louvre, Paris; Eddy van der Veen

"**MEEKLY BOW** thy proud head....
Adore what thou hast burned,
burn what thou hast adored!"

The baptism of Clovis, chief of
the Franks, at Reims in 496 marked
a new era. He became the first
barbarian king in the West won to
the church of Rome. The conversion,
long sought by his wife Clotilda,
a Burgundian princess, came after
her God granted him a signal victory.
Three thousand Frankish warriors
followed him into the faith.

Brutal and shrewd, Clovis
destroyed the last remnant of
Roman rule in Gaul, drove the
heretic Visigoths from Aquitaine,
began the conquest of Burgundy.
But his Merovingian descendants,
mired in murder and debauchery,
degenerated into mere shadows.
Power was wielded by the mayor
of the palace, a hereditary office.

Finally, in 751, the pope agreed
with the mayor, Pepin the Short:
"It is better to give the name
of king to him who has the wisdom
and the power." So Childeric III,
shorn of his royal locks, was put
into a cloister and King Pepin
began the Carolingian dynasty.

His son Charlemagne would have
the power to extend the Frankish
kingdom into an empire (opposite)
and the wisdom to rule it well.

The coronation dramatized the pope's dependence upon the Frankish king and gave hope to dreams of an *imperium christianum*, a Christian empire. As savior of the pope, defender of the faith, and now as emperor of the West, Charlemagne would reign over a domain that was both church and state.

As I traveled his empire, seeking glimpses of Charlemagne's world, I toured a realm as diverse as his. But he had ruled as one land what we know as many: France, Belgium, Luxembourg, the Netherlands, Switzerland; much of Germany, Austria, and Italy; part of Spain. Yet at heart he remained a Frank, heir of a powerful family that long had linked its fortune with the Christian faith.

As a lad he heard tales of his grandfather Charles—nicknamed Martel (the Hammer)—who had routed the Moslem invaders near Tours. At nine he no doubt saw his father, Pepin the Short, crowned by the great Anglo-Saxon missionary Boniface. Later the pope himself journeyed across the Alps to consecrate Pepin and anoint his sons as successors. Soon the boy who would become Charlemagne was to learn how a priest dies for his faith, and how a king pays for his crown.

Not long after Pepin's coronation, Boniface, worn by 35 years of missionary work in Germany, retired to Fulda, his favorite monastery. But when he heard worrisome reports about his fledgling church in Frisia, he hurried north to take up again the task of preaching and converting. Where the Dutch town of Dokkum now stands, a pagan band slew the old man and 53 of his companions.

Fulda's monastery lay "amongst woods in a wide and lonely tract." When I came upon the site, I found a cathedral wearing a warm baroque smile. Under the black altar table in the crypt a marble Boniface in bishop's miter rose out of his 18th-century sarcophagus. Little marble angels with determined faces strained to hold up the heavy lid. Just beyond, in the cathedral museum, I saw the *Codex Ragyndrudis,* a large manuscript volume of church fathers' writings. It bore deep slashes, for Boniface held it when the Frisians hacked him to death. Not all the pleasant baroque decorations that surround the relic can obliterate the spell of that savage moment nearly 1,200 years ago.

In his teens Charles rode with his father when Pepin, paying for his papal blessing, marched into Lombardy to subdue "that stinking people . . . the source

From Germanic forests rose a Christian empire welded by Charlemagne's iron will

Frankish lands inherited by Charlemagne

Lands he conquered

Lands he made tributary

0   200
STATUTE MILES

DANES

Dokkum
Verden
Elbe
FRISIA
SAXONS
GERMANY
Weser

Paderborn
Cologne
Geismar
Aachen
(Aix la Chapelle)
AUSTRASIA
Rhine
Fulda
SLAVS
Ingelheim
Frankfurt
Mainz
Soissons   Reims
Worms
St. Denis
Verdun   Lorsch
Paris
Meuse
Danube
BRITTANY
NEUSTRIA
Seine
BAVARIA
Orléans
Salzburg
AVARS
Tours
Lech
St. Gallen
AUSTRIA
HUNGARY
BURGUNDY
FRANCE
ALPS
Loire
Great St. Bernard
Pass
Venice
AQUITAINE
Rhone
Pavia   Po
Garonne
LOMBARDS
Ravenna
Pisa
BASQUES
Roncesvalles Pass
ADRIATIC SEA
BASQUES
PYRENEES
ITALY
Pamplona
SPANISH MARCH
ARABS
Ebro
Tiber
CORSICA
Rome
Barcelona
MEDITERRANEAN SEA
DUCHY OF
BENEVENTO
Naples
SPAIN

BACKBONE OF EMPIRE, *the Rhine cradled the Frankish nation, carried its commerce, shielded it from Saxons to the east. Charlemagne's armies crossed many times; he bridged the Rhine at Mainz, but failed in his try to link it by canal to the Danube. Here the storied river sweeps below Cat Castle and distant Lorelei Rock.*

THOMAS NEBBIA

of leprosy," the *Langobardi*, or "Longbeards," under papal curse. A Germanic people that had swept out of Austria and crossed the Alps in the sixth century, these Lombards held much of the Italian peninsula. They flanked Rome, defying papal claims to territories purportedly conveyed to the papacy by Emperor Constantine. Pepin's defeat of the Lombards gave the pope a real claim—and sealed an alliance between the Frankish kingdom and the church.

Pepin died in 768. Because families, not first sons, inherited Frankish thrones, Charlemagne for three years had to share the kingdom with a younger brother. As their rivalry neared open warfare, the brother fell ill and died. Now Charlemagne alone ruled Frankland, the forerunner of modern France and Germany. But his realm had yet to become a unified, loyal kingdom. Christians "little better

CHARLEMAGNE WEEPS *as his rear guard falls like tenpins, ambushed at Roncesvalles on the return from Spain in 778. Three centuries later troubadours of a crusading era glorified the clash and gave chivalry a hero in the* Song of Roland.

Betrayed by his jealous stepfather, Count Roland refuses to summon aid lest he lose renown. He "makes an exit for the soul with his lance" in heathen foes, and glories in the bright blood that paints his sword. But one by one Roland's comrades, the "paladins," are overwhelmed.

Lean-faced Basques (opposite) till Pyrenean slopes where moaned a companion in arms, "Your prowess, Roland, has been our undoing."

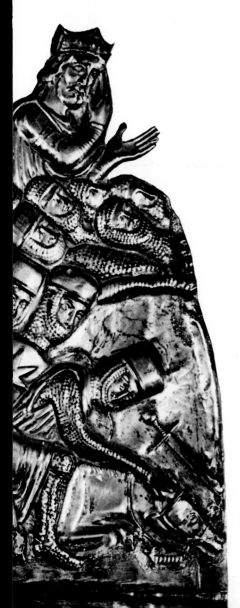

than heathens" cherished old customs and tribal laws. Aquitanians and Bavarians brewed rebellions. An unruly kingdom, its borders bristling with foes, swiftly molded Charlemagne into a warrior-king.

His father and grandfather had bequeathed him three enemies: to the north and east, the Saxons; to the southeast, the Lombards; to the southwest, the Arab invaders of Spain, against whom he marched with a great army in 778.

Dissident Arab chieftains south of the Pyrenees had led him to believe that he would be welcomed in Spain. Instead its people refused to be "liberated" and he withdrew northward. In a high pass he was ambushed—not by Moslems but by fiercely independent Basques who scorned his rule.

Einhard, a monastery-schooled courtier who became Charlemagne's biographer, recorded the disaster: Basques, hidden on a wooded mountaintop, "rushed down on the rear of the baggage train and forced the rear guard down to the bottom of the valley." They "killed everyone . . . plundered the baggage and took off swiftly in all directions under cover of the approaching dark."

Legend seized on the incident, multiplying details, elevating the skirmish into a great battle, bestowing fame on the pass of Roncesvalles as the site, and enshrining the name of one who fell, Count Roland. The legend finally took poetic form as the *Song of Roland*, an epic glorifying the chivalric virtues of the warriors of feudal Europe.

Charlemagne never again personally led his army into Spain. But by the end of his reign his troops had staked

49

out the Spanish March (from the Germanic *marka,* border), a military district that stretched from Pamplona in the west to Barcelona on the Mediterranean.

N O SUCH BUFFER ZONE separated the Franks and the Saxons. Along that northeastern frontier, wrote Einhard, "there was no end to the murders, thefts, and arsons on both sides." For each raid on Frankish border settlements, Charlemagne's troops retaliated with vengeance. The punitive thrusts into Saxon territory soon evolved into a war of conquest.

"No war ever undertaken by the Franks," Einhard continued, "was carried on with such persistence and bitterness, or cost so much labor, because the Saxons,

like almost all the tribes of Germany, were a fierce people, given to the worship of devils, and hostile to our religion...." The Saxons fought not only for their land but their way of life. They knew that bowing to Charlemagne's crown also meant kneeling to his Christian god. His was a holy war, which he decreed upon "the perfidious and oath-breaking Saxon people until they were conquered and converted to the Christian religion—or totally annihilated."

During his first campaign, in 772, Charlemagne

"HIGH ARE THE MOUNTAINS and the valleys dark ... the defiles mysterious." The Frankish rear guard, like tight herded sheep, magnifies in the Song of Roland *to 20,000 knights; Basque raiders become 100,000 mounted Saracens. Roland emerges as the champion of Christendom —"there is not such a vassal under the vault of heaven." He cleaves a Pyrenees pass, Brèche de Roland, with his magic sword Durendal, girded on him by his liege lord Charlemagne, white-bearded and "more than 200 years old."*

51

marched to the Saxons' sacred grove near Paderborn, in Westphalia. There he tore down the Irminsul, the tall wooden column the Saxons revered as the symbolic bearer of the universe. He had been born to a tradition of ax-and-sword missionary zeal: Saintly Boniface, guarded by Charles Martel's troops, years before had chopped down the pagans' holy oak near Geismar. With the very wood of that tree of Thunor the thunder god, Boniface had built a chapel. On his raid, Charlemagne looted the heathen gods' hoard of silver and gold.

For 32 years, no matter how deep he penetrated into Saxon territory, no matter how many leaders submitted to him, no matter how many forced baptisms he exacted, the moment he withdrew his army the Saxons rose up again. "Like a dog that returns to its vomit," said a Carolingian annalist, "they returned to the paganism they had once thrown up."

When conversion at sword's point failed, Charlemagne wielded his sword for slaughter. Once he rounded up 4,500 Saxons and beheaded them all in one day. Then, say the annals, "the king went into winter camp . . . and there celebrated Christmas and Easter as usual." In time, he could celebrate the obliteration of Saxon society and the spread of his kingdom across their blood-sodden land.

As the Franks trampled down their centuries-old borders and massacred old enemies, new foes confronted them. Beyond the Frisians and Saxons loomed the pagan Danes and Slavs; beyond Bavaria ranged the Avars, nomadic horsemen of the Asiatic steppes who had surged into Europe in the sixth century. Their oppression of the conquered made *slave* of Slav. Slavic women the Avars "harnessed like beasts to their wagons, violating them systematically, destroying their family life, and indeed reducing their whole existence to the level of brutes." Avar horsemen drove Slavic men into battle as human shields.

The Franks all but wiped out the Avars in seven years of savage war. Where once stood the palace of the Avars' khakhan—khan of khans—"there is not so much as a trace of human habitation," Einhard wrote. Fifteen wagons, each drawn by four oxen, hauled the khakhan's treasures to Charlemagne.

The king needed such booty to make his ceaseless warfare profitable—and to pay off his vassals. Exchanging royal gifts of loot and land for military service,

"**W**herever capable men are found," Charlemagne ordered, "give them woodland to clear." His command felled forests and opened new fields for manorialism— "no lord without land, no land without lord." For centuries serf would toil and lord would dwell (manoir), first in wooden manor house, then in stone castle. A military vassal to his overlord, the lord of the manor was protector, governor, and judge to his serfs, the villeins (whence our villains!) whose village derived from the Roman villa.
Heavy soil yielded to new deep-biting wheeled plow and iron-toothed harrow (opposite). Iron shoes and a collared harness that no longer choked the animal when he pulled made workhorses of steeds. In places crop rotation rested one field in three, reaping wheat and rye from fall planting, oats and barley from spring. But hand-sown seed produced sparse crops; the lord's mills and ovens monopolized the grain; war and famine ever threatened. Bound to lord and land, serfs married only at his will, worked his fields before theirs. They paid rent in kind and coin, rendered homage with Easter eggs and Christmas geese, and lamented, "What the peasant produces in a year, the lord wastes in an hour."

"SEPTEMBER" IN A FLEMISH CALENDAR, C. 1500; BRITISH MUSEUM, LONDON

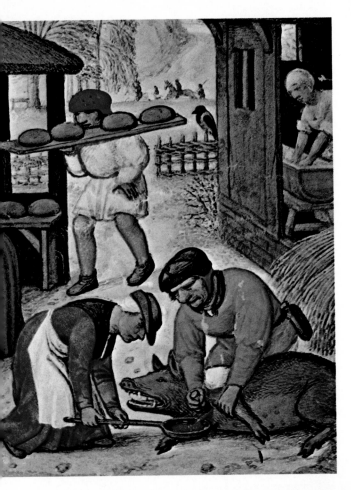

Up at dawn, to bed at dusk, serfs bend to a calendar of toil Charlemagne named in his Frankish tongue: Plow month (June), Hay month (July), Harvest month (August), Wind month (September), Vintage month (October). . . . They chop wood, butcher pigs for winter, harvest grain for bread and beer (safer than water or milk)—a seesaw of work, this day for themselves, that day for their lord. Stewards watch lest they "wander off to visit markets and fairs."

Hole-in-roof heating blackens early dirt-floored, rush-bed huts, and "nothing but rainwater" washes peasant faces. Time brings chimney and hearth to half-timbered village homes shared with the livestock. Windmills and churches widen a world once seen as an acre—the measure of a day's plowing.

Picturing heaven's hierarchy in terms of the feudal pyramid, peasants pray to saints to intercede for them with God—just as they petition their manor court, not the king. The superstitious turn to a witch or the spirit of a gnarled tree. After six days of toil, men disturb Sabbath and clergy with "ballads and dancings and evil and wanton songs and such-like lures of the devil."

Women sin most often in disobeying their husbands. Pondside ducking stools douse naggers, and men have "the right to beat their wives" but "not to kill them thereby."

"DECEMBER" (UPPER) AND "JANUARY" (OPPOSITE) FROM FLEMISH CALENDAR; BRITISH MUSEUM. "JULY" FROM FRENCH CALENDAR, ALSO C. 1500; BIBLIOTHÈQUE NATIONALE, PARIS

IN ALPINE MEADOWS, *where cheery face greets morning sun, where horse and ox tug summer's last hay, man, woman, and child still tend their beloved land.*
"O Earth, our mother!" sang serfs in Charlemagne's realm, seeing in the soil the marvel of birth.

Here in Austria—eastern march of his empire—mother earth even proffered salt to preserve meat for winter's cruel days. Salt also sustained royal purses, for only the crown mined it. Troops kept peasants penned in the Salzkammergut—Salt Crown Lands—to thwart smuggling. Travelers needed passes to enter; not until the 19th century were visitors welcome.

Salzburg, made a bishop's see by Boniface, guarded salt for Charlemagne. Boniface in 748 charged an Irish abbot there with "perverse and sinful" belief: that the earth was round.

VOLKMAR WENTZEL, NATIONAL GEOGRAPHIC STAFF

Charlemagne created a hierarchy of powerful nobles. As they swore fealty to the king so did lesser men render homage to the nobles. Landholders not only had to join campaigns but also equip themselves. A vassal would be ordered to an assembly point "so prepared with your men that you may be able to go thence well equipped in any direction which our command shall order.... Each horseman is expected to have a shield, lance, sword, dagger, bow, quiver with arrows, and in your carts.... axes, planes, augers, boards, spades, iron shovels and other utensils...."

A lord's "man," though technically free, vowed obedience to the lord, to serve him, to bear arms for him. A man could be absolved from his oath of fealty if the lord tried to kill him or make him a slave, stole his property, or seduced his wife. But the man had to find another lord and swear a new oath to him, for each man must have his lord.

The nobility's power was rooted in the land—almost the only form of wealth in those days of little commerce or industry, and certainly the only way of acquiring influence. Most of Charlemagne's subjects lived on the land as peasants who either toiled on their own plots or worked as tenants on the nobles' great holdings. Some managed to break their bondage to the land. The son of a serf freed by Charlemagne became the archbishop of Reims. Once he enraged a nobleman, who sneered, "The emperor has granted you freedom, but not nobility, for that is impossible!"

The king himself held vast royal *vills*, estates that supplied his court and his army. The vills also served as way stations on his almost continuous tours of the realm. Indeed it was easier for the court to go where the food was than to bring the food to the court.

"For the sake of ornament," Charlemagne ordered every estate adorned with "swans, peacocks, pheasants, ducks, pigeons, partridges, and turtledoves." He laid down a host of other orders to the stewards who managed his vills. One that caught my eye: "See to it that . . . our grapes are not squashed out by foot." He wanted his larders stocked with "bacon, smoked ham, sausages, freshly salted meat . . . mustard, cheese, butter, malt, beer, mead, honey. . . ." And he demanded that the vills be self-sufficient, each with its own "blacksmiths, a goldsmith, a silversmith, shoemakers, turners, carpenters, sword-makers . . . men who know how to make beer . . . bakers to make pastry for our table. . . ."

But as his kingdom expanded he could no longer rule it solely from horseback; diverse peoples, languages, and traditions challenged his hope of unity. So he ruled through several hundred "counties," each governed by a resident count directly responsible to the king. Generally scions of old-line Frankish families, the counts

could amass enough land and power to threaten the crown. To check them, Charlemagne, who also used the church as an arm of government, often played off bishops against counts. And to keep watch over their conduct of local affairs — levying the militia, collecting royal dues and tolls, administering justice — he dispatched *missi dominici*, "the lord's emissaries," as royal inspectors.

The missi, usually traveling in twos (one layman and one ecclesiastic), spent a few weeks each year in a territory comprising several counties. Charlemagne ordered his missi to "make a diligent investigation whenever any man claims that an injustice has been done to him by anyone," for he demanded that his laws should protect the weak as well as the strong. "No one shall dare to plunder or harm the holy churches of God, or widows, orphans, or foreigners. . . . Nor shall anyone be kept back from the right path of justice by . . . fear of the powerful."

Long before his coronation Charlemagne had dreams of imperial grandeur. Like Constantine, he would build a new Rome. He would rule from a permanent capital with a "sacred palace," in imitation of the Byzantine court. He chose for his Rome a town of the Frankish heartland, Aachen, between the Rhine and Meuse rivers southwest of Roman-founded Cologne. Einhard, "a small body containing a great spirit," helped build the palace, which had a marble pool big enough for a hundred swimmers. "No one could be fairly regarded as his superior in swimming," he wrote of Charlemagne. To this day Cologners insist that the monarch would have picked their proud city if he had not been lured to Aachen by its warm medicinal springs and his fondness for swimming.

Charlemagne held court in a marble-decorated hall 150 feet long, his maps of empire inlaid in tables of silver and gold. Nobles preened for court. We hear of a deacon "who followed the Italian custom and resisted the course of nature.

THRONE OF EMPIRE *dominates Charlemagne's chapel in Aachen (opposite). Plundered pillars and the octagonal style of Ravenna's San Vitale church brought Byzantine splendor to the Frankish capital. Crown of light, Emperor Frederick Barbarossa's 16-turreted chandelier, symbolizes a heavenly Jerusalem.*

Crown placed on Charlemagne in Rome in 800 (right) produced a dilemma to vex the centuries. If the pope crowned the emperor, was not the church paramount? Countered Germany's Holy Roman Emperors and France's Most Christian Kings, heirs alike of Charlemagne: How could they reign in God's name without being supreme? And what of the emperor in Constantinople claiming to rule over Christendom?

14TH-CENTURY FRENCH MINIATURE IN MUSÉE GOYA, CASTRES, FRANCE; GIRAUDON
OPPOSITE: WALTER MEAYERS EDWARDS, NATIONAL GEOGRAPHIC STAFF

58

For he went to the baths and had himself closely shaved, polished his skin, cleaned his nails, and had his hair cut as short as if it had been done by a lathe."

The king, favoring old Frankish dress—high gilt boots laced with red thongs, embroidered linen breeches and shirt, long cloak—reigned as the head of a clan. He gave audiences while he dressed in the morning. If a dispute needed to be settled, "he had the litigants brought before him, heard the case, and gave a decision as though he were seated on the judgment seat" instead of on his bed.

The palace swarmed with children, whom the king royally spoiled. He had 14 of his own—six by concubines—and he brought up the five daughters of his son Pepin, who had died of plague. The children, dining and traveling with the king, "gladden the father's heart, like fresh shoots of vine," wrote a courtier. Charlemagne festooned his daughters with jewels, crowned them with coronets, robed them in ermine. He loved them so much, we are told, that he would not let them get married. But he tolerated their love affairs and illegitimate children.

One tale told of the king, who often had trouble sleeping, seeing a predawn tryst from his window. He did not punish his daughter or her lover "since they are so young." Besides, he himself preached chastity more than he practiced it.

*T*HOUGH HIS COURT might scandalize visiting churchmen, Charlemagne attracted the best Christian minds of his day. They found a barely literate king, but one who cherished learning. Einhard reports that Charlemagne kept writing tablets "under his pillow, so that during his spare time he might accustom his hand to draw letters." He studied Latin, Greek, arithmetic, logic, rhetoric, astronomy. And what he wanted for himself he wanted for his empire.

He believed that Christianity could unite that empire. But how could an ignorant mind know the Scriptures? "Strive to learn," he besought his churchmen. In a letter to abbots and bishops he complained of illiterate monks: "What pious devotion had faithfully prompted in their hearts, their uneducated tongues could not put into words without stumbling." Hardly a Bible existed that was not riddled with the gross errors of untutored copyists. Paganism and superstition stalked his realm. He needed teachers and schools to light again the torches of learning—or the Christian empire entrusted to him would die in darkness.

In Italy, where a tradition of secular learning still lingered, he recruited Peter of Pisa, who brought literature to the court school, and Paul the Deacon, a Lombard who later wrote a major history of his people. From Spain came Theodulf, a poet, theologian, patron of the arts, and caustic social critic: "A bishop who himself is stuffed with food should not try to stop others from being gluttons; and he should not preach sobriety when he himself is drunk."

WONDERS OF ARABY *come to Aachen in 802 as gifts from Harun al-Rashid, Baghdad Caliph of* Arabian Nights *fame. The elephant, Abu al-Abbas, won Charlemagne's heart and lumbered beside him on treks through the empire. Brought along to panic Danish foes in 810, the beast died—contradicting bestiaries, which said elephants live 300 years. With it went Charlemagne's luck. A plague decimated cattle, his Rhine bridge burned, three in his family died, then he did. Tomb remains indicate he stood six feet four.*

Charlemagne's greatest teacher, Alcuin of York, came from the British Isles, whose monasteries kept learning alive in the continent's darkened age. Alcuin sent forth pupils who would carry to the next generation his terse lesson in the difference between words of the tongue and words of the pen:

Pupil: What is the tongue? *Alcuin:* Something which whips the air. . . .

Pupil: What is writing? *Alcuin:* The guardian of history. . . .

In the court school the sons of royalty, nobility, and commoners sharpened their minds with problems such as: A ladder has 100 rungs. On the first sits one pigeon, on the second two, and so on to the 100th, where 100 sit. How many pigeons sit on the ladder? The pupils could not use algebra to solve this problem in arithmetic progression; the Arabs' gift of algebra would not enlighten Europe for centuries to come. But they did not have to rely on counting, for Alcuin taught a solution through logic: The number of pigeons "pair" to make a total of 100 on steps 99 and 1, steps 98 and 2, and so forth. Only step 50 and step 100 have no "pairing" steps. Thus, there are 49 pairs of steps, each pair adding up to 100. The result: $49 \times 100 + 50 + 100 = 5,050$ pigeons.

The palace school trained many of the next generation's clergy and became a model for schools Charlemagne established in monasteries and episcopal churches. There children learned the Psalms, simple reckoning, elementary Latin grammar, and the chanting of the liturgy. No one could become a priest unless he had some familiarity with the creed, the Gospels, certain devotions—and could write.

10TH-CENTURY IVORY; KUNSTHISTORISCHES MUSEUM, VIENNA. MONOGRAM, 775; ARCHIVES NATIONALES, PARIS. "D" FROM 9TH-CENTURY BIBLE, ALCUIN'S REVISION; BRITISH MUSEUM. GOSPEL BOOK OF CHARLEMAGNE, 783; BIBLIOTHÈQUE NATIONALE, PARIS. GATEWAY BY WALTER MEAYERS EDWARDS, NATIONAL GEOGRAPHIC STAFF

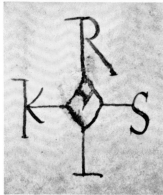

"LET SCHOOLS be established in which boys may learn to read,'' urged the king who could scarcely sign his own monogram, ''Karolus'' (above). Yet his lust for learning brightened his age and ours.

Dove at his ear, St. Gregory the Great bends to bookwork (opposite) in the 6th century. Scribes of his day wrote on parchment (more durable but more costly than papyrus), crowding the Latin CAPITALS of their ''majuscule'' script. Merovingian clerics evolved a scrawl that began John 1:2 thus:

hoc erat Inprincipio

Charlemagne's savants shaped a ''Carolingian minuscule'' that rendered the same phrase:

hoc erat in principio

—clear to readers today as hoc erat in principio, ''the same was in the beginning.''

The text opposite is printed in letters derived from this script. We call this type ''roman'' because Renaissance scholars and printers mistook classics in this script for Roman originals. Most of our Latin classics came to us through Carolingian copies. (The italic type you are reading first appeared in an edition of Virgil published in Venice in 1501.)

Famed Carolingian monastery of Lorsch (left above), in Germany, preserved nearly 600 works, sacred and classical, in its library. As artists embellished such houses of God, monks adorned His Word with Celtic-Germanic illuminations (left).

63

Alcuin fostered a corrected text of the Bible. From Rome came approved versions of canon law, the liturgy, and works of the early church fathers. Monastic *scriptoria* discarded the scrawls of old. Throughout the realm men would read The Word in an elegant, legible handwriting—Carolingian minuscule.

Charlemagne thrived in the genial society of his scholars, who dubbed him King David, flattered him as a new Cicero, and bestowed on each other nicknames derived from the great figures of antiquity. They shared good food and good talk: "And father Albinus [Alcuin] would sit, ever on the point of uttering pious words and freely partaking of food with lips and hand," wrote Theodulf. "In the midst David presides with scepter, dealing out mighty portions...." We can almost hear Charlemagne, discoursing on poetry and dogma in Latin, calling out in Frankish to the hunters who bring in roasts on spits.

BELOW his hilltop palace at Aachen rose a "beautiful basilica," which he "adorned with gold and silver lamps and with rails and doors of solid brass." His palace is gone, but the chapel still stands, an eastern-style octagonal edifice surmounted by a cupola, with a gallery around the interior. As I stood in the golden light of the chapel, I looked up and saw a marble throne. There he had sat. And beyond, high in the cupola, his people could see, as I did, Christ enthroned in golden mosaic. Their emperor reflected God's majesty.

But in his last years, aging, ill, dwelling on his soul, he came troubled to the chapel, haunting it at all hours. He believed that his sins had brought God's wrath upon the empire. In one last effort to appease his Lord, he willed three-quarters of his treasury to the archbishoprics and bishoprics of the realm.

"The soil is everywhere losing its fertility," he lamented in a decree in 807. Famine threatened. Epidemics raged. But he could do little more than preach against priests who "buy land and serfs and other property" with church money and "spend their time on banquets, oppression, and robbery."

On January 28 in the year 814 Charlemagne died. Within two generations his empire and educational reforms collapsed, victims of civil war. The empire became a patchwork of fiefs controlled by nobles who passed title and land to their heirs. In a sundered realm without a strong king feudalism took root.

Within little more than a century after his death Charlemagne's line disappeared. But he would cast a long shadow down the ages, inspiring chivalric legends and quests for the ideal of a Holy Roman Empire. Otto III would open Charlemagne's tomb at Aachen, don the imperial cross that gleamed on the body —and die in 1002 at 21. Emperor Frederick Barbarossa proclaimed Charlemagne a saint; Napoleon would hark back to Charles as "my great predecessor." The reality of a united empire eluded them all. Only Charlemagne created that single society under God, that Christian empire at once so mighty and so fragile.

For even the stones of empire—churches, monasteries, towns—would crumble. Out of the north swept death and destruction. Defenseless, the Christians of a shattered holy empire huddled in their churches and prayed: "*A furore Norman-norum libera nos, Domine*—From the fury of the Northmen deliver us, O Lord!"

"THE GOLDEN BOOK," *a legacy of Carolingian hands and minds that illumined a Europe long darkened, enshrined holy words in splendor worthy of sacred relics. But, like the chronicled meteor that portended the death of Charlemagne, the age "flashed . . . with a great blaze"—and vanished in new darkness.*

From rockbound fjords fierce Northmen sailed in search of plunder, striking terror in lands they ravaged. National Geographic's Howard La Fay unfolds a stark saga as he wends to far shores

In the Wake of the Vikings

"ON 8 JANUARY THE HARRYING OF THE HEATHEN miserably destroyed God's church in Lindisfarne by rapine and slaughter." That single terse sentence in the Anglo-Saxon Chronicle for the year 793 marks the explosion of the Vikings into the mainstream of history.

The heathen who sacked that tidal island off Britain's east coast had sailed across the wintry sea in fragile ships with perilously little freeboard. They had come from misty reaches beyond the Christian pale, and outlandish heads of serpents and dragons glared from their ships' prows. Their feats of navigation astounded Europe; so did their barbarity.

"Never before," protested the scholar Alcuin, "has such a terror appeared in Britain." Those Vikings slew unarmed monks, looted sanctuaries of sacred ornaments and vestments, plundered libraries that preserved the

Viking raiders overtake lateen-rigged merchantmen in the Mediterranean; painting for National Geographic by Tom Lovell

literary legacies of the ancient world. What they could not carry off, they burned.

The Viking Age spanned 250 turbulent years—years of bloodshed, of discovery, of colonization; years of epic heroism, epic poetry, and epic tragedy. Years when Swedes, Danes, and Norwegians surged out of their frosty fastness at the top of Europe in a giant pincers that eventually encompassed the known world. Born merchants as well as warriors, they traded as often as they raided; and with increasing frequency as the age waned, they settled where they conquered.

Nor were they indifferent to the unknown world, these bearded giants who worshiped strange gods and avidly sought glory in death rather than peace in life. As their power waxed, so did the quality of their ships and their seamanship. In those simpler times, some thought that the gray mystery of the North Atlantic led only to a turmoil of monsters fringing the edge of the flat world. Right-minded mariners rarely ventured out of sight of land. Yet generations of Norse skippers pressed relentlessly toward the sunset. In that oceanic waste, they discovered and colonized the Orkneys, the Shetlands, the Faeroes, the Hebrides, Iceland, Greenland. And, just before the end of the first Christian millennium, adverse winds blew Greenland-bound Bjarni Herjulfsson past his destination. Before making his way back, he coasted a new land "well-wooded and with low hills"—America.

My own explorations of the Vikings' world led me from piney Newfoundland forests to windswept Caspian shores, from the long arctic nights of Iceland to the soft breezes of the Bosporus. And I found their faint traces—a runic inscription, a crumbled longhouse, a magnificently resurrected ship of war. I found too a spiritual heritage—common, to be sure, to all mankind, but perhaps best realized among the Norsemen. Once a Frankish messenger hailed a Viking band sailing up France's Eure River. "Who is your master?" he demanded.

"None," came the reply. "We are all equals."

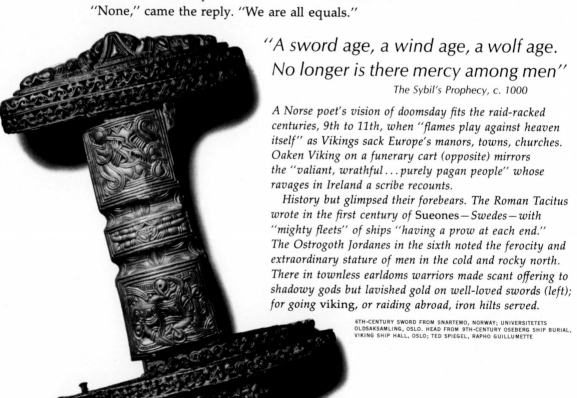

"A sword age, a wind age, a wolf age. No longer is there mercy among men"

The Sybil's Prophecy, c. 1000

A Norse poet's vision of doomsday fits the raid-racked centuries, 9th to 11th, when "flames play against heaven itself" as Vikings sack Europe's manors, towns, churches. Oaken Viking on a funerary cart (opposite) mirrors the "valiant, wrathful . . . purely pagan people" whose ravages in Ireland a scribe recounts.

History but glimpsed their forebears. The Roman Tacitus wrote in the first century of Sueones—Swedes—*with "mighty fleets" of ships "having a prow at each end." The Ostrogoth Jordanes in the sixth noted the ferocity and extraordinary stature of men in the cold and rocky north. There in townless earldoms warriors made scant offering to shadowy gods but lavished gold on well-loved swords (left); for going* viking, *or raiding abroad, iron hilts served.*

SEVEN SISTERS FALL *trails 1,500-foot veils into Norway's Geiranger Fjord.*
Farmers brave landslides to till ledges, tethering tots lest they fall off.
Goats trim sod roofs like those on Viking houses. Along such glacier-carved
clefts Vikings fished, farmed, cut timber in tune with seasons.
When land ran short, they sailed the sea fingers to fairer shores.

ANDREW H. BROWN, NATIONAL GEOGRAPHIC STAFF

THE VIKINGS SPRANG from a primitive society in which men lived by farming, hunting, and fishing. Norway's innumerable fjords, Sweden's network of lakes and streams, and Denmark's 500 islands had early turned their people seawards. An affinity for ships, in fact, marks every phase of the Scandinavians' history. When a Viking died, a ship bore him into the dark eternity of the burial mound.

Three sixth-century kings lie in huge man-made mounds at Gamla—or Old—Uppsala, royal seat of pagan Sweden; 300 smaller barrows arc toward the horizon. Visiting them, I saw children slamming down the snow-mantled mounds in red and yellow sleds. But there was no gaiety in the scene. Kings once burned here, and the smoke of the pyres seemed to linger in the air. Neither snow nor frolicking children can soften the stark, heathen grandeur of these tombs.

Near the royal mortuary I entered a grove surrounding Old Uppsala Church, remnant of a 12th-century cathedral built on the ruins of a pagan shrine. Inside had reigned Thor, mightiest of the gods; Odin, god of war; and the god Frey, source

RAIDERS' RETURN *brightens a misty morn as a Norse settlement pours out to welcome menfolk, beach ships, unload spoils. Stocky horses will haul heavy goods in a high-wheeled wagon over bumpy terrain; finely carved cart (below left) probably served as a ceremonial carriage.*

Joy and dread tug housewives' hearts. Some will mourn sons or mates this night while others stow bright booty in chests whose keys jingle at their belts. A Norse wife enjoyed rights her medieval sisters dreamed of; denied the family keys, she might divorce her husband. Many owned land, ran farms when men went viking. Brides had a say in choosing mates, kept maiden names, forged the bond—or sundered it— simply by telling witnesses. Women spun wool from distaffs under the arm, wove at stand-up looms, kneaded dough in troughs of wood their daughters know today (below).

Viking men, tough and ruthless, could give wives away, expose unwanted babes, have concubines and slave girls, claim a refund of the "bride price" if a wife walked out.

WOMAN OF BINDALSEIDET, NORWAY; TED SPIEGEL, RAPHO GUILLUMETTE. BEECH-AND-OAK CART FROM 9TH-CENTURY OSEBERG SHIP BURIAL, VIKING SHIP HALL, OSLO; MITTET FOTO. PAINTING FOR NATIONAL GEOGRAPHIC BY TOM LOVELL

73

VIKING SPORT *flourishes still on the Swedish isle of Gotland. Athletes hurl metal disks in* varpa, *a game like pitching horseshoes; Vikings tossed stone disks. Feasting and carousing livened the long, gloomy winter nights. An earl and his lady watch from the high seat (right) as two slave girls tussle; a prankster tries to quench their wrath with mead, fermented honey and water. Norse royalty had an awesome capacity for strong drink as well as a chilling propensity for finding death in the dregs of a cup. Sagas tell of four kings who perished violently after long stints at the drinking bench.*

74

of "peace and sensuous pleasures." Every nine years, an 11th-century historian related, the people flocked to a festival at Uppsala to witness "the slaughter of nine males of every creature, with whose blood the gods are placated. The bodies are hung in a grove near the temple." Strolling through the trees, I glanced up, half expecting to see the same grisly fruit silhouetted against the sky.

The ancient religion of the North held no promise of salvation. But if you died fighting, the warrior-maids called Valkyries would carry you to Valhalla to banquet on mead and pork until the distant day when the gods themselves fell in battle before the powers of darkness. Of all the desirable qualities a man might possess, luck ranked first. Some won renown for woman-luck or weapon-luck. A Norseman bent on raiding sought a chief famed for victory-luck. Priests were notorious for their lack of weather-luck. Even after Christianity came, crews hurled many a priestly passenger screaming into the sea at first sight of an ominous cloud.

The Vikings balanced their murky superstitions with a passion for poetry; no self-respecting king would make war without a complement of *skalds*—court poets —to memorialize his deeds. In the elaborate metaphorical style of the skalds a battle became "the reddening of spears"; blood was "wound-dew" and to slay enemies was "to feed the ravens" or "sate the eagles."

Pursued by thoughts of ringing epics and blood-reeking sacrifice, I left the grove of the old gods. From a window at the inn of Odinsborg—Odin's Fort—

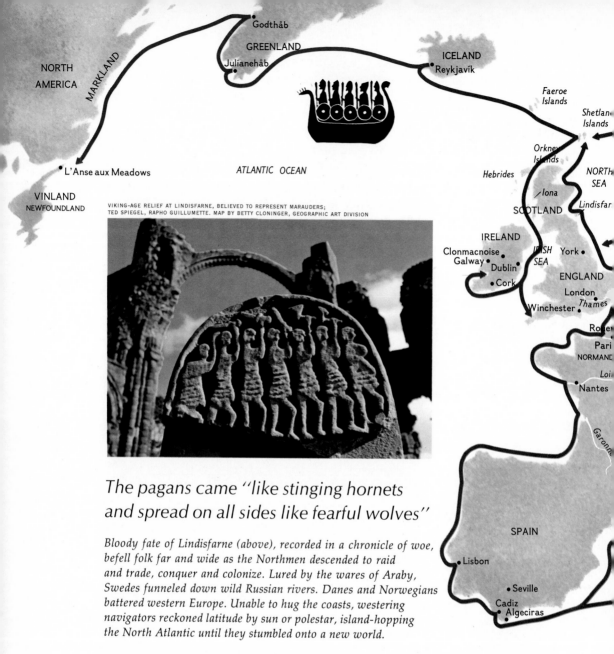

The pagans came "like stinging hornets and spread on all sides like fearful wolves"

Bloody fate of Lindisfarne (above), recorded in a chronicle of woe, befell folk far and wide as the Northmen descended to raid and trade, conquer and colonize. Lured by the wares of Araby, Swedes funneled down wild Russian rivers. Danes and Norwegians battered western Europe. Unable to hug the coasts, westering navigators reckoned latitude by sun or polestar, island-hopping the North Atlantic until they stumbled onto a new world.

I looked out across the sinister barrows of Gamla Uppsala and silently toasted the buried kings with a specialty of the house—a horn of foaming mead.

"Pre-viking scandinavia was a self-contained society," said Dr. Arne Emil Christensen, Jr., curator of the Museum of Antiquities in Oslo. "Swedes, Norwegians, and Danes shared a common language and culture, and knew little of the world outside. Just preceding the Viking Age, we find evidence of a population explosion—more burials, more place names. But the land couldn't support more people. So they took to their ships—the finest in the world at that time and for centuries to come—and solved the problem by raiding richer lands to the south."

As we entered the vaulted silence of the Viking Ship Hall, the serpent prow of the Oseberg ship sailed inexorably, miraculously out of the past. "Almost

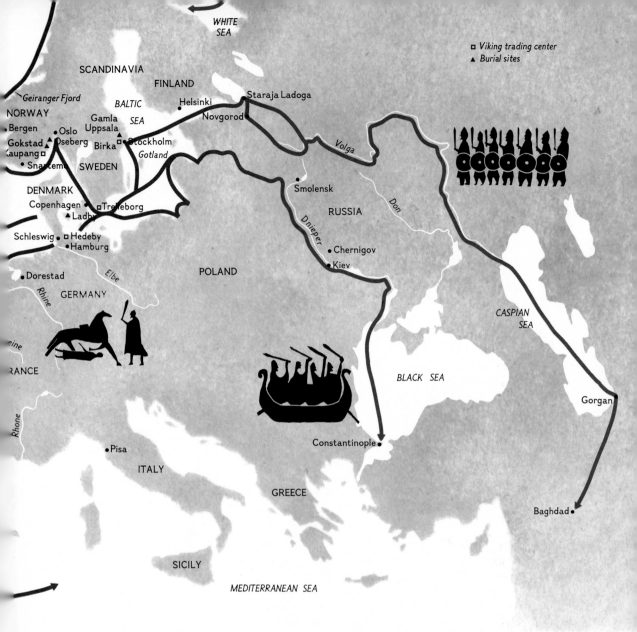

WHITE SEA

Viking trading center
▲ Burial sites

SCANDINAVIA

FINLAND

Geiranger Fjord

Staraja Ladoga

BALTIC SEA

Helsinki

NORWAY
Bergen
Gamla Uppsala
Oslo
Gokstad ▲ Oseberg
Birka ▲
Kaupang □
Stockholm
Gotland

Novgorod

Volga

Snartemo

SWEDEN

DENMARK

Copenhagen □Trelleborg
▲Ladby

Smolensk

RUSSIA

Don

Schleswig □ Hedeby
Hamburg

Dnieper

Chernigov
Kiev

Dorestad

Elbe

Rhine

GERMANY

POLAND

CASPIAN SEA

Seine

FRANCE

BLACK SEA

Gorgan

Rhone

Constantinople

Pisa

ITALY

GREECE

Baghdad

SICILY

MEDITERRANEAN SEA

certainly this was the type of vessel that raided Lindisfarne in 793," said Dr. Christensen. Nearby stood the less ornate Gokstad ship; both had served as sepulchers beside the Oslofjord. Built several generations later, the Gokstad was much more seaworthy, my companion explained. "The shipwright gave Gokstad's hull a more efficient shape, improved the mast, and added two feet of freeboard. All the strakes are of solid oak, naturally curved, and the grain runs with the curve. Planking and ribs are lashed together with whalebristle, giving the ship a tremendous flexibility in heavy seas. It's a classic."

Incredibly, the Viking art of boatbuilding survives. Beside a fjord in the Norwegian village of Lysekloster near Bergen, Alfred Søvik led me into his shop where piles of wood shavings curled shoulder-high against the walls. A gleaming, graceful boat lay on stocks—a virtual twin to the small boats dug up with the Gokstad,

PAINTING FOR NATIONAL GEOGRAPHIC BY TOM LOVELL

NORSE MARAUDERS WREAK MAYHEM *at Clonmacnoise, most celebrated of Irish monasteries. Scorning the cross, pagans hack holy men to death, defile sanctuaries, rob golden objects that made churches the treasuries of medieval Europe. Swift assault lets few reach haven in the round tower, its entry accessible only by ladder.*

St. Patrick had carried Christianity to Erin in the fifth century. Monasteries flourished; in the 6th century Irish monks settled at Iona off Scotland, whence sprang the center at Lindisfarne. In time Celtic outposts of piety and learning stretched from Iceland to the Danube.

even to the *steor,* or steering paddle, at the right rear that gave us our word "starboard." Straddling a plank, the gray-haired craftsman swung an ax in graceful, almost metronomic strokes, showing how he hews the naturally curved wood into its final, impeccably smooth shape.

In the Viking tradition, he uses no plans, relying on hand and eye to shape the exquisite shell. And his unit of measurement is the all-but-forgotten *alen* (about 21 inches) employed by Viking shipwrights. The art had been passed to Mr. Søvik by his forebears. But he has no son and cannot find an apprentice. What will happen after he retires, I asked. He smiled wryly. "After me—plastic."

THE BRITISH ISLES, with their moistly fertile fields, drew the land-starved Vikings like a lodestone. First came the Norwegians, doubling the hook of Scotland in their long-ships and scudding down the Irish Sea. They settled the Orkneys, the Shetlands, and the Hebrides. But Ireland was the goal of most, and there they ravaged without mercy. "The sea spewed forth floods of foreigners over Erin," reported the Annals of Ulster for 820.

By 845 the Norwegians held fortified harbors from Galway to Cork. They also founded one of the first towns known to Ireland—Dublin. The Gothic splendor of Dublin's Christ Church Cathedral looks down on the remains of the original settlement, found under 14 feet of debris.

Entering the dig, I noticed that the first streets had been constructed of planks, in the fashion of every Viking town ever uncovered. I looked at an irregular floor outlined by the remains of a wicker and mud daub wall, the home of a combmaker. Archeologists have found his combs and the antlers from which he carved them. Other workers in bone produced chessmen, dice, and whistles. Leather scraps in one of the jammed-together houses indicated a shoemaker's shop. Brooches and pins have turned up, even a mold for casting silver hammers—the symbol of Thor.

One searches in vain for any imprint of the Vikings on Irish life. A few family names hark back—Searson to

79

Sigurdsson and Sugrue to Siegfried—and two persistent folk beliefs: that the Vikings brewed the finest beer ever tasted in Erin, and that foxes are Viking dogs maliciously left behind when Brian Boru, High King of Ireland, drove their masters from the land in 1014.

In Iceland, by contrast, I found a nation whose people, alone among Scandinavians, still speak the Old Norse language of the Vikings. Locked in its medieval loneliness, Iceland immortalized the Viking Age in the sagas—one of the world's great literary forms. And here the Old Norse system of patronymics still lives. Consider a hypothetical example: When Halldora Benediksdottir marries Eirik Jonsson, she does not take his name; the marriage produces a boy, Bjorn Eiriksson, and a girl, Elin Eiriksdottir—four "family names" in a single household.

In the pitch darkness of 10 a.m. on a December day I called on Dr. Kristjan Eldjarn, famous historian and President of Iceland, in his office at Reykjavik. Icelanders, he told me, still fish and farm for a living, as they have since the Vikings first settled here around 875. "Nor has the structure of our community changed in any essential way," he continued. "You might recall that in the year 1000 the Althing—the legislative body of Iceland—adopted Christianity. It was a pagan, Thorgeir of Ljosavatn, who announced that all should be baptized. And all were. There was no bloodshed, no persecution. Icelanders are still just as devoted to democratic procedures."

In 835 Danish Vikings first appeared in force, raiding both sides of the English Channel. In France they sailed up the Loire and sacked Nantes, up the Seine to plunder

SAILING THE AGES, the Oseberg ship looms in Oslo's Viking Ship Hall. Serpent head rears from the stem, tail coils above the stern—a sublime work of art which served as sepulcher for a ninth-century Viking lady and her sacrificed slave.

Scholars believe that vessels like this carried the first raiders. Yet, for all her beauty, Oseberg reveals serious flaws. Scant freeboard left her vulnerable to swamping; towering stem and stern would make her unstable in high winds. But Viking shipwrights, most skilled of their age, soon hewed safer craft. By the year 1000 they had created a variety of shapes—long, swift vessels for war, squat cargo ships that could dare the oceans.

Boy Scouts of Jutland (above) row a replica of the keel-less Ladby ship, first Viking vessel found in Denmark. Eager to probe their heritage, Scouts built the ship, guided by experts who studied Ladby's fragments. The boys showed she could haul cattle and horses, and survive a buffeting by wind or wave. They also learned their forebears sailed as equals—Ladby had no special place for a chieftain.

Paris. The words of a chronicler echo down the centuries like a litany of dread: "Everywhere Christ's people are the victims of massacre. . . . They seize Bordeaux, Périgueux, Limoges, Angoulême, Toulouse; Angers, Tours, and Orléans are made deserts. . . . Rouen is laid waste. . . ."

In 859 a Viking fleet of 62 ships ranged south from its winter lair in the Loire, looting the Iberian coast and sacking Moorish Algeciras in the shadow of Gibraltar. Then, perhaps for the first time, the terrible dragon ships nosed into the Mediterranean, pillaging the North African littoral where the marauders captured the first Negroes—Vikings called them "blue men"—they had ever seen. In Italy they put Pisa to sword and brand, and one Arabic source indicates that they reached Alexandria. By the time the fleet returned to the Loire in 862, 40 ships had been lost; but the survivors of this epic voyage had gained wealth and glory.

By 900 little plunder remained along the French rivers. Nonetheless, a band of Danes led by a Norwegian named Hrolf—known to history as Rollo—ravaged what was left in the lower Seine Valley. In 911 the Frankish king, Charles the Simple, ceded to Hrolf and his raiders all the lands they then occupied. Their name, *Nordmanni,* passed to their newly won territory as Normandy.

Across the Channel, England felt the fullest Viking fury: London, Rochester, Canterbury, Winchester fell. Though King Alfred the Great saved England, he could not expel the Danes from the northeast, which became known as

"This is a lovely place and here I should like to make my home"
The Greenlanders' Saga

Norwegian archeologist Helge Ingstad strips sod and studies a time-warped nail at L'Anse aux Meadows in Newfoundland, first proven site of a Norse colony in America. Aided by the National Geographic Society, Dr. Ingstad unearthed artifacts and traces of longhouses dating from the Viking Age.

Sagas say Bjarni Herjulfsson first sighted the New World in 986. Leif Ericson explored it around 1000, delighted in its rich pastures, called it Vinland. Settlers came, but "Skraelings"— Eskimos or Indians—harried them with war clubs and stone-tipped arrows (opposite). Why did the colonies fail? "Simply because Viking weapons were no better than those of the natives," Dr. Ingstad told author Howard La Fay, "and the natives far outnumbered the newcomers."

83

the Danelaw. Legacies of the Danelaw still linger in England, in such Old Norse suffixes as -*by* (town), -*bec* (stream), and -*thorp* (hamlet). Driving through the old Danelaw one day, I passed towns called Skirpenbeck and Lumby. The following day I found myself in Normandy, visiting towns called Bolbec and Hambye. I had gone from one nation and language to another; yet where each shared a Viking ancestry, I found the place names virtually interchangeable.

When Viking raids intensified late in the tenth century, England's King Ethelred *Unraed* (usually mistranslated as the "Unready" rather than the true "Uncounseled") fatally erred; he pacified the raiders with the proceeds of a special tax—the Danegeld. Scenting easy treasure, Vikings poured into England. In 1009 a Norwegian fleet tore down London Bridge with grappling irons and plundered the fair valley beyond. By 1012 the English could endure no more. Ethelred fled. Four years later an able Dane, Knut (Canute), was consecrated king and eventually welded England and most of Scandinavia into a short-lived North Sea empire.

Historians theorize that England fell not in a series of haphazard campaigns but in a carefully organized war. The existence in Denmark of four strategically scattered military camps, all commanding vital waterways and dating from about 1000, lends weight to this theory. One of these, the excavated camp at Trelleborg, strikes the visitor like a sudden clang of arms. Primitive and powerful, an earthen bulwark more than 55 feet thick rises from the plain in a huge circle. My eye traced the outline of 16 long, boat-shaped barracks on the surface of the craterlike interior.

In the nearby fjord of Roskilde the Danes have salvaged five crushed, wave-worn Viking vessels, including an ocean-going *knarr*, or cargo ship—the first ever found. Archeologists believe the tubby ship, little more than 50 feet long, probably resembles the "wave-plungers" that colonized the New World. As I peered across the Schleifjord from the city of Schleswig, now in Germany, I wondered how many knarrs had knifed through these Baltic waters to moor at Hedeby across the way. I could see the 60-acre townsite protected by its earthen rampart, once a throbbing Viking mart where Slavs, Franks, Saxons, Celts, and even Arabs converged to barter slaves for silver, furs for silks, swords for amber.

W HILE DANES AND NORWEGIANS harried the fat and ill-defended coasts of western Europe, the Swedes thrust across the Baltic into the vast birch forests and steppes of Russia. Their ships plowed ever southward down the Volga and the Dnieper toward the wondrous marts of Baghdad and Byzantium. As they advanced they founded such cities as Smolensk and Chernigov. Most prized of their wares were fair slaves to trade for the silks and silver of the Orient.

The energetic Swedes swiftly gained supremacy over the native people, and in their principal northern trading center, Novgorod—which they called Holmgard— their leaders ruled as princes. Contemporary documents refer to these merchant-traders as the *Rus,* probably from the Finnish word for Sweden, *Ruotsi,* or Rowing Way. Eventually they gave their name to the entire country—Russia.

GLITTER OF A PAGAN AGE *reflects the brilliance of Viking smiths and carvers. Norse sites yielded golden brooches, festooned with filigree, that tied shoulder straps to buttonless dresses; silver bracelet, coiled gold serpent, tiny silver Valkyrie thrusting a drinking horn. Viking fancy formed an endless variety of "gripping beasts" like this amber bear hugging himself. Pop-eyed glass figurine roamed a gaming board.*

"Send me a merchant who will buy
... and ... not dispute anything I say"

Ibn Fadlan, 10th century

Viking prayers before a carved pole are swiftly
answered as Mongol and Persian caravaneers
arrive at a Volga River mart to haggle with
brawny Swedes over piled pelts and slave girls.

Skull of a sacrificial ox hangs at right. Easterners
pay with the bright silks of China, an ornate brazier
of Araby, and carefully weighed silver coins—so
highly treasured that Vikings hid them in hoards
in their homelands. To Arab chronicler Ibn Fadlan the
Northmen on the Volga seemed the "filthiest of God's
creatures," yet the most perfect physical specimens
he had seen—"tall as date palms, blond and ruddy."

In time Scandinavian power centered at Kiev on the Dnieper. From there, dragon fleets crossed the Black Sea in futile assaults on Constantinople. Impressed by the valor of the Rus, the Byzantine emperors recruited a special corps of Northmen for their army, the Varangian Guard. Many a runestone in Norway and Sweden mourns a warrior who *vard daudr i Grikkium*—died among the Greeks.

Kiev is now the third largest city in Russia and capital of the fertile Ukraine. Over glasses of tea one evening I discussed the city's early history with Professor Vassili Dovzhenok of the Ukraine's Academy of Sciences.

"It's notable that the early rulers of Kiev had Norse names," he told me, "but the names of the last and probably the greatest princes, Vladimir and Yaroslav, were Slavic. I think what is true of the Vikings in Kiev is true of the Vikings everywhere: in the end they were assimilated into the

SAINT VLADIMIR, prince of Kiev, guards the tranquil Dnieper and the city he Christianized. With Viking help, the pagan Vladimir in 980 gained the Russian realm Norse settlers had built; he butchered foes, kept some 800 concubines. Turning from human sacrifice, he studied faiths of his neighbors. Amid splendors of Constantinople's churches his envoys "no longer knew whether we were in heaven or on earth." Vladimir chose Byzantium's faith and the hand of its princess Anne.

The Byzantine heritage glimmers in Kiev's St. Sophia Cathedral (left), founded by Vladimir's son, Yaroslav the Wise.

TED SPIEGEL, RAPHO GUILLUMETTE

local population. Vladimir, however, who came to power in 980, most certainly determined the future course of the Russian nation."

Vladimir made Christianity the state religion. One report says he drove the entire population of Kiev into the Dnieper for mass baptism; a rear guard of soldiers clubbed reluctant converts to death. *Kreshatik,* or Christening, Street recalls the day when all Kiev followed it to the river to be baptized.

Under Yaroslav the Wise in the 11th century the Rus court attained its golden age. Yaroslav filled the treasury with the profits of the lively north-south trade. He took a Swedish princess to wife and his offspring became prized consorts for European royalty. So much so that Kievans grumbled at the shortage of brides: "Every European king marries a princess of Kiev."

*I*N THE TWILIGHT OF THE VIKING AGE one of Yaroslav's daughters caught the eye of the most ferocious, cultured, and vivid of the sea kings—Harald Sigurdsson, called Hardraada, or Hard Ruler. Harald was born into a northern world convulsed by chaos. War raged endlessly among the Scandinavian states. In Ireland the Celts

DRAGON SHIP SAILS *a sea of flame in the Shetland Islands'*
Up Helly Aa *festival, marking the end of Yuletide with
rites of the Vikings who colonized here.*

*On such a pyre many a Norseman voyaged to Valhalla;
some believed "the higher the smoke ... the higher would be
raised the man ... the more goods were burned with him,
the richer he would be." Scribe Ibn Fadlan saw one dead
Viking dressed in brocade and fur and set in his longship
with food, weapons, and sacrificed animals. While warriors
beat shields to drown the screams, an old woman—"the
Angel of Death"—stabbed a slave girl destined to share
her master's last journey. A torch touched the pyre,
a fearful wind blew, all burned to ash.*

*In Valhalla, a Valkyrie (right) offers drink to an arrival
who will fight beside Odin on* Ragnarok, the Last Day.

had brought a bloody end to Viking suzerainty over Dublin. With the collapse
of Knut's North Sea empire, Anglo-Saxon monarchs re-ascended the throne of
England. More effective armies had arisen in western Europe; no longer could a
harrying fleet expect to find unprotected coasts.

At 15 Harald was blooded in battle at the side of his half brother King Olaf,
fighting to regain the Norwegian throne. Severely wounded, Harald managed to
slip away to Russia where he found refuge in the glittering court of his kinsman
Yaroslav. There too he found the princess Yelisaveta. Harald fought valorously for
Yaroslav. But heroism and love could not win a princess; Yaroslav rejected the suit
of the throneless Norwegian. So Harald sailed down the Dnieper to fabled Constantinople, joined the Varangian Guard, and soon became its commander. For
11 years Harald wielded his sword for the empire, campaigning from Sicily to
Asia Minor, from the Caucasus to Palestine. A fearful figure, he towered almost
seven feet tall. His saga reports him as fair of hair and beard but "one eyebrow
was slightly higher than the other." He won incredible booty and, with it, Yelisaveta's hand. They sailed to Norway, where the combined thrust of Harald's gold
and personality brought him the crown in 1047.

In colors muted by a thousand years, three daughters of Yaroslav stare from a
mural in Kiev's Cathedral of St. Sophia. I looked at those royal maidens for a long
time. All have a certain loveliness. In the end it is Yelisaveta who lingers in the
memory—she of the wide, haunted eyes, the mouth touched by tragedy. Yelisaveta,
gentleborn but destined to live out her life amid the blood quarrels, primitive
wooden dwellings, and drunken, gluttonous revels of the North.

Within his kingdom Harald ruthlessly caused rivals to "kiss the thin lips of
the ax." On his longship *Dragon* Harald bore his banner *Land-Waster* throughout
Scandinavia, reddening spears, spilling wound-dew, feeding the ravens.

Then, in 1066, the "Thunderbolt of the North" turned his gaze on the greatest
prize of all—England, where Earl Harold Godwinson had seized the crown upon
the death of Edward the Confessor. William of Normandy laid claim to the throne,
but so did Harald of Norway. And in the autumn of that year, within the space
of three weeks, Harald Hardraada, the archetypal Viking, Harold Godwinson,
himself of half-Viking ancestry, and William, descendant of Vikings, fought two
climactic battles that determined the fate not only of England but of all Europe.

90

To capture a crown, a scion of Vikings brings England to her knees—
and into the mainstream of Europe. Kenneth M. Setton re-creates the
bloodstained panorama of 1066 as he journeys from Normandy,

TRACING WILLIAM
THE CONQUEROR

"LOOK AT ME WELL! I am still alive and by the grace of God I shall yet prove victor!" His harsh voice rising above the din of battle, William pushes back his helmet and bares his face to retreating troops who thought him slain. "Inflamed by his ardor," exults the warrior's chronicler, William of Poitiers, "the Normans then surrounded . . . their pursuers and rapidly cut them down so that not one escaped."

This episode marked the turning point of a blood-splashed October day nine centuries ago—a day which so changed the course of events that it is impossible to reckon our history without those few furious hours. For when darkness fell on Senlac Hill, near the seaside town of Hastings on the southeast coast of England, William, Duke of Normandy, had earned the lasting sobriquet of "Conqueror." And a flow of concepts began that would

The sight of William spurs Normans to victory at Hastings; detail from the Bayeux Tapestry, courtesy the city of Bayeux

influence men's lives for centuries to come. William's victory at Hastings made England once more a part of Europe, as it had not been since the better days of the Roman Empire. The Scandinavian influence on England began to give way to the political and cultural ideas of the Latin world. Besides feudalism and a new aristocracy, the Normans implanted in England much of their law, architecture, and social customs. Ultimately, the Conquest would affect the New World. Such terms as "justice," "liberty," and "sovereign" crossed the English Channel with William. Indeed, the Conquest left its mark forever on the language you are now reading.

To RELIVE THE EVENTS OF 1066, and to sense the forces and personalities that shaped them, I journeyed to that corner of France where William was born. I spanned the Atlantic in less time, and obviously with less peril, than William spent crossing the Channel. But he was making history; I was merely writing it.

I went first to Bayeux, where the Conquest is immortalized in the incomparable Bayeux Tapestry. Stitched shortly after William's victory at Hastings, it hangs now in the former bishop's palace across from the historic cathedral. On its 77 yards of embroidered linen the drama of the Conquest comes alive. Scanning every inch,

GEORGE F. MOBLEY, NATIONAL GEOGRAPHIC PHOTOGRAPHER. 11TH-CENTURY COIN FROM
SUSSEX ARCHAEOLOGICAL MUSEUM. PAINTING FOR NATIONAL GEOGRAPHIC BY BIRNEY LETTICK

I walked its length oblivious to the clamor of touring schoolchildren. Perhaps to them it appeared as an oversized cartoon strip—which, in fact, it was to the simple folk of the 11th century. I saw it as a masterwork of medieval artistry, an epic poem on linen. Its embroidered images would flash across my mind again and again as I followed the Conqueror's footsteps.

His heroic bronze figure on a horse greeted me at his birthplace, Falaise. Thrusting a bannered lance forward, it stands in the Place Guillaume le Conquérant and guards the approach to the restored ducal palace.

Here history rides on the wings of legend. The guide will show you the window from which the young duke of Normandy, Robert I "the Magnificent," first saw the fair Herleve, also known as Arlette, the daughter of a tanner. She was washing clothes in a stream. Another story relates that Robert met her while returning from the hunt. But there

JESTER, *juggler, and minstrel make William's meal merry in the ducal palace at Caen. Duchess Matilda enjoys the antics from the women's gallery as trenchermen feast on joints of pork and mutton, grilled fish, tasty pheasant, crusty bread. Knives and fingers serve as tools; forks will not appear until the close of the Middle Ages.*

Castle at Falaise (opposite) recalls the romance of William's birth. From an earlier citadel here, Duke Robert spied the lovely Herleve at the stream. In time she bore his child—the future conqueror of England, pictured on a silver penny struck by his Pevensey mint.

can be no doubt what happened next. A castle chamber is pointed out as the place where the girl spent her first night with Robert. William was the child of their union.

She was later married off to a viscount, to whom she bore two famous sons—Bishop Odo of Bayeux, who fought beside William at Hastings, and Count Robert of Mortain, who became one of the richest landholders in Britain.

Surely Clio, Muse of history, tries her hand at roulette. How else can we explain the fact that the illegitimate son of a tanner's daughter left an impress on England, and much of Europe, that has lasted to this day.

We know nothing of William's earliest years, probably spent at his mother's home in Falaise. He began his reign in 1035, at about seven, when Robert died while returning from a pilgrimage to Jerusalem. Before his departure Robert had prudently secured William's succession. But it was one thing to be recognized, another to rule. Even in peaceful times a boy was subject to the vagaries of guardianship.

In 1046, as William approached his majority, his cousin Guy of Burgundy led a large-scale revolt. Desperate, William appealed to his overlord, King Henry I of France—then little more than the region around Paris—who came to his vassal's aid the following year. At Val ès Dunes, southeast

APPLE BLOSSOM BEAUTY *veils the violent past of Normandy, named for the Northmen who ravaged the land, settled in it, and created the dynasty whence William emerged. Fat cows and lush orchards yield a bounty which Normandy transforms into creamy Camembert cheese and the fiery apple brandy called Calvados; amid the Perche hills breed sturdy Percherons, descended from steeds that carried Norman knights.*

Gothic spires (opposite) cap the Romanesque Abbaye aux Hommes in Caen, built by William to lift the ecclesiastical ban which fell upon his marriage, possibly because he and Matilda were distant cousins. Here his body lay until Huguenots in 1562 scattered his bones. Matilda's marker (lower) survives in the companion Abbaye aux Dames. Exhumed in 1961, her bones show she stood a petite four feet two. William, by contrast, appeared "great in body . . . but not ungainly."

96

of Caen, William first proved himself one of the century's greatest warriors. "Hurling himself upon his enemies," noted William of Poitiers, "he terrified them with slaughter...." So many were pushed into the Orne River that "the mills at Borbillon were stopped with corpses."

THROUGH NORMANDY'S green fields and pink orchards I traced William's struggles: Alençon, which he seized in a murderous night attack; Domfront, marked by the ruins of the fortress he besieged and by the little church where he heard Mass; Mortemer, where Normans defeated a royal army after William and King Henry had fallen out; Gerberoy, where in later years William would nearly lose his life against rebels led by his son Robert Curthose (short-hose).

About 1051 William married Matilda of Flanders, and his power grew rapidly. In 1063-64 he conquered the rich county of Maine, securing his southwest border. If his ascendancy was of recent origin, so were the wealth and position of the men around him, who replaced Norman rebels slain in the struggles that marked his rise.

Scarcely 150 years had passed since William's forebear Rollo and his Vikings had taken over lands along the lower Seine. When a weak king of the Franks recognized Rollo as count of Rouen, the title cloaked the raider with legitimacy and introduced him into the rough-hewn feudal system that was emerging amid the remnants of Charlemagne's empire.

Rollo accepted baptism and took on the obligations and rights of a royal vassal. His heirs expanded his holdings, won the title of duke, and sought to suppress the warring bands of lesser nobles. They rebuilt abbeys destroyed by their ancestors, and grateful churchmen helped them unify and administer the duchy.

The descendants of Rollo's Northmen became Normans, who spoke French, wrote Latin, and embraced Carolingian concepts of law. Yet they retained Viking vigor and independence of spirit. Their society remained fluid, mobile, adventurous. Not until William had imposed a feudal structure on England after 1066 was he emboldened to do the same in Normandy.

ALAIN PERCEVAL. OPPOSITE: PAINTING FOR NATIONAL GEOGRAPHIC BY BIRNEY LETTICK. MAP BY GEOGRAPHIC ART DIVISION

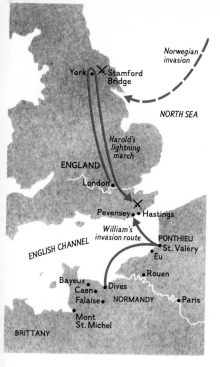

MEANWHILE, in England, events moved toward the climax of Hastings. King Edward the Confessor, born of the royal West-Saxon line, was pro-Norman, being related through his mother to the Norman duke. Opposing Edward was the powerful Saxon earl, Godwin of Wessex, who controlled most of southern England.

In 1051, when Earl Godwin and his sons revolted unsuccessfully, King Edward banished them. Childless, he named William of Normandy his heir.

But the rebels returned and drove out Edward's Norman supporters. England now felt the rising power of Godwin's son Harold, whose sister had married the Confessor.

According to chroniclers, Edward sent Harold Godwinson across the Channel, probably in 1064, to confirm William's right to the throne. Strong winds chanced to carry him to the coast of Ponthieu, whose count imprisoned him.

William secured his release and "sumptuously refreshed him," obligating him to support William's claim. The Bayeux Tapestry shows Harold swearing an oath of fealty to the duke, a grave impediment to his own royal aspirations. It also shows Harold on campaign with William, rescuing Norman soldiers from quicksands near Mont St. Michel.

Rivals for a crown trade wary glances at a peaceful parley

Harold of Wessex, his falcon signifying peace, and William, head shaved Norman fashion, meet in Ponthieu. Harold swore to support William's claim to England, even fought beside him near Mont St. Michel (opposite). But when King Edward died, Harold reneged, courting invasion by William and another rival, the king of Norway. Harold raced north to defeat the Norsemen near York, sapping the army he would lead against William.

Once a center of Druid rites, Mont St. Michel lured Christians with a chapel built in response to a visionary command of the Archangel Michael. In 966 a forebear of William founded an abbey at the seagirt shrine, whose inrushing tides killed many a pilgrim. Today a causeway funnels tourists to a concert of spires and turrets spanning nine centuries of French architecture.

Although I rescued no one, I did save my car there. Tourist buses crowded the causeway connecting the island shrine with the mainland; I had to park on the beach below. I had just started dinner when the sea began to rise rapidly. Outside, the wind blew so hard I could hardly stay on my feet. But, inspired by Harold's exploit, I drove the spray-drenched little Renault through a foot of water to the causeway. Just in time; 20 minutes later I saw four cars awash.

Edward the Confessor died on January 5, 1066. There were now three contenders for his crown—William, Harold Godwinson, and King Harald Hardraada of Norway, whose ambitions symbolized the ties which had bound Normandy, England, and Scandinavia for generations. Which would reign? Which would shape England's future?

Momentous questions these, and men did well to ponder the celestial meaning of the "star with hair" which suddenly appeared on April 24, 1066, and "shone for seven days with an exceeding brightness." It was Halley's Comet, a once-in-75-years visitor due to return in 1986. According to one chronicler, "many thought this portended a great change in some kingdom." They were right. On the very day of Edward's burial, Harold Godwinson was crowned king in the new abbey of Westminster. Whether by change of heart or under duress, Edward in the end, according to the Anglo-Saxon Chronicle, designated Harold his heir.

The quickness of Harold's act must have taken William by surprise, but the lords of Normandy soon pledged their support for an invasion of England. William secured the pope's censure of Harold for breaking his oath of fealty. He recruited his feudal levies from Normandy and his mercenaries from all parts of France, Flanders, and the Norman territories in southern Italy. He built a fleet and provisioned it. By August the ships had assembled at the mouth of the River Dives. In early September they sailed to St. Valéry sur Somme, whence an easterly wind could carry them to the south coast of England.

In St. Valéry, as in so many European cities, street names of today preserve the history of long-dead yesterdays. The Quai du Romerel derives its name from Rome Relais, meaning "the place where pilgrims stopped on the road to Rome." On this street my hotel, the Relais Guillaume de Normandie, stands where William moored his ships. Had I planned, like William, to cross the Channel by boat, I too should have had to wait. As my plane left Le Touquet, violent seas lashed the beaches.

WHILE NORTH WINDS held William at St. Valéry, and Harold Godwinson kept watch in London, startling news came that the Norwegian king Harald Hardraada had launched an invasion of northern England. Pushing up the Humber and the Ouse, he defeated the northern earls at Fulford on September 20, 1066, and occupied nearby York. Swiftly, Harold Godwinson marched north to meet this last Viking invasion of England. On September 25, he surprised and overwhelmed the Norwegians in the Battle of Stamford Bridge on the Derwent.

But the encounter weakened the English, and now came a greater foe.

Two days after Harold's victory the winds over the Channel shifted and the Normans set sail. "Thus with a favorable wind," says William of Poitiers, "they all reached Pevensey, and there without opposition they freely disembarked."

William raised a fortification at Pevensey, doubtless within the Roman walls, which then stood much closer to the sea. He pushed on to Hastings, which offered a safe anchorage, and there built another castle. *(Continued on page 121)*

Soon after the Battle of Hastings, deft hands stitched in color the dramatic events that led to William's triumph. The rhythm of life in a violent age pulses yet in this

Epic Tale in Tapestry

For nine centuries the Bayeux Tapestry has preserved the glory of the Norman Conquest of England and the drama of Harold of Wessex and William of Normandy.

Picture story for an unlettered public, this pageant on linen embroiders the Norman view that Harold Godwinson, having sworn to help William become king of England, had no right to accept the throne himself. His fall came in retribution for breaking that oath. The Anglo-Saxon Chronicle, however, states that King Edward "entrusted the realm . . . to Harold"—hence an English belief that the Saxon earl died defending his country against the "invader."

What were they like, these two great peoples the tapestry shows confronting each other? The chronicler William of Malmesbury, writing some 60 years after the Conquest, looked back and drew these portraits:

"The Normans . . . were at that time, as they are now, exceedingly particular in their dress, and delicate in their food, but not to excess. They are a race inured to war, and can hardly live without it, fierce in attacking their enemies, and when force fails, ready to use guile or to corrupt by bribery. . . . They weigh treason by its chance of success, and change their opinions for money. . . .

"The English at that time wore short garments, reaching to the mid-knee; they had their hair cropped, their beards shaven, their arms laden with gold bracelets, their skin adorned with punctured designs; they were wont to eat until they became surfeited and to drink until they were sick. These latter qualities they imparted to their conquerors. . . ."

The Old English, or Anglo-Saxon, society of Harold's day grew out of invasions by Germanic tribes from the North Sea coasts after Rome's legions abandoned Britain early in the fifth century. Called Saxons for their short sword, *seax*, these mercenaries and raiders became settlers, carving farms out of lowland forest. Briefly they were checked in the west by a Celtic chieftain later romanticized in legend as King Arthur. But soon the south of Britain was divided among West Saxons (Wessex), South Saxons (Sussex), and East Saxons (Essex).

The forest spirits that held these Saxons in thrall gave way before twin currents of Christianity—from Celtic monasteries on

Listening to a recorded commentary, Bayeux visitors witness William's fleet sailing for England; George F. Mobley, National Geographic photographer

101

the northern islands of Iona and Lindisfarne, and Roman missionaries that came to Kent City—Canterbury. The cross-fertilization produced an intellectual flowering in abbeys of Northumbria, illumined by the historical scholarship of the Venerable Bede.

Yet Germanic deities would live on in our days—Tiw (Tuesday), Woden (Wednesday), Thunor (Thursday), and Frig (Friday). And as petty Saxon kingdoms fought for supremacy, we hear men "smashing their shining swords, their bloody, hammer-forged blades onto boar-headed helmets, slashing and stabbing with the sharpest of points." For this is the warrior society of *Beowulf*, glorying in combat, prowess, loyalty to kin and chief.

Alfred of Wessex, greatest of Anglo-Saxon kings, loved to hear a minstrel sing such epics, a log fire casting shadows in the great hall as he and his men quaffed mead from horns.

Only Alfred succeeded in stemming the Danish tide that threatened to engulf England in the ninth century. But he could not drive it back far. The invaders settled behind a line roughly from the Thames estuary to modern Liverpool. Since Danish law and custom prevailed therein, all territory north of this line became known as the Danelaw.

Successive kings of Wessex conquered the Danelaw, but new incursions brought Canute, a Dane, to the throne of a united realm in 1016. England seemed locked within the Scandinavian sphere, for soon Canute also reigned over Denmark and Norway.

The portentous act that triggered the Norman Conquest: Harold Godwinson, crowned and enthroned at Westminster, holds orb and scepter

But when his line ended in 1042, the throne reverted to the West-Saxon dynasty with Edward the Confessor, whose concern about his successor opens the tapestry's tale.

Edward inherited a realm that combined features from the Danish north and the Saxon south. He kept the housecarls, Canute's bodyguard, as a standing army paid for by a special tax. The tapestry shows these professional household troops as the backbone of Harold's army. The Danish *jarl* became an earl, who controlled a major region, such as Godwin's earldom of Wessex. His deputy in each shire was the shire reeve, or sheriff. Below him stood the thanes, warrior nobles, each supported by an estate of five hides

The Raven and the Fox and other medieval fables decorate borders

Amid battle at Hastings, scavengers pull mail from the fallen

(farms), perhaps with a church, a kitchen, a bell house, and a gate. Unlike the Norman knight, the thane usually owned his land. One held 70 villages, most inherited from his father.

Peasants in the villages lived in wattle-and-daub cottages where the family cooked and slept in a single room. The three main classes were the churl, or freeman (who bore arms in the militia and could move up in rank if he acquired a five-hide estate); the serf, obliged to till his lord's land; and the slave. Crop failure might force a freeman to sell his family into slavery.

Leading thanes sat in the Witan, a council of bishops and nobles which advised the king and traditionally "elected" him. In practice, they accepted and acclaimed the person with obvious hereditary right—or power, as in the case of Harold (left).

The English tradition of rule by discussion and consent had its roots in local assemblies that administered "customary" law for the "hundred," originally a district that could support a hundred warriors. Men versed in local custom sat in the open with their reeve, or king's deputy, every four weeks to settle tax disputes, hear pleas, and bring charges against thieves—as well as those who had not been zealous enough in their pursuit. Kinsmen who failed to produce the accused paid fines.

Homicide could be paid for by a wergeld, or "man price," which went in compensation to kin or lord. A thane was worth six times more than a churl. A slave had no wergeld. A runaway slave could be stoned to death.

Courts in the Danelaw (and comparable

while nobles, archbishop, and populace acclaim him king of England.

Carolingian inquests) herald our modern jury. In each district the 12 leading thanes, swearing on relics that they would neither accuse the innocent nor protect the guilty, brought suspected lawbreakers to trial for God's judgment. Oath helpers could support a man's sworn innocence; often ordeal by fire or water determined guilt. If he held a red-hot iron without being burned, he was innocent. If he was thrown into a pond and floated, he was guilty—the water had rejected him. If he sank, he was innocent.

Not until the 12th and 13th centuries did regional law in all its variations give way to a uniform royal law, the "common law" shared by all Englishmen. Judgment by one's neighbors, similarly, came to supersede trial by compurgation, ordeal, or combat.

*L*ife in the countryside followed the rhythm of the seasons, changing little through the Anglo-Saxon centuries. Peasants tilled strips in the fields surrounding the village and from their collective labors paid a rent in produce to king or lord. Typical payment from a Wessex manor: 10 vats of honey, 300 loaves of bread, 42 ambers (casks) of ale, 10 wethers (sheep), 10 geese, 20 hens, 10 cheeses, an amber of butter, 5 salmon, 20 pounds of fodder, and 100 eels.

The tapestry reflects such husbandry. The only work of its kind to survive from this period, it presents a moving panorama of medieval life, often with a tree or tower ending an episode, a punctuating device tracing to classical and Carolingian times. Men plow and harrow, sow grain, shoot birds with a sling, work with block and tackle, wield hammer and adz. Norman ships knife the seas; single masted and high prowed, they hark back to Viking dragon ships.

Transporting some 3,000 horses across the English Channel was a monumental feat —but necessary, for William based his power on cavalry. The mailclad horseman had come into his own in Carolingian days, following the introduction of a heavy charger and the stirrup from the east. But it cost a lot to equip a mounted knight. Society had to be shaped to support a force of aristocrats in the saddle.

The knight's fee or fief linked the personal bonds of military feudalism to the economic base of the manor.

Harold's housecarls, in contrast, rode to Hastings on horseback but dismounted to fight on foot, as the tapestry shows. They favored the battle-ax introduced by the Danes, while William put lance, sword, and archer to telling effect on that "fatal day for England." He later subjugated his conquered realm by the Norman genius for castle building.

Whereas the Old English fortification had been the *burh*, a walled town or borough, the Norman's compact motte-and-bailey castle enabled a commander to hold a large tract of country with a small number of horsemen. The tapestry depicts several timber forts, each atop its motte, or mound, and with a cleated bridge spanning the moat to the bailey (an outer, palisaded court not shown). One of these castles is at Bayeux.

Long attributed to William's wife Matilda, the Bayeux Tapestry in fact was probably commissioned by his half brother, Bishop Odo of Bayeux, for display in the city's cathedral, consecrated only 11 years after Hastings. Although it is a Norman document, the style of the figures stitched in colored wools leads some scholars to believe that English hands from Canterbury made it. Odo was also earl of Kent.

The first specific mention of the tapestry comes in a 1476 inventory of Bayeux Cathedral. In 1792 French revolutionaries used it as a wagon cover until a local lawyer rescued it. Two years later it was almost cut up to decorate a festival float. Scholars believe two missing panels at the end may have portrayed William on England's throne.

To bring this priceless masterpiece to you, the National Geographic Society sent a team of color craftsmen to France. By permission of the mayor and the city of Bayeux, the glass casing was removed from the 231-foot-long tapestry so that Milton A. Ford and Victor R. Boswell, Jr., could achieve the finest reproductions of the work ever made. Now the tapestry stretches before you in its entirety—a magic carpet to waft you back to the stirring days of the Conquest.

On a bluff overlooking the pleasant seaside resort of Hastings, I explored the stone fortress that replaced William's wooden one. From here I roamed the countryside that he pillaged to encourage Harold to attack him. Lacking supplies, William could ill afford to let weeks pass without a trial of arms.

Harold rushed south, arriving in London about October 6 and setting out for Hastings on the 11th. He would have done well to avoid battle as long as he could. But inspired by the success of his tactics at Stamford Bridge, he wanted to surprise William and detach him from the Norman fleet at Hastings. He drove his tired army the 65 miles from London to the Sussex Downs in three days, reaching the ridge of Senlac, seven miles from Hastings, on Friday night, October 13. William of Poitiers notes that the English thus gained the higher ground; but Harold's men were exhausted and William's men too vigilant to be taken by surprise.

In the early morning hours of Saturday, October 14, William rode out of Hastings with some 7,000 men and made for Telham Hill. Across a valley on Senlac Hill stood the enemy, equal in number. England's fate hung in the balance.

To "THE TERRIBLE SOUND OF TRUMPETS" William advanced, bowmen in the van, followed by infantry in armor, and finally the mounted knights. Harold's soldiers formed a wall of shields, 600 yards long, 10 to 12 men deep.

William's left wing struck the Saxon line first, flinging spears and stones. Then the knights moved in, swords swinging. The shield wall held. Now the Norman left broke, exposing a flank. A rumor spread: William was dead.

Seeing his forces disintegrate, William rode into the midst of battle, pushed back his helmet, and rallied his men. Twice, says William of Poitiers, the Norman knights feigned retreat, then turned to cut down their pursuers. At last the English line weakened. William directed his archers to shoot high so that the arrows would plummet down on the heads of the English. At this point, apparently, Harold fell. It was four o'clock in the afternoon. "The bloodstained battleground was covered with the flower ... of England." William had triumphed.

William built Battle Abbey on the site of his victory. His church has long since disappeared, and children's laughter rang in my ears as I looked out upon the peaceful meadows where that carnage took place. But the scene is hallowed by one of history's greatest events, and my heart and mind were stirred.

In the weeks that followed Hastings, William received the submission of Sussex, Kent, and southern Hampshire. He cut a swath around London, then entered the city. On Christmas Day 1066, Archbishop Aldred of York "set the royal crown upon the duke's head" in the church of St. Peter — Westminster Abbey.

William's coronation filled my mind as I entered the abbey. The church of his time has been replaced by the beautiful structure we know today, final resting place of royalty and genius. Inside, determined shepherds kept flocks of tourists moving in a babel of English and foreign languages. I thought of that scene nine centuries ago when those at the coronation were asked, according to custom, whether they would accept William as their king.

Such a clamor of "yeas" broke out in English and French that the Norman cavalry stationed outside believed the English were assaulting William. Rashly loyal, they sought to draw off the supposed attackers by setting fire to nearby houses. In the turmoil, poor William received the crown but lost his audience.

PAINTING FOR NATIONAL GEOGRAPHIC BY TOM LOVELL. ABOVE: GEORGE F. MOBLEY, STAFF PHOTOGRAPHER

"Stand fast! Stand fast! . . . fear nothing, for if God please, we shall conquer"

With word and deed, William's half brother
Bishop Odo spurs his knights to crack the
Saxon shield wall. Astride a white horse,
he flails with a mace, good for bashing armor.
A cleric, he chose a weapon that "might
shed no blood." Few others felt such qualms;
blood drenched the field of Hastings on a day
England will never forget: October 14, 1066.

For most of that day Harold's line — tough
housecarls flanked by raw militia — held firm
"at the hoary apple tree" on Senlac Hill.
Norman arrows thudded into Saxon shields;
back flew axes, javelins, "stones fastened
to pieces of wood." William's determination
never wavered. "Thrice," says a chronicler,
"his horse fell . . . thrice he quickly avenged
the death of his steed." At last, fooled
by feigned retreats, showered by shafts aimed
in a high arc, hit again and again by cavalry,
the English sank to defeat.

On the site rose the town of Battle (above).
Railroad overpass marks William's command
post; Battle Abbey school at upper right
stands near the spot where Harold fell —
"unconquerable," wrote Churchill, "except
by death, which does not count in honour."

122

William spent most of 1067 in Normandy, returning to England in December to continue the subjugation of his kingdom. He besieged Exeter, gained Gloucester and Bristol. In 1068 he secured Warwick, Nottingham, and York, then swerved south to occupy Lincoln, Huntingdon, and Cambridge. When Danish raiders and hostile Yorkshiremen tried to destroy the Norman establishment north of the Humber in 1069, his "harrying of the North" was swift and terrible.

THE CONQUEST destroyed almost completely the old Anglo-Saxon nobility. Thus William was able to build in England a feudal state to his own liking. Land was the principal form of wealth, and with it he rewarded his followers. William held a fifth of the kingdom directly, the church a fourth, and he granted fewer than 200 Norman barons conditional tenure to estates confiscated from more than 4,000 Anglo-Saxon thanes. In return for their fiefs, the barons had to supply William with a set number of mounted soldiers. This provided William with an army of some 5,000 knights. At this time a knight was anyone, landholder or mercenary, who fought on horseback.

At first the barons maintained their knights from their own households, but this was expensive and troublesome. So they began to grant them sub-fiefs from which to support themselves. A vassal owed his lord armed service, attendance

at court, payments on special occasions; and he must get approval when he or his children contracted a marriage.

Thus grew the feudal pyramid that would characterize much of Europe—except that in Norman England it was capped with a strong king whose heavy demands for knight service from his barons gave him mastery of the military organization. To control his barons, William let them build castles only by his license and forbade private war.

Year after year William rushed back and forth across the Channel to meet crises. He was trying to weld duchy and kingdom into an Anglo-Norman state. But enemies encircled him: Scots, Flemings, Angevins, Bretons, and above all, the French. Misfortune dogged him. His son Robert Curthose revolted. He fell out with his arrogant half brother, Bishop Odo, now also earl of Kent. His Matilda died.

In 1085 William desperately needed money and assurance of the loyalty of his subjects. The Danes were planning another great invasion of England (which never came off).

GLEAMING AT THAMESIDE, *William's square White Tower (left center) haunts the capital he conquered. Entering London three months after Hastings, he granted it a charter it still cherishes; at the same time, he set a wooden citadel at the city's eastern edge. Here in 1078 Bishop Gundulph of Rochester, a skilled churchbuilder, began the classic Norman keep of white Caen stone, its walls 15 feet thick. The centuries added a battlemented maze of royal apartments, armory, dungeons and torture chambers, all known now as the Tower of London.*

Today amid the ghosts of kings and executioners, visitors gaze on crown jewels, weapons, and the lovely Chapel of St. John—which William would recognize instantly.

124

William customarily wore his crown three times a year, feasting with his magnates in Winchester at Easter, in Westminster at Pentecost, and in Gloucester at Christmas. That year in Gloucester, after "deep speech with his wise men," he decided to hold an inquest of the kingdom's landed resources for tax purposes. The result, the famous Domesday Book, would be the most remarkable statistical record ever produced in a medieval kingdom.

While the royal commissioners were going into every shire to gather the information, William traveled through southern England. At Salisbury in August 1086 he held a great court. The Anglo-Saxon Chronicle records that there came to him "all the people . . . of any account over all of England, whosoever's vassals they might be; and they all submitted to him and became his vassals, and swore oaths of allegiance to him. . . ." The proceeding was as unusual as the Domesday survey. Both acts strengthened the English monarchy.

WILLIAM SPENT his happiest days hunting, and in the England of today there is no more picturesque reminder of the Conquest than the New Forest. In Hampshire south of Salisbury he found tens of thousands of thinly settled acres which he took as a private preserve. Not satisfied, he "afforested"

125

additional areas by evicting some 2,000 men, women, and children. The Anglo-Saxon Chronicle states: "He preserved the harts and boars and loved the stags as much as if he were their father." As I drove through the New Forest, wild ponies ambled along the road, forcing many a car, including my own, to a stop.

In 1087 William, now 60 and heavy with fat, attacked and burned Mantes in a campaign against the French. As he rode through the debris, his horse stumbled, throwing him against the saddle and inflicting a fatal rupture.

Half a century later a chronicler represented the dying king as saying: "I tremble, my friends, when I reflect on [my] grievous sins. . . . I . . . am stained with rivers of blood. . . . I direct my treasure to be given to the churches and the poor. . . . I appoint no one my heir to the crown of England, but leave it to the disposal of the eternal Creator. . . . For I did not attain that high honor by hereditary right, but wrested it . . . in a desperate battle." William died near Rouen on September 9, 1087, after the great bell in Rouen's cathedral of St. Mary had struck Prime, the hour of sunrise. The hardships of his life were over, and so was my journey.

Despite his disclaimer, William had given his crown, scepter, and sword to a son, William Rufus (the Red). Rufus was succeeded as king by his younger brother Henry. It was during the long reigns of this first Henry and his grandson, Henry II, that the common law developed under which we live today.

One may wonder much about William, as I did, but of his greatness there can be no question. Great men and great nations supply the themes for great history. But history is the creative construct of the historian; it does not just happen.

REVOLT IN THE NORTH *woke William's wrath. "Like a ravening lion" he pounced on balky York, whose Shambles, old butchers' quarter (right), retains a medieval air. He slew thousands, laid waste the land. Corpses rotted by roadsides. "Barbarous homicide," Normans conceded—but Yorkshire quieted.*

William bought off invading Danes, repelled Welsh raiders, brought King Malcolm of Scotland to heel at Abernethy, near the River Tay (opposite). He dotted the realm with castles, most of wood, and manned them with vassals by fealty bound.

In 1086 tax-hungry William "sent his men over all England" to survey resources. The result, men later said, would match in comprehensiveness data kept for the Last Judgment; so they called it Domesday (Doomsday) Book. The dean of Exeter Cathedral scans the Exon Domesday report on southwestern shires (upper).

LITTLE SHAMBLES

SCOTLAND

Tay

Abernethy•

Newcastle-
on-Tyne

Durham

York

ENGLAND

WALES

Gloucester

Colchester

London

Thames

Salisbury

Canterbury

Winchester

Exeter

Pevensey

Hastings

■ WILLIAM'S CASTLES

The Conqueror had been generous to the church, and its "clerks" were generous to him. They extolled his accomplishments and so helped preserve his memory. It is as Master Wace reminds us in his rhymed chronicle of the Norman dukes:

> All things to nothingness descend,   Nor long shall any name resound
> Grow old and die and meet their end;   Beyond the grave, unless 't be found
> Man dies, iron rusts, wood goes decayed,   In some clerk's book; it is the pen
> Towers fall, walls crumble, roses fade....   Gives immortality to men.

We turn now to churchmen who recorded great deeds—and shaped them as well.

DAY OF RECKONING *for an English town: Holding a scroll, the sheriff details the wealth of his shire. While a monk records and a mounted knight keeps the king's peace, Domesday commissioners cluster in the shade. Foreshadowing our jury system, the kingdom-wide survey summoned jurors to give verdicts, or truthful statements. At the end, says a chronicle, "there was not one hide [about 80 acres of cropland] nor even ... an ox, cow, or swine that was not set down in the writ." William now had a base for a tax to replace the Danegeld, first levied for tribute to Danish raiders. Preserved in the Public Record Office in London, the two parchment volumes of the Domesday Book provide an incomparable picture of 11th-century England being reshaped by Norman nobles and clergy. Saxon nobility lay shattered, but life changed little for freeman or serf. If French echoed in the great hall, English prevailed in kitchen and cottage. In time English conquered the conquerors.*

PAINTING FOR NATIONAL GEOGRAPHIC BY BIRNEY LETTICK

By Urban T. Holmes

THE WORLD OF BERNARD OF CLAIRVAUX

HORTLY BEFORE EASTERTIDE in the year 1112, a band of young nobles streamed through the dark forests of Burgundy. Their leader was a handsome youth, slight, of middle height, with blond hair and large eyes that seemed to burn with a special passion. When the men reached Cîteaux, "a new monastery in a vast solitude, chiefly inhabited by wild beasts," they were questioned at length and then taken before Abbot Stephen Harding.

"What do you seek?" he asked according to ritual.

The young man with the blond hair fell prostrate.

"God's mercy, and yours. . . ."

The suppliant's name was Bernard. In time all Europe would know him as Bernard of Clairvaux, then as Saint Bernard. Driven by the love of Christ, endowed with a brilliant mind and a restless soul, he would shake the medieval world with his moral force, choose a pope and chastise kings, shape history with a sermon, and electrify common men with his vision of a warm and compassionate God.

His white-robed Cistercians would spread across Europe, pushing back the forests, creating pioneer farms, reforming and revitalizing a church troubled by heresy and laxness. Like Francis of Assisi, another great mystic, Bernard would reaffirm the power of faith in

Abbot with church and staff at La Bussière-sur-Ouche in Bernard's native Burgundy symbolizes the saint, founder of holy houses, shepherd of the faithful, "soul of his century"; Jonathan S. Blair

an age shaken by change and new ideas. In two men so different—one the stern reformer, the other a gentle mendicant—we see mirrored the religious aura that enveloped medieval man like the air he breathed. In the 12th century life was short, often cruel—a brief span between the dark mysteries of birth and death. Heaven and hell were real, and men worried much about their souls.

I STOOD on the castle hill above the Burgundian hamlet of Fontaine-lès-Dijon and looked down on its stone cottages. Perhaps 400 people. There could have been scarcely more when the third of their seven children was born here to the noble Tescelin and his wife Aleth. His home would have been a castle with a great hall and adjacent family room surrounded by a wall of sharpened pales.

Young Bernard would have watched his father ride off to battle as a loyal vassal

of the duke of Burgundy, and his brothers ride and hunt and trade hard blows in preparation for a warrior's life. But he was marked for the church by his mother and sent for schooling to the canons at Châtillon-sur-Seine some 40 miles away. There he studied the *trivium* (grammar, rhetoric, logic) and perhaps began the *quadrivium* (arithmetic, geometry, music theory, astronomy). He read a great deal, particularly in the Bible.

When he was about 16, his beloved mother Aleth fell ill with a deadly fever. The memory of her last hours—the family gathered around her bed, the chanting of the priests, her weakening responses—must have burned itself into

LIKE MONKS *marching to Mass, paired pillars pass the centuries in silence at Sénanque. Sited by Cistercians seeking God in lonely places, the 12th-century abbey graces an arid Provençal ravine.*

Around the cloister a monk spent silent hours in study and meditation. He sought communion with the Lord through a life of renunciation, interceding for mankind with praise and prayer. And within the green garth he might be laid to rest, shielded as in life from a sinful world.

WALTER MEAYERS EDWARDS, NATIONAL GEOGRAPHIC STAFF

"**HE WHO LABORS** as he prays lifts his heart
to God with his hands." Bernard's wisdom
guides a lay brother at Aiguebelle,
tending his flock in a field of Dauphiné.
For his fellows in choir (below) Bernard
urged: "Let the chant be full of gravity."
Cistercians worshiped and worked with a will,
believing idleness the enemy of the soul.
Their husbandry awed the medieval world;
wealth flowed to abbeys that had abjured it.

St. Benedict, rule-maker of monasticism,
laid a heavy burden on the keeper of stores:
He must display maturity, prudence,
and temperance. Tippling cellarer above
seems the exception that proves the rule.

his mind. Later, it was said, the saintly Aleth would appear to her son in visions. "Play the man," she would tell him, "Play the man. . . ."

For the next few years Bernard studied and enjoyed the company of his peers. When at the age of 21 he announced his intention to become a monk, few were surprised. Only the church offered an outlet for a man of contemplative bent.

Close to hand stood the great monastery of Cluny, which had burgeoned as a leader in monastic reform. Its magnificent abbey church, breathtaking today even in ruins, its splendid music and endless services, its many daughter houses flourishing across Europe, all attested to its fame and influence.

But Bernard chose instead the humble house at Cisteus, now Cîteaux, founded not long before among the reeds—cistels—of the Saone River. In this wilderness half-starved Cistercians struggled to live and worship God in accord with the austere discipline of the sixth-century Rule of St. Benedict. "I was conscious," wrote Bernard, "that my weak character needed a strong medicine."

When friends and family tried to dissuade him, his zeal, magnetism, and eloquence converted them; 30 young men, including four of his brothers, accompanied him to Cîteaux. Some left wives. His father and youngest brother would follow later.

With the "White Monks" Bernard found the medicine he sought. "They wear nothing made with furs or linen," noted the chronicler William of Malmesbury,

"neither breeches, unless when sent on a journey, which at their return they wash and give back. They have two tunics with cowls, but no additional garment in winter. . . . They sleep clad and girded, and never after matins return to their beds." Meals consisted of two dishes and only the sick ate meat. "They never leave the cloister but for the purpose of labor, nor do they ever speak . . . save only to the abbot or prior." On such austerity Bernard thrived; in 1115 he was chosen to lead a dozen Cistercians to found a new monastery at Clairvaux in Champagne. They raised a shelter and slept on the floor; the abbot enjoyed no privileges.

The monks ate what they could find, beech leaves, vetch, roots. Bernard welcomed the harsh life, but the wretched diet almost killed him. He developed a painful gastric complaint, perhaps an ulcer. One story has it that he had a hole dug beside his abbot's chair because of his frequent need to vomit. Once, it is said, he was so absorbed in his adoration of Christ and the Virgin that he drank a cup of lamp oil, thinking it water — and never noticed the difference.

But Bernard's driving zeal could not be cloistered: "Nothing that concerns the glory of God is a matter of indifference to me." He began to pour out the hundreds of letters that would propel him to Europe's center stage.

ｈE NURTURED a grim disapproval for the black-robed monks of Cluny. It erupts in a letter written after his young cousin Robert was enticed from Clairvaux by the Cluniacs. "Everyone made merry over him as though they were victors dividing the booty. O good Jesus, what a lot of trouble was taken for the ruin of one poor little soul!" He deplored the luxurious life at Cluny: "Does salvation rest rather in soft raiment and high living than in frugal fare and moderate clothing? If warm and comfortable furs, if fine and precious cloth, if long sleeves and ample hoods, if dainty coverlets and soft woolen shirts make a saint, why do

SERMONS IN STONE *impressed on unlettered men lessons from Scriptures they could not read. At Autun, they gaped at Judas's fate (right). Demons yank ropes as the Betrayer screams his last; the pay for his perfidy dangles in a round purse.*

Hearts swelled at the scene opposite: Mary hugging her Babe on the Flight into Egypt. The troubled saw in her a tender, approachable link to an awesome God. Fostered by Bernard, her cult grew. France dedicated nearly every church to Notre Dame. Itinerant sculptors adorned many, often in anonymity. Not so at Autun: "This is the work of Gislebertus," proclaims an inscription.

Bernard decried sumptuous decor as vanity. "The church clothes her stones in gold and leaves her sons naked."

CARVINGS BY GISLEBERTUS ON CAPITALS OF 12TH-CENTURY
ST. LAZARUS CHURCH IN AUTUN, BURGUNDY; YAN AND (OPPOSITE) ZODIAQUE

In a Rule that guided Bernard, St. Benedict sought
"some degree of goodness in life and a beginning of holiness"

*A*s wealth turned monasteries toward luxury, reformers like Bernard yearned for the rigor and simplicity of the Rule of St. Benedict, compiled in the sixth century and still a model today.

Born at Nursia (today Norcia) in central Italy, Benedict saw a world brutalized by barbarians, Christianity torn by schism. Monks roamed, obedient only to their whims. At 20 Benedict quit his studies and fled Rome for a cave in a cliff near ruins of a villa where Nero once frolicked. For three years he prayed and meditated, garbed in a hair shirt and fed by a friend who lowered bread in a basket.

Time changed Benedict's mind. Turning his back on a hermit's life, he banded his disciples into a community where they could learn together "how to fight against the devil." They settled atop Monte Cassino (right) and there he wrote the Rule. Wars becloud the mount's history; in 1944 Allied airmen left the monastery in rubble. But a new one rose to crown the Benedictine Order.

In a medieval illumination (above) the monastery looms behind Benedict and Abbot Desiderius (still living when portrayed, hence the square halo).

Benedict's book symbolizes the Rule that helped calm a violent age, gave dignity to labor and respect to learning. A sampling from it mirrors a stern yet compassionate shepherd, wanting only "to do now what may profit us for eternity":

Let no one presume . . . to have anything as his own . . . for monks should not have even their bodies and wills at their own disposal.

Monks should practice silence at all times.

[A monk] should always have his head bowed and his eyes downcast, pondering always the guilt of his sins.

Let monks . . . bear with the greatest patience one another's infirmities, whether of body or character.

Wine is no drink for monks; but since nowadays monks cannot be persuaded of this, let us at least agree upon this, to drink temperately and not to satiety.

Let the use of baths be afforded to the sick . . . but to the healthy . . . let them be granted seldom.

In administering correction, let [the abbot] act with prudent moderation, lest being too zealous in removing the rust he break the vessel.

And let the abbot realize that the shepherd will have to answer for any lack of profit which the Father of the family may discover in his sheep.

138

I delay and not follow you at once? But these things are comforts for the weak. . . . Wine and white bread . . . benefit the body not the soul. The soul is not fattened out of frying pans!" In another attack on his Benedictine rivals one passage seems almost wistful as the pain-wracked abbot lashes out against Cluniac cuisine: "Who may tell of the eggs alone, in how many ways they are tossed and vexed, how busily they are turned and turned again, beaten to froth or hard-boiled or minced, now fried and now baked, now stuffed and now mixed. . . ?"

He turned furiously on the "vast height of your churches, their immoderate length, their superfluous breadth, the costly polishings, the curious carvings and paintings which attract the worshiper's gaze and hinder his attention." As for their Romanesque sculpture, "To what purpose are those unclean apes, those fierce lions . . . those fighting knights, those hunters winding their horns? . . . For God's sake, if men are not ashamed of these follies, why at least do they not shrink from the expense?" Though the centuries would bring change, Cistercians of Bernard's time shunned even stone belfries and stained glass.

Bernard's eloquent fervor touched the heart of the famed Abbot Suger of the royal abbey of St. Denis, near Paris. Though Suger continued to embellish his church with gorgeous glass and precious ornaments, he gave up his many fine horses and splendid livery, traded his spacious house for a cell so small that "men were amazed," and made his monks follow suit. The severe Cistercians acquired a certain glamor. They were, according to Marie de France, writer of lays and fables, "closest to heaven." Zealous young recruits hammered on the doors of their monasteries. Monks from other orders deserted to Clairvaux. Bernard wrote to their abbots, defending the monks or sending them back with appeals "to your loving heart for this little sheep of yours who has strayed from the fold."

Bernard, the "hawk of Rome," never hesitated to address himself to the great and powerful in defense of God's establishment. When the cardinals split into factions in 1130 and chose two popes in irregular elections, this clearly endangered Christian unity. Scandalized, Bernard plunged into the dispute, supporting Innocent II as pious and morally worthy and castigating the rival Anacletus II, a clever politician who had once been a monk at Cluny.

"We all expect your support," he wrote the archbishop of Tours, "late though it may be.... We do not blame your slowness, because it savors of gravity.... But I ... who am your friend say to you: 'Do not try to be more wise than it behooves you to be wise.'" France quickly backed Innocent, but Henry I of England hesitated. Confronting him on the Continent, Bernard asked, "Is it that you are afraid of sinning by submitting to Innocent? Just think of your other sins and leave this one to me." Henry submitted at Chartres.

The conflict ended with Anacletus's death in 1138. But the ascetic abbot with the blistering pen would never again find the seclusion he so desired. "I am forced to move in affairs that trouble the peace of my soul," he wrote his brethren at Clairvaux, "and are not perhaps very compatible with my vocation." He traveled widely now, arbitrating disputes between Louis VII of France and his vassals, or between the maritime cities of Genoa and Pisa. He drafted a rule for the Knights Templars similar to that of St. Benedict; they would follow a monastic way of life but with their swords defend the Christian states established in the First Crusade.

Common folk saw him as a saint in his own lifetime, a maker of miracles, and trekked to Clairvaux to be healed by his touch. His visage now appeared "pale, emaciated ... almost ethereal ... so impressive that the mere sight of him convinced his hearers before he had even opened his mouth."

BERNARD TAUGHT that physical love, natural to man, can be transformed into a saving love, a passion for Christ. Men must first know themselves, then progress with humility and charity to a knowledge of God, and finally—their physical nature disciplined—they would achieve union with the Spirit of God. Excited by the warmth and emotion of his faith, men would drop to their knees and exult with him, "My God, my Love, how You love me!"

Bernard would tolerate no challenge to that faith, even by the keenest intellect of the day: "Read, if you please, that book of Peter Abelard which he calls a book of theology.... See what sort of things he says there about the Holy Trinity."

Abelard jolted his age by questioning ideas long taken for granted. As a student in Paris he had plunged into the conflict over universals, a debate with roots in Plato and Aristotle. Are the things we see every day, like a chair or a dog, only imperfect copies of perfect, universal models that exist in the mind of God? "Realists" held that individual things perished, thus reality lay in the universal models. "Nominalists" said that a universal model was merely a *nomen*, or name; reality lay in the chair. Abelard attacked both *(Continued on page 149)*

Above the world's din men still hear, as Bernard heard,
the hallowed harmony, the promise of inner peace in

The Call of the Cloister

The Cistercian way offers "a model for all monks, a mirror for the diligent, a spur to the indolent"

William of Malmesbury

Bells toll the canonical hours at Aiguebelle, an abbey in southeastern France that Bernard visited. Three hours before dawn the pealing of Vigils, or Matins, seems to echo the words of St. Benedict: "Up with us . . . for the Scripture arouseth us."

In the centuries since Bernard, Cistercians have known decline, persecution, and the temptations of affluence. But today, once again, the abbot of Clairvaux would feel at home among his spiritual descendants, called Trappists after the 17th-century revival of the order at La Trappe in Normandy. Toil, prayer, and penance fill their lives.

In deepest night they quit their hard pallets, mindful of Benedict's holy Rule: "When they rise for the Work of God, let them gently encourage one another, on account of the excuses to which the sleepy are addicted." From the austere dorter, or dormitory, they troop to the church to chant the Night Office.

All through the day bells summon the silent brethren to worship—at daybreak, and three, six, nine hours later: Lauds, Tierce, Sext, None. Toward evening come Vespers. With nightfall Compline completes the day. Before the majestic tones of Gregorian chant have died away, the monks have prayed for the six hours of sleep ahead: "From all ill dreams defend our eyes. . . ."

A little bread and coffee serve for breakfast. Midday sends monks to a meatless dinner (opposite) where the Rule says "there should not fail to be reading. . . . And let there be the greatest silence, so that . . . no voice but the reader's may be heard there."

Cooks no longer rotate. It was more practical, wrote Thomas Merton, a modern Cistercian writer, "as well as more merciful to make this . . . important office a more permanent appointment."

Often the brethren gather in the chapter house (next facing pages) to hear a chapter

"The fifth degree of humility is that he humbly confess...." Rule of St. Benedict

from the Rule so that none "may excuse himself on the ground of ignorance." The abbot, in his central chair, hears admissions of Rule breaking and leads discussions of the community's affairs.

At confession (left) a monk shares the burdens of his soul with a priest. Surely Trappists have little to confess; sin must wither in such antiseptic soil.

Morning and afternoon, monks work in field and shop, for Benedict saw sloth as sin. The fruits of pious labor have spread beyond the cloister. To a 16th-century Benedictine dabbling with medicinal elixirs, we owe Bénédictine liqueur. Each bottle bears the initials D.O.M., *Deo Optimo Maximo*—To God, most good, most great. Cistercians in America sell their excellent bread and cheeses.

A Cistercian's day includes hours of solitary study and meditation, often in the scriptorium, or library (below). In such chambers medieval monks copied holy texts, encouraged by Bernard: "Every word that you write is a blow that smites the devil." Today typewriters have joined the battle.

Each day these quiet men who have given themselves to God join together at Mass (opposite) to relive the sacrifice of Christ, Who gave Himself to mankind.

WALTER MEAYERS EDWARDS, NATIONAL GEOGRAPHIC STAFF (ALSO OVERLEAF)

camps with his dialectical rapier. The universal and the individual both exist, he proclaimed; our concept of chair derives from our study of individual chairs.

Abelard's great sin, in Bernard's view, was to apply this hot light of reason to matters of faith. "He defines faith as private judgment," Bernard fumed, "as though . . . the mysteries of our faith were to hang uncertainly in the midst of . . . varying opinion. Is not our hope baseless if our faith is subject to inquiry?" Abelard, proud, pushy, confident, demanded a confrontation.

On a May day in 1140 eager spectators crowded Sens, where a great cathedral was slowly rising in Gothic splendor, to see the hawk of Rome meet the Aristotle of Paris. Ranged on one side were bishops and abbots; across from them, Louis VII with his magnates and barons. Bernard rose, a gaunt figure in a plain white habit, and swiftly read out the passages he considered damning. His overpowering attack swept away any thought of debate.

Stunned, the scholar protested: "I refuse to be judged thus like a guilty clerk. I appeal to Rome." On the way there he learned that the pope had condemned his teachings and ordered him to a monastery. A year later he fell ill, but before he died Bernard is said to have visited him and exchanged a kiss of peace.

Bernard's letters hounded Arnold of Brescia, Abelard's pupil, from land to land: "The enemy of Christ. . . . His tongue is a sharp sword, his words are more sweet than oil, but in reality they are death." Arnold also was condemned, and in time hanged and burned. To Bernard and other church leaders heretical teaching threatened men's everlasting souls and could not be met with compromise.

IF I COULD ASK Bernard what he considered the crowning event of his life, he probably would answer (with a certain brusqueness, perhaps, for so foolish a question) that it came in 1146 on the hillside at Vézelay, below the wonderful Romanesque basilica that still stands. There, with Louis VII at his side, Bernard spoke fiery words in a sermon that launched the Second Crusade. I can visualize the great throng, spellbound as he preached, then surging forward, crying out for the cross, badge of the Crusader. So many came that the supply of cloth gave out, and Bernard cut up his own habit to meet the need.

For a year Bernard traveled, preached, and wrote letters to stir up support. When a renegade Cistercian monk found in the Crusade an excuse to persecute Jews in the Rhineland, Bernard denounced his "hellish wisdom," tracked him down, and forced him to return to the cloister. In 1147 Louis and Conrad III of Germany led thousands to the Holy Land. The Crusaders marched from disaster to disaster; some were captured, some forced to embrace Islam. What terrible irony that the Moslem sons of the Second Crusaders may have fought against their own cousins in the Third Crusade a generation later.

One of Bernard's letters reveals the temper of these days of defeat. Returning Crusaders, he complains, are again planning "those accursed tournaments," and two nobles "have agreed regardless of all law to attack and slay each other. Notice with what sort of dispositions they must have taken the road to Jerusalem when they return in this frame of mind!"

Lectio divina, *spiritual reading, absorbs a monk between work and prayer;*
Walter Meayers Edwards, National Geographic Staff

Bernard sought yet another crusade, but for once the people and the nobles balked. "Go milk cranes," a wag admonished him.

His prestige shaken, Bernard retired to live his last months as a simple monk. "The only sort of pleasure I have is in eating nothing," he wrote. "So that suffering may never be absent from me, even sleep has left me." According to custom, a mat was placed on the ground at Clairvaux for the abbot to lie on as his hour neared. In August 1153 the voice of the "Mellifluous Doctor" was stilled.

A prison stands today on the site of Bernard's beloved abbey of Clairvaux. Lines of trees mark the old abbey church; a cellblock covers the cloister. But at the mother house at Cîteaux, some 70 monks yet worship and labor. For me it was a stirring experience to see this great house still occupied, still used as it was intended. I thought of the young man who came here so long ago. When

PALACE OF THE POPES, by the Rhone at Avignon, recalls the "Babylonian Captivity" of the church.

Locked in a struggle for supremacy with emperors, the medieval church was very much of this world. It was the chief landlord of the age. Its bishops were territorial magnates as well as spiritual lords; the investiture controversy raged over whether king or pope should choose them. Its tax on every household—Peter's Pence—extracted coin from kingly realms. Papal power reached its pinnacle under reformers Gregory VII (1073-85) and Innocent III (1198-1216), who excommunicated and humbled the greatest princes in Christendom.

The nadir came when pontiffs became puppets of the rising French monarchy. French-born Clement V moved here to Avignon in 1309. Clement VI (holding St. Peter's keys and taking the tiara at left) drained papal coffers sending crusaders to Smyrna (now Izmir, Turkey) and embellishing Avignon. A return to Rome spawned the Great Schism in 1378. Rivals, hurling anathema at each other, claimed the papacy. In 1417 a council restored unity.

Threats to "God's business"—heresy or schism—brought Bernard sallying from his cloister. "There is only one church," he maintained, "the ark in which lies the salvation of the world."

he joined, there was only one Cistercian house; at his death there were 343. He had led the White Monks to greatness and strengthened the church for the conflicts ahead. Strength of a subtler kind would come soon from a vastly different saint.

THERE APPEARED before Pope Innocent III in 1210 a young man of Assisi, Giovanni Francesco Bernardone, son of a wool merchant. He was "of more than middle height," with a "delicate and kindly face, black eyes, a soft and sonorous voice." He proposed something revolutionary: a brotherhood of monks who would live in absolute poverty and seek their salvation not in the cloister but

GENTLE FRANCIS OF ASSISI,
renouncing earthly riches,
sheds even his clothes (above)
to wed "Lady Poverty."
A friend stays Francis' father,
enraged when his son sold cloth
from their warehouse to repair
the Church of St. Damian.

Turning from happy-go-lucky
days of his youth in Italy,
Francis created a brotherhood
to pursue the pure life of the
Gospels. But his Friars Minor
(Francis hoped his brothers
would "always be less than all
others") followed a path far
different from that of Bernard.

Where Cistercians gathered
in silent, regulated abbeys,
Francis and his mendicant band
roved the countryside singing,
begging, working at whatever
tasks came to hand.

Bernard debated with kings
and prelates; Francis preached
to simple folk, even urged
"my little brethren birds" (left)
to love God, for "ye do not
sow, neither do ye reap,
yet He keeps and feeds you."

His humility, his innocent
love of all creatures, cast a
glow across the centuries whose
radiance warms mankind yet.

in town squares and highroads, preaching and tending the sick. Pope Innocent, strongest of medieval pontiffs, was a pious man, but also tough and realistic. He had heard much about Francis, and much of it was disturbing. . . .

Francis was born in his father's house, close by the Piazza del Comune. He received some Latin schooling but became more familiar with the romantic songs of the French troubadours. His father did business over the Alps and doubtless had many visitors from France. The tales of chivalry and fair damsels deeply impressed Francis. When in 1202 the men of Assisi rode forth to battle the men of Perugia in ancient dispute, Francis rode with them, an elegant young man "of knightly manners." Assisi took a fearful beating, according to a poet's account:

Fallen are the Lords of Assisi, and their limbs are all mangled,
Torn apart and defaced, so their own cannot know them;
There is no head where the foot is, the entrails are scattered,
The eye no longer looks from the socket, its one-time window.

Francis survived the carnage and was imprisoned for a year. Long after, he would still remark "how much wrong that the men of Perugia did to the men of Assisi."

But he regained heart and rode forth once again to a new war in Apulia. Just before leaving, however, he gave his fine coat of mail to a poor soldier. Then on the first night out he had a vision, and he returned to Assisi a changed man. He made a pilgrimage to Rome, later began to care for lepers.

153

When a voice told him to repair "my house, which is falling down," he obeyed literally. Using funds from the sale of his father's cloth, he began to repair three churches at Assisi: St. Damian's, where he heard the voice, St. Peter's, and the tiny Santa Maria della Porziuncola. The task would take him three years.

His father was so distressed that he kept Francis chained up for a time. Finally, Francis went before the bishop and denounced his parent, claiming in his place "the Father who is in heaven." He gave up all he possessed, even the clothes on his back. He wandered now, praying, meditating, uncertain of his mission.

One day in the Porziuncola he heard a priest reading from Matthew 10: "And as ye go, preach, saying, The kingdom of heaven is at hand. . . . Provide neither gold, nor silver, nor brass in your purses, nor scrip for your journey, neither two coats, neither shoes, nor yet staves. . . ." In these words Francis found his vocation. He

154

BUTTRESSED BY FAITH, *Assisi lifts men's eyes into the hills of Umbria. Here Francis began his days, and here his tomb rests in the massive Basilica and Convent of St. Francis (left foreground). Basilica of St. Mary of the Angels (below) enshrines the Porziuncola, "little portion," tiny sanctuary where he welcomed the noblewoman Clare, locks shorn in renunciation. He helped found her order, the Poor Clares, in the Church of St. Damian, where he had hearkened to the voice of God. Its garden (lower) keeps green the memory of Francis' delight in nature.*

JONATHAN S. BLAIR

AGELESS ASSISI *preserves its tranquil face behind a veil of modernity. Street lamps bathe stones in harmony with the quiet garb of Francis' friars. Auto lights reflect in winding streets* il santo *might have trod. Souvenir shops and snack bars serve a sea of pilgrims who read his timeless message in the shrines.*

Like the wild creatures that flocked fearlessly about him, a snowy dove flies into the saint's arms (above) in a corridor of the Basilica of St. Mary of the Angels. Legend blooms anew in roses from a bower nearby. There he hurled himself naked into thorny rosebushes when Satan tempted him with pleasures of the flesh.

Now the bushes grow thornless, and on leaves splashed with red the faithful see the stain of blood from one of the most beloved saints.

cast off his sandals, discarded purse and staff, and began to preach. Soon others joined him, their uniform the simple dress of the peasant—a loose, undyed wool cloak with a protective hood and a belt of cord.

When Francis sought Rome's blessing for his brotherhood, Pope Innocent hesitated. Then the cardinal-bishop of Sabina counseled: "If we reject the petition of this poor man as something novel . . . when all he asks is that the law of life of the Gospel be confirmed to him, let us beware lest we offend against the Gospel of Christ." Innocent yielded, and Francis returned to Assisi. He and his friars were allowed to use the Porziuncola as a headquarters.

He was a joyful leader. "Let the brothers take care not to appear sad or gloomy," he wrote. God's troubadour, the peasants called him, for "drunken with the love and pity of Christ" he would often take two sticks and pretend he was "drawing a bow across a violin and with fitting gestures would sing in French of the Lord Jesus Christ."

His preaching moved a young noblewoman, Clare Sciffi. She talked with Francis often and finally, in defiance of her father, took vows and founded an order of nuns, the Poor Clares. Francis obtained for them the Church of St. Damian. They lived on alms, sewed, spun, nursed the sick. In his chivalric manner, Francis always called them "ladies," not "sisters." Clare he addressed simply as "Christiana."

FRANCIS' FAME GREW and stories about him proliferated. The collection called the *Fioretti*, Little Flowers, tells of him preaching to birds and gentling a huge man-eating wolf, turning it into a village pet.

In 1219 Francis appeared among the knights of the Fifth Crusade, then encamped before Damietta near the Nile's mouth. In an attempt to make peace, Francis crossed the enemy lines and was brought before the sultan of Egypt, Malik al-Kamil. The sultan, a mild and tolerant man, listened patiently to Francis' preaching for several days, finally sent him back with the gift of a carved ivory horn, today preserved at Assisi. Francis had won respect, but neither Crusader nor Saracen was ready for peace.

When Francis returned to Assisi, he found turmoil among the brethren. His order had grown too large, too complex. The gentle mystic stepped down as its leader.

I drove from Pavia to Monte La Verna, the retreat high in the Apennines where Francis retired. The mountains

were beautiful, the road winding. Like other pilgrims, I walked the last few hundred yards. The monastic buildings, raised after the saint's time, seemed almost empty; a few friars, a few sisters scurried about. Almost instinctively, I found my way into a small chapel where Mass was being said. A small plate marked the spot where, we are told, Francis received on his hands, feet, and side the wounds that Jesus knew on the cross. No one can adequately explain the stigmata. Yet when his body was examined after his death, substantial witnesses told of seeing his wounds—black, swollen, like "nailheads in the flesh."

Tortured with pain, Francis came down from the mountain, traveling through Umbria on an ass, while crowds came to see him and listen. Often, dazed by pain or meditation, he did not see them. At last, as his days seemed numbered, companions brought him to St. Damian's. There Clare nursed him. When he gained strength, she built him a wattle hut in the garden. And now, as the sight of earth and sun and sky grew dim, he composed the beautiful "Canticle of the Sun." He wrote not in Latin, but in the everyday Italian of Umbria:

> Praise to Thee, my Lord, for all Thy creatures,
> Above all Brother Sun, who brings us the day and lends us his light;
> Lovely is he, radiant with great splendor,
> And speaks to us of Thee, O Most High.
> Praise to Thee, my Lord, for Sister Moon and the stars
> Which Thou hast set in the heavens, clear, precious, and fair.
> Praise to Thee, my Lord, for Brother Wind, for air and cloud,
> For calm and all weather by which Thou supportest life in all Thy creatures. . . .

Not long after, weakened by fasting and illness, Francis had himself carried to the Porziuncola, stripped, and laid on the ground. He wished to die as he had lived, in absolute poverty. As he died, those present said, larks swirled around the tiny church. All knew a saint had left their midst.

Bernard and Francis, each in his own way, kept bright the flame of faith, and their spirit lives on in the hush of cloisters and in the tolling of Franciscan mission bells, in the United States and over the world. Their orders, as well as the Benedictines, Dominicans, Carmelites, and others, would help staff the emerging universities, heal the sick and bury the dead, and by their simple presence constantly remind man of God's love.

Few things reflect the soaring faith of the age better than the Gothic cathedrals then rising in Europe, their lofty lines lifting the eye from arch to arch as the soul itself strives always toward heaven. It was in the 12th century that stonemasons began to build with their hands what the great mystics taught with their tongues.

Harnessing his arts to the vaulting Gothic spirit, medieval man
raised hymns in stone that glorify God and exalt mankind.
An age of faith finds its noblest expression

Building the

Medieval sculptor in stone supports St. Lorenz Tabernacle, Nuremberg; from "The Flowering of the Middle Ages," © *Thames and Hudson, London*

Great Cathedrals

"Crowding upward before the eye…a vast symphony in stone" Victor Hugo

It rises on an island where the Seine cuts the pulsing heart of Paris: Notre Dame. Sculptured pinnacles and flying buttresses, bathed in light, reflect the glowing faith that fashioned them 800 years ago.

Stone by stone, this "sublime and majestic edifice" reflected the upsurge of the Capetian dynasty (successors to the Carolingian kings), spreading from the Paris basin to French nationhood in an age of Crusades, growing towns, quickening commerce.

As the millennium passed, northwestern Europe underwent a revival in spirit and architecture. A monk who witnessed the year 1000 wrote: "It was as if the whole earth, having cast off the old … were clothing itself everywhere in the white robe of the church."

Society expressed this zeal in *morbus aedificandi,* a fever of building—first in the earthbound Romanesque style, then in a bold

BRUCE DALE, NATIONAL GEOGRAPHIC PHOTOGRAPHER

architecture that, in Henry Adams's words, "gave this effect of flinging its passion against the sky." Between 1170 and 1270 the French alone raised 80 cathedrals in the new style that Renaissance architects would disparage as "Gothic"—crude, barbaric.

Crude? Columns mount breathtakingly high, then blossom out to support soaring vaults.

Barbaric? Pointed arches, like hands touched in prayer, seem to supplicate heaven.

Each cathedral, site of a bishop's throne *(cathedra),* drew to it the surging life of its community. Its bronze bells tolled the populace to worship, weddings, feast days that spiced the calendar of toil with pageantry. Center of order in a chaotic age, the church sanctioned merchants' contracts and judged kings' edicts. Teacher, nurse, guardian of medieval man from cradle to grave, it gave him the joyful prospect of eternal life.

Focus of faith, witness to the march of history, Notre Dame is the living symbol of France

Soaring nave of Notre Dame has embraced worshipers since the vaulting stood but a skeleton against the sky. Then the singing of Mass mingled with the clamor of workmen. In the choir would sit aging Maurice de Sully, peasant-born bishop of Paris, seeing his life's dream take shape. In 1163 he had watched the cornerstone being laid, perhaps the pope himself mixing the holy water and mortar. Completion would take nearly two centuries.

Maurice poured into the work revenues from Notre Dame's extensive holdings; donations came from king and serf. Women of Paris, mindful of Our Lady, gave so often they prompted a legend that Notre Dame was "built with widows' mites." Rich were the rewards they found in the glow of votive candles in its chapels. Commented a 14th-century visitor: "On entering one feels as if ravished to heaven, and ushered into one of the most beautiful chambers of paradise."

In Gothic tradition, Notre Dame forms a cross. The long nave runs east toward Jerusalem with arms—transepts—extending north and south. Entering a main west portal, worshipers face the high altar in the apse, beyond a partly enclosed choir and the bishop's throne. Lacking pews or chairs, medieval congregations stood.

Notre Dame's paving has echoed the tread of history. Here Heraclius, Patriarch of Jerusalem, preached what would become the Third Crusade. Here Philip IV in armor spurred his charger up to the altar to thank the Virgin for a victory. Here England's Henry VI became king of France. And here Napoleon, bowing to no man, waved the pope aside and set the crown of empire on his own head.

In the French Revolution citizens toppled statues from the west portal, mistaking Biblical monarchs for kings of France. They declared the cathedral a Temple of Reason and stripped it. Only Robespierre's fall saved it from demolition. Lovingly restored by architect Viollet-le-Duc, it endures, in the words of Pope Paul VI, as "a pure jewel of Gothic art."

"Every pound of weight is adjusted, divided, and carried down from level to level till it touches ground... as a bird would alight" Henry Adams

Whips crack. Teamsters shout. Oxcarts from Left Bank quarries creak across the Seine on the Petit Pont—the Little Bridge—loaded with limestone blocks. At the Rue Neuve Notre Dame they turn right and thread the crowded Cité to the mason's yard, already humming on this bright morning in 1190.

Entire communities, driven by fervor, helped build cathedrals. "Men and women ... bowed their haughty necks to the yoke and harnessed themselves like beasts of burden," observed an abbot; "sometimes a thousand ... attached to one cart—so vast is the mass, so weighty the load." But more than fervor, it took the daring and imagination of a master builder—and the skills of smiths, masons, carpenters, and glaziers who here swarm over half-finished Notre Dame.

Stonecutters lay templates to stone and chisel decorative corbels and bosses. Workers overhead tread a huge wheel, reeling up timbers. Earlier, stone drums had been winched up to form piers along the nave.

From atop each pier rise slender columns, up past the triforium, or gallery, past the clerestory, where tall windows beckon the sun. Carpenters bridge the nave with scaffolding and build wooden frames on which masons arc intersecting ribs, locking the arches with a keystone. Weighted ropes hold slabs of stone as mortar dries. Six inches thick, the vault ceiling will support a man 115 feet above the paving.

The ribs carry the vault's weight down to the columns. But this outward thrust would splay the columns if there were no buttresses to counter the pressure. Slender stone bridges do this, leaping down and out from one pier to another, each junction capped by a pinnacle.

Later the intermediate buttress will disappear and the bridge of stone will "fly" 50 feet. Men call the device a flying buttress. It channels the thrust down and the eye up— up past the steep roof, past the spire, and on to the height of man's aspirations.

PAINTING BY ROBERT W. NICHOLSON, GEOGRAPHIC ART DIVISION

*Stained glass, glory of the
glazier's art, transformed dim
cathedrals into radiant vaults
of jeweled light and learning*

God is light, says Holy Writ, and Gothic
builders fused the two in a new art form
born of faith. Their towering vaults and
pointed arches needed only slender columns
and outer buttressing—not the massive walls
that bolstered round Romanesque arches.
So vast windows lighted Gothic cathedrals,
and filling them were luminous scenes that
awed and instructed the beholder. Looking up,
he saw favorite Bible stories, great events
of history, even details of his own life;
the grain harvest opposite glows above
the west portal of Notre Dame.

   Abbot Suger of St. Denis, who pioneered
the Gothic style when he rebuilt the choir
of his royal church in 1140, noted that
"we caused to be painted, by the exquisite
hands of many masters from different regions,
a splendid variety of new windows." The art
budded in 12th- and 13th-century naves and
flowered in rose windows like that adorning

BRUCE DALE, NATIONAL GEOGRAPHIC PHOTOGRAPHER, AND (ABOVE) JONATHAN S. BLAIR

Notre Dame's north transept (below);
it survives intact from 1255. The French
dismantled and stored it during two world
wars. Virgin and Child shine from the center
of this 43-foot stone web: its petals portray
Old Testament figures; 18 kings of Judah,
ancestors of Mary, stand in a row beneath.

   In days when few could afford glass for
their homes, guilds of cobblers, tanners,
and furriers vied in donating rich windows
to God's house. The patron picked a subject
and approved a design. From it the glazier
made a pattern showing in what shapes to cut
the various colors. A hot iron snipped
the pieces from sheets previously tinted
by mixing metallic oxides into the molten
glass—cobalt for blue, copper or gold for red,
iron for yellow. Artisans painted on details
and shadings and kiln-fired them. Then they
assembled the pieces in grooved lead strips.
A glazier in Reims (above) uses the same
techniques to repair a window today.

   Nowhere is the art better illustrated than
at Chartres, whose 13th-century glass is
"the pride of France." Less fortunate was
Canterbury, English shrine of martyred Thomas
à Becket. Many windows fell when a Puritan
divine mounted a 60-foot ladder and zealously
"rattled down proud Beckett's glassie bones."

"Mankind has thought of nothing important that it has not written in stone"
Victor Hugo

Brooding malevolently, they line the gallery along the façade of Notre Dame— scores of grotesques, part beast, part bird, part hideously human. They were driven out of the cathedral, says the legend, when Our Lady moved in. No wonder they stare so balefully at the rooftops of Paris!

Though these are copies replacing time-ravaged originals, they show the skill and whimsy that sculptors brought to church ornaments. They transmuted rainspouts into gaping gargoyles (below) that guard against evil spirits. And in the figures that step from columns flanking the portals of Chartres Cathedral (opposite) they achieved a grace and nobility that speak to us across the centuries.

In their carved catechisms, sculptors followed rigid rules. God, angels, and the apostles go barefoot; other saints are shod. St. Paul must be bald and long-bearded. St. Peter always wears a tonsure, curly hair, and short beard. The Christ child must lie on an altar. The three Magi represent youth, maturity, and old age. In the Crucifixion Mary appears to the right of the cross, St. John to the left. A scene depicting the Resurrection always shows Jesus emerging from an open tomb, cross in hand. Jews invariably wear cone-shaped hats.

The cathedral's north portal, facing a region of gloom and cold, generally portrays the Old Testament. The south portal, warmed by sunlight, presents the New. Often on the western facade, facing the setting sun, the Last Judgment unfolds. The saved rise triumphantly to paradise; the doomed shrink from tormenting devils, toads, and serpents, and tumble writhing into the jaws of hell.

Conceived by clerics, such mute dramas were the work of *imageurs,* image makers. These men rose from the rank of masons, the elite of medieval craftsmen. All had served seven-year apprenticeships and belonged to a mason's lodge, a shed where they took their midday nap and afternoon break. Here they kept their tools— axes, chisels, mallets, tracing boards.

A symbolic pair of gloves revealed that the master builder—architect and construction supervisor of the Middle Ages—was himself a mason. Besides wages, he might be given a house to live in, some land, and a pension. He was a man of great dignity.

His achievement strikes wonder in the visitor today, as it did in pilgrims of old.

For a thousand years the wondrous shrine of St. James
in a remote corner of Spain has held high a beacon for believers.
With Michael Kuh share an adventure of faith on a

Pilgrimage to
Compostela

Our single file of pilgrims stretches 70 yards back into the vaulted cavern of Compostela's great cathedral. The Frenchmen, Spaniards, Germans, Portuguese, Japanese, whatever, ahead of me inch toward the stairs behind the altar. Candle smoke and incense permeate the 800-year-old nave. It is July 25, the feast day of St. James. Outside, in the huge stone square, fiesta rockets explode. We hear them—*pop, bang, pop-pop-pop*—faintly, as though we were fish underwater.

Finally my foot reaches the first of the 15 steps, and five minutes later the French priest in front of me is hugging the silver back of St. James's statue in the traditional embrace. *"Merci, Saint Jacques,"* he whispers in a granite ear and completes the message that has brought him across two countries and 20 centuries. Now it is my turn to give the *abrazo*. I have no message but feel my heart lift strangely as I touch Santiago's jewel-encrusted mantle.

Who are you, Saint James, and how did you get here, so far from Galilee? How did you find this westernmost corner of Europe, where some in the Middle Ages

"James, thy very own Galicia,
Famous for its path of glory,
Trod by weary-footed throngs" Codex Calixtinus

Pilgrims for a thousand years have hymned Spain's patron, whose shrine rivaled Rome and Jerusalem as Christendom's greatest. Their song survives in the Codex Calixtinus, *12th-century guidebook for the traditional journey from France (right). Joining pilgrims at the waystop Rocamadour, the author lights a starry taper. Faith recalls the star that led ninth-century diggers to the apostle's remains, miraculously wafted from Holy Land to Spain; his vision led Christian armies against the Moors. In time half a million pilgrims came each year to Compostela, among them the 11th-century Spanish hero El Cid and in the 20th century the future Pope John XXIII. Age, ailments, bad water, and brigands took a toll: "I had rather go five times to Rome," a pilgrim wrote, "than once to Compostela."*

Santiago de Compostela

Lug

GALICIA

OVERLEAF: FIREWORKS SHOWER THE SKY ABOVE THE CATHEDRAL AT SANTIAGO DE COMPOSTELA ON THE EVE OF ST. JAMES'S DAY; MICHAEL KUH (AND ABOVE). MAP BY BETTY CLONINGER, GEOGRAPHIC ART DIVISION

thought the earth ended and an infinite ocean of malevolent spirits began? There are no sure answers; tradition and faith pick up the story where Scripture leaves it.

James, the Gospels tell us, was one of the Galilean fishermen whom Christ turned into "fishers of men." He witnessed Christ's Transfiguration, and His agony at Gethsemane, and became the first of the 12 apostles to suffer martyrdom. Tradition adds that James traveled widely, preached the Word throughout Roman Hispania, finally returning to Jerusalem and death. Then in a miraculous seven-day voyage his disciples transported his body to Galicia, near present-day Santiago de Compostela. The story of the journey appears in the *Codex Calixtinus,* a 12th-century compilation devoted to his cult and named for Pope Calixtus II. It includes hymns, rituals, and advice to French pilgrims to Compostela.

I have coffee and *coñac* at the Café Avenida with Abelardo Moralejo, retired vice-rector at Santiago's university and a professor of Latin. As a translator into Spanish of the Codex, he is uniquely qualified to comment on the apostle's

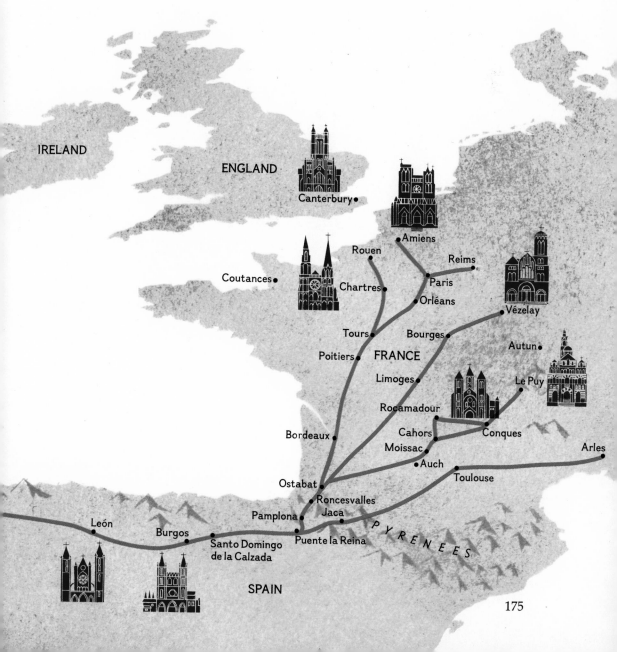

posthumous return to Spain. "These are not scholarly questions," says the professor, "but the story is fairly clear. Upon landing, the disciples were received near here, near this cafe, by a lady named Lupa, a sort of local queen, who allowed them to bury St. James and mark his grave. Then there is a gap of 800 years.

"In the ninth century the grave was rediscovered. Presently, within another 300 years, the cathedral as we now see it was begun. Pilgrims began to come from every point of Europe's compass. Kings and queens, knights and saints, butchers and bakers—all the pious people of a devout age thronged the Road to Santiago. And so significant did this road become that we Spaniards still refer to that galaxy, your Milky Way, as *El Camino de Santiago*.

"Three main goals," he continues, "drew medieval pilgrims: the Holy Land, a long, arduous, expensive, and dangerous expedition; Rome, a powerful magnet but perhaps lacking in mystery; and Santiago de Compostela, not as far as Jerusalem and, being at the end of Europe, more romantic than Rome. Perhaps this aura of

romance, this blend of faith and adventure, can best explain what was a medieval compulsion and remains even now a journey with purpose."

For a pilgrimage to Santiago, university scholars won sabbaticals; sinners, absolution; debtors, more time to pay. They returned wearing a cockleshell badge on hat or cloak, sign of a successful pilgrimage and a reminder of the miraculous power of St. James. A local horseman, a story goes, was engulfed by waves as he rode along the shore to his wedding. When the bride appealed to St. James, her groom reappeared, adorned with cockleshells.

"Our cockleshell badge," says Professor Moralejo, "made men proud of themselves, of having physically reached a spiritual goal. Psychologically, this combination produced the kind of motive most of us miss today. Unfortunately."

"How right you are!" I thought to myself, remembering the restless yearnings of the spirit that drove me, 17 years before, to forsake New York for the quiet, beautiful places of Europe. I too had found moments of fulfillment, of spiritual

WASHED BY RAIN, *blessed by a rainbow, Le Puy (the peak) thrusts skyward its volcanic and man-made spires. Pilgrims assembled here, prayed in the Cathedral of Notre Dame (right) before the "Black Virgin," a statue tradition says crusading Louis IX brought from Egypt. French Revolutionaries burned it; a copy replaces it. Colossal Madonna (left), cast of cannon captured in Crimean War, beckons today.*

DEAN CONGER, NATIONAL GEOGRAPHIC STAFF

Golden-visaged St. Foy drew pilgrims to Conques and its splendid abbey

A statue sheathed in gold, encrusted with precious jewels, holds the skull of the patrician girl who died for the faith (la foi) in the last Roman persecution in Gaul. Legend tells how she rode forth on a light-stepping horse, serenaded with cymbals and flutes, to work the miracles sought by pilgrims.

Relics buttressed faith. Men took oaths on them, through them sought to cure illness, avert the evil eye, stop a plague, ensure a good harvest. Greatly valued (merchants of Venice paid the king of Jerusalem 20,000 gold coins for a newly found piece of the True Cross), they were often housed in costly reliquaries. Louis IX built an entire church, Paris's beautiful Sainte Chapelle, to house a thorn from the crown Christ wore.

Romanesque church of St. Foy (below) rose in the 11th century. Its steps, a classroom for catechism, still know the tread of pilgrims bound for Santiago who pause to seek the saint's "many mercies."

WALTER MEAYERS EDWARDS, NATIONAL GEOGRAPHIC STAFF (ABOVE), AND MICHAEL KUH

joy: the nightingale in the moonlit lemon tree, singing through the roar of falling water by a Moorish mill; the curlews whistling through mist and loneliness once behind the rainbows in Connemara; the partridges at dawn in Andalusian sierras; the clacking of storks in Castilian steeples.

STARTING MY OWN ROAD to Santiago was a moment of awareness. Of the traditional pilgrim routes, I had chosen the one that winds from the volcanic cliffs of Auvergne through southern France to the Pyrenees. In the remote valley of Conques, as I climbed the steeply cobbled Rue Charlemagne and first glimpsed the ruddy stone Romanesque spires of the church of St. Foy, I could feel, almost see, centuries of predecessors in pilgrim habit: cloak, sandals, staff hung with water gourd, broad-brimmed hat cocked up in front.

The feeling grew stronger when I arrived at the village inn and found its dining room, with its heavy oak beams and bright copper, filled with pilgrims—even though they had come to Conques in a large blue bus instead of on foot. And here I enjoyed the first of many flawless French meals, in this misty green valley where the chocolate-colored, rain-swollen River Dourdou carries its cargo of trout, one of which ended up as my lunch.

How did Conques, off the map of history since the first hermits came to meditate in religious solitude here 1,600 years ago, become a must for medieval pilgrims tramping the *Route de Saint Jacques* from Burgundy to Spain? I talk to Père Camuls, one of the priests in charge of the church and the bejeweled reliquary of St. Foy. Well wined and dined, a fine raconteur, the embodiment of the "jolly friar," Père Camuls tells me that in early pilgrim days Conques was just a minor way station—"*Evidemment*, a major attraction was lacking."

So one of the monks at Conques thought of the girl martyred for her Christian faith—*la foi*—whose treasured remains lay in the neighboring town of Agen. "And

Cattle fair livens lonely farmers' lives as in medieval times

Pilgrims knew the sights and sounds of market days, introduced in Gaul by the Romans and revitalized by Charlemagne. In St. Christophe Vallon, near Conques, farmers assemble on the 21st of each month to trade cattle. Men in berets get the feel of livestock, calculate, make bids. "Of a truth, by all the saints, no man will give thee so much as I," medieval swindlers told a seller. When an accomplice arrived offering less, simple farmers quickly sold.

Early fairs were sometimes held in cemeteries or by a church in hopes that sanctity of the site would keep traders from fighting. Today buyer and seller still haggle eyeball to eyeball (opposite), clinch the deal with a nod, then relax over wine while maman *gossips. Festive spirit of these local gatherings reminds us that "fair" stems from Latin* feriae, *"feasts."*

MICHAEL KUH

the thought was father to the deed," Père Camuls continues, "though it required ten years' patience. This monk entered the Agen community and set such a good example that after ten years he was named guardian of St. Foy's tomb. Then one night while the community slept this fine fellow packed up the saintly relics and made off. Of course there was a tremendous row, with people from Agen searching the countryside, but the monk made it safely to Conques with his holy loot. Thanks be to God, we've had the relics ever since.

"*Alors,* when the word went around that Conques had St. Foy, pilgrims came in hordes and *tout le monde était enchanté,* except for the people in Agen, who after more than one thousand years are still a trifle bitter."

With which we had a glass of rosé and looked once again at Heaven and Hell frozen in stone over the portal. Until a troupe of children romped into the square and finally subsided on the church steps for a dose of catechism. Père Camuls was as tolerant of their mischief and mistakes as he'd been of the covetous monk's pious purloining of St. Foy's remains.

At St. Christophe Vallon I find the monthly cattle market in progress. Strolling through the throng of haggling farmers, listening to their shrewd Auvergne patois as they prod and pinch bawling calves, is to live again in the 12th-century France of Aymery Picaud, the voluble cleric of Poitiers to whom we owe so much of the *Codex Calixtinus.* Picaud refers with pride to his sweet land of France where wine,

181

food, and water were fine and abundant. And I see it in the golden calves, the amber wine of Auvergne, the Rabelaisian laughter of beet-faced locals in navy-blue denims.

After St. Christophe's bonhomie, Rocamadour in its stern, stone setting seems a chastening place. No matter that pilgrims no longer mount on their knees the punishing height of its Penitents' Staircase. Rocamadour is a sanctuary, and sanctuaries, wherever you find them, speak the same language. They speak of sacrifice and piety; they lower your voice as they raise your hopes. Marble plaques here make a mosaic of gratitude from those whose hopes were answered. As I read the plaques by the Chapel of St. Marie, a late band of English pilgrims arrives. Their layman guide confides to me that he witnessed a miracle here several years ago.

"This Englishwoman, about 30, had advanced tuberculosis in her left leg," he tells me. "She could barely hobble. Doctors had done her no good. Here she prayed for a cure. And she walked out of this chapel as well as you or I. The cure has lasted. She returns every year to give thanks."

I approach Cahors by a lovely old road that bathes its

MICHAEL KUH

"Gascony...covered with forests...rivers and pure springs"

Codex Calixtinus

The graceful Pont Valentré, a 14th-century fortified bridge, bore pilgrims across the River Lot from Cahors toward Gascony. At the abbey of Moissac they found respite, like the modern pilgrim (opposite), amid cloister columns. Once over the Garonne, they met the Gascons: "verbose, cynical, lecherous, drunken, gluttonous, and down at heel"— but courageous fighters and "remarkable' in their hospitality." Faith of the Gascons lives on in the cathedral at Auch, guarded by saints in Renaissance glass.

feet in the River Lot. To medieval pilgrims rivers, streams, and fountains were as service stations today. Nothing could match the exquisite pleasure of bathing and drinking after a day's march of 10 or 15 miles.

A calendar sunset bathes the back road to Cahors, a narrow, twisting, and deserted lane. Soon the high country of the Périgord envelops my headlights. Then all at once there are lights and a bridge, and under the bridge, by lamplight, the sportsmen of Cahors are pitching iron balls down sandy aisles, playing *boules*. One short bald man is *formidable*. He never misses!

Cahors in the 13th century was like Zurich today—a banking center of Europe. Popes and kings sent emissaries to borrow. But financial decline set in as the Hundred Years' War came to an end in 1453 and France found herself bankrupt. Ever since, the good red wine and the Pont Valentré, the turreted bridge across the Lot, have been Cahors' local attractions. I quaff the first and photograph the latter. Both are magnificent, especially the bridge by night, a golden

"This mountain is so high that it seems to touch the sky"

Codex Calixtinus

Mist veils Roncesvalles Pass, gateway to Spain, where pilgrims reflected on Roland's grim fate and their own perils. Flimsy ferries plied raging rivers. "Cursed be their boatmen!" railed the Codex at locals who overloaded boats and rejoiced as they stripped drowned victims. Tollmen robbed many a traveler, "searching him to his underpants." How welcome, then, the sight of the Roncesvalles abbey (below). There "the door is open to all . . . and virtuous ladies undertake the duties of nursing."

MICHAEL KUH

184

span of medieval romance admiring itself in the river's slow surface. The chirrup of crickets conjures up the ghostly tread of Burgundian pilgrims.

Moissac to the southwest I find flat, hot, and stagnant until I dive back 900 years into its cool, columned cloister— a marble forest of 76 arcades, each different. A bestiary of griffins, phoenixes, and unicorns adorns the stylized capitals. Through one of the arches juts the russet beard of a young Toulouse painter, Jacques Joos, en route to Santiago at a connoisseur's pace. "There are so many things to admire along the way," he explains, "that I begin to doubt if I'll ever make it. I should be in the Pyrenees now, not here. But why go as the crow flies? After all, one is not a crow."

By direct road, if not as a crow, I leave Moissac and stop for the night at Auch. Though an old *voyageur* of the by-roads of France, I knew Auch only as a name on a map. But it provides travel's best pleasures, the sort Aymery Picaud and his friends must have known at nightfall when they happened by chance on exactly the right place: an honest inn, a warm welcome, good food and wine, and beautiful girls to admire around a splashing fountain. What better setting to sip a Bénédictine and reflect on the goodness of life?

AFTER AUCH I began the gradual green climb into the Pyrenees. Around me fat cows slouched about in luscious pastures. At Oloron I was within the bounds of the old kingdom of Navarre; still in France by my road map but within sight, almost hearing, of Spain.

Inside the church a three-day-old boy was being baptized. "He is called Jean-Pierre," his grandmother told me. "*Comme il est beau, n'est-ce pas, monsieur?*" Then she posed beneath the portal for the camera of Jean-Pierre's father.

The whole medieval cosmos gleams in the 12th-century Pyrenean marble of this portal. Here 24 jolly old men play a string ensemble; countrymen hunt stags, catch salmon and smoke them, make cheese, trim vines. Goblins and devils leer in comic frightfulness, like Halloween masks. Their sculptor was a comfortable man, with good digestion like Père Camuls back in Conques.

I am eager to press on. Twisting up and down abrupt green valleys I come upon a village that lives off contraband. Then suddenly the frontier, one guard's "*Bonsoir, monsieur*" followed by another's "*Buenas tardes. Vaya con Dios.*" And so into Spain I go with God.

Up out of Valcarlos, I climb now in earnest, into a rougher age and country. The road gives but a tenuous hint of the 20th century through the steep, sheep-strewn slopes near

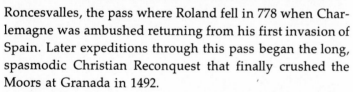

Roncesvalles, the pass where Roland fell in 778 when Charlemagne was ambushed returning from his first invasion of Spain. Later expeditions through this pass began the long, spasmodic Christian Reconquest that finally crushed the Moors at Granada in 1492.

Darkness comes on and with it an opaque curtain of mist. As I grope for an approaching summit, I wish for the great bell of Ibañeta that used to guide mist-blind pilgrims the last miles, like ships lost at sea, to the monastery of San Salvador, founded, legend says, by Charlemagne. But now there is no monastery, no great tolling bell, only the ruins of a church. Suddenly I am surrounded by phantoms and tinkling bells. I stamp on the brakes.

A shepherd sticks his cut-throat grin inside my window. I expect the knife, remembering Aymery Picaud's curse on the savage mountaineers who preyed on pilgrims. "Do you have tobacco?" the shepherd shouts. So we smoke together in the middle of the road and the bawling sheep.

"Carlomagno was here," I say, thinking of Charlemagne, making talk. "Carlos *who?*" he asks. "I know no Carlos."

Bedlam breaks loose in Pamplona during the Fiesta of San Fermín as bulls for the corridas *stampede through streets to the arena. Youths brave horns and hoofs. Crowds jostle* gigantes, *giant effigies of Moors, Indians, royalty. Pilgrims noted Navarrese piety— but warned of tainted streams (like spring at left) where locals bade them water their horses, then skinned the dying beasts!*

In the hamlet of Roncesvalles, where millions of pilgrims stopped to rest and pray, canons chant their Mass in the 13th-century abbey and the air is filled with peace. But in Pamplona, my next stop, I find a blaze of red berets and bursting rockets. It is the eve of San Fermín's fiesta, the most feverish in Spain. A bacchanal of bulls and blood-red wine. For seven days and nights no one sleeps.

Each morning the bulls stampede through the streets, the men of Pamplona one step ahead of the murderous horns. Not always ahead. One boy gets a horn through his thigh like a hot knife through butter. "Why do you do this thing?" I ask a runner, who holds in his hand the rolled-up newspaper that distracts the bull.

"*Hombre.* Because. Because my father and grandfather did. In Pamplona we live for the running of the bulls. Why do you Americans play golf and baseball?"

MICHAEL KUH

"We have heard the cock crow, We have reached comfort"

Pilgrims' song

Balm of a bountiful landscape cheered pilgrims on the **Camino Francés**, *the French Way. Ahead lay Santo Domingo de la Calzada, named for its founder, St. Dominic "of the causeway," who built roads to aid travelers. Here schoolgirls kneel at his tomb, where chickens in an ornate cage recall a miracle: Unjustly hanged, a youth survived and two cooked fowl flew to life. Pilgrims would offer them crumbs. If the birds accepted, it meant the donors would reach Santiago.*

188

Deafened by noise, aching from dancing the *jota*, I head for Estella, relieved to get back to the *Codex Calixtinus*, to trade Ernest Hemingway's world for Aymery Picaud's. But before Estella comes Puente la Reina, "whence all roads to Santiago become one." From this junction pilgrims proceeded eagerly to "Estella *la belle*," tree-shaded city on the River Ega, "filled with every sort of felicity." Picaud described it perfectly. When I reach Estella, the Ega proves shaded and fragrant and full of children swimming. How little 800 years count in Spain!

Beyond Estella I meet the first parched hints of Castile's plateau. Navarre's green hills flatten out to ocher and gold. Wheat is well mixed with vines at Logroño. Nájera is red sandstone; Santo Domingo de la Calzada, a traveler's prize. In the friendly comfort of the government hostel, Carlos Gómez, innkeeper extraordinary, tells me, "Hospitality is an old tradition here, ever since St. Dominic himself built highways and bridges to help the pilgrims."

In the cozy cathedral by the road, Don Carlos's three little daughters tell me the story of the famous miracle here. A chambermaid, it seems, fell in love with the handsome son of a pilgrim couple passing through, but he wouldn't notice her. So

*"Castile...rich in gold
and silver....Bread
...milk, and honey"*
Codex Calixtinus

*Massive gate of Santa Maria,
adorned by figures of the Virgin,
heroes, and Emperor Charles V,
greets visitors to Burgos, heart of
Old Castile. Founded in the ninth
century as a bastion against the
Moors, it flourished as a pilgrim
center and capital of kings of
Castile and León. Here came
creaking oxcarts (left) bringing
golden harvests of wheat. Nearby
was born Spain's national hero,
Rodrigo Díaz de Vivar—El Cid,
from* sidi, *Arabic for lord.
He lies in the cathedral near a
crucifix so realistic that, awed
pilgrims said, it sweated and bled.*

she hid a silver cup in his knapsack and accused him of stealing it. Authorities seized the boy, found the cup, and he was hanged. The parents cried, but went on to Santiago. Returning, they found their son still hanging and cried again. But the boy said, "Don't cry, mother and father, because I am fine."

The parents ran to tell the judge of Santo Domingo, but he scoffed at them. He said he would as soon believe that the roast cock and hen he was about to eat would fly off the table and crow. "And what do you think?" says one of Don Carlos's daughters. "As soon as he said that, the two roast chickens flew up into the air. The hen cackled and the rooster crowed. So everybody ran down the road and let the boy go. . . . Look up there, in that chicken coop, and you can see a white hen and rooster alive to remind us of the miracle." I looked, and just as the three little sisters promised, there they were. The rooster raised his head, full of ego. *Cock-a-doodle-doo* throughout the cathedral.

I MOVE ON TO BURGOS, crossing an area of Old Castile which Picaud praised with a forked tongue: "This land is full of treasures, rich in gold and silver . . . forage and powerful horses. Bread, wine, meat, fish, milk, and honey are abundant. However, there are no trees and many bad and vicious men."

Just to show that 800 years can make a difference, this land today has little treasure, no gold or silver, nor horses of much value. No meat but lamb, little milk and less honey. Still no trees, he's right. But nowhere in Spain, perhaps, are there fewer "bad and vicious men."

Burgos has a pretty riverside promenade along the Arlanzón, and most of the city's inhabitants stroll it after sundown, as the Spanish say, "to take the freshness." At one end stands the Arch of Santa Maria, through which I approach the vast Gothic wedding-cake cathedral. One cannot help being impressed by the

"Galicians . . . by their customs most resemble our French race"

Codex Calixtinus

Promise of congenial folk heartened French pilgrims
on the last leagues to Compostela. Outside town,
they customarily bathed "for love of the apostle."
Galicians still welcome visitors with snippets
of octopus, peppers sold by handfuls, cups of wine,
and skirling of the gaita gallega, Galician bagpipe.

MICHAEL KUH

man-hours that went into its trimming, but I agree with Francisco, the one-armed guard of the car park before it. "A great cathedral," he observes. "Maybe too great. And neglected. Bulbs burn out, carvings rot, rats as big as cats run through the cloister." With which he leaves the cars in his custody to fend for themselves and walks me around, finding faults.

"Where shall we eat?" I ask Francisco.

"Down the street where the priests go. Priests and truck drivers know where the food is good." And they apparently do. The roast lamb comes out of a baker's oven crisp and delicious.

Castile in July is like Kansas in August—wheat and more wheat. In Castrillo Matajudíos I find the men of the town *trillando*—threshing—in ancient style, mules drawing sledges around on the harvested grain. One man sings as he makes the circle; another sleeps in the shade of a high-wheeled cart. One telephone and one television set connect this adobe hamlet with Burgos 30 miles away.

For Aymery Picaud, Burgos to León was a long flat stretch broken by hostels and monasteries, including one at Sahagún which grew into the Spanish Cluny. Now, grandeur gone, the stretch is merely long and flat.

During the 700-year Moorish rule, León was one of the first cities retaken; in 914 it became the principal city of Christian Spain. Today its medieval splendor glows in its golden Gothic cathedral. Not a bulk like Burgos, too big for the eye to encompass; León's cathedral is Bach in stone. *Tiene gracia,* as the Spanish put one of their highest compliments—it has grace. Some of the finest stained glass in Spain plays bejeweled fugues through its vaulted twilight.

A WINDING MOUNTAIN ROAD brings me to Ponferrada, named for the bridge strong as iron that was built nine centuries ago for the convenience of pilgrims. The remains of a mighty castle—drawbridge, moat, walls—evoke the proud Knights Templars, who once held the town. Standing in the shade of the citadel's overweening bulk, I sense how Templar chivalry curdled into the arrogance that finally destroyed the order. This is not one of those nostalgic castles that make you wish for a bygone age. The countryside has little to remind you of all those armored athletes charging across newly planted fields challenging each other. This is mining country, about as close to drabness as Spain can get—a palette of browns, grays, and blacks, contouring steeply, where dun-colored donkeys pull cartloads of coal along the horizons.

From somber Ponferrada I emerge into a green highland of trees and white-water trout streams, then climb past gorse-cluttered gorges to the eight-family hamlet of Cebrero. Its gray cluster of thatched barns and cottages sits on a 3,500-foot balcony looking down on the promised land of Galicia.

No way station until this on my long journey has spoken so clearly the thanksgiving that pilgrims must have felt on arrival. From Cebrero's stone perch extends the whole rolling green-and-gold province of Lugo, crisscrossed by dusty roads, all seeming to lead, like strands of a spiderweb, to Saint James. This is the second of three literally high moments along the itinerant symphony of Compostela, moments that build from the Pyrenean overture to Spain, past this Galician climax of the first long movement, to crescendo on the hill of San Marcos, from which pilgrims first see the towers of Santiago.

At Lugo, the provincial capital, as I promenade atop the Roman perimeter wall, clouds of swallows ricochet through a vermilion sunset. Filigreed silhouettes of cathedral turrets rise into the lowering night. And decorating an archway stands a stone St. James—a reminder that Santiago lies but a few hours' ride away.

I drive through pines, over rivers, passing farmers in wooden shoes and screech-axled oxcarts that patiently shamble through tall fields of corn. The closer I come to Compostela the more I feel in Ireland. I see it in the faces, the houses, the green lay of the land—evidence on every side that this is a Celtic bastion never broached by the Moors. In Arzúa I see a sun too bright for Ireland; but the look and the walk, the sly humor of these Galicians is pure Cork or Connemara.

In Lavacolla, at the last granite crucifix along the pilgrim's route before Santiago —now but a 15-minute drive—I am in another Celtic country. Such crosses stand starkly on the skyline of Brittany. Thinking of this, of France, and of the long road I've followed in the footsteps of Aymery Picaud, I start at the sudden sound of French at my elbow. I turn to meet Père Georges, kneeling behind me at the cross —a priest from Picaud's own city of Poitiers!

"This has been the dream of my entire life," Père Georges smiles gravely. "Twenty-nine days I have walked from Poitiers, never leaving the path of my predecessor Picaud. I cannot express, monsieur, the joy this has given me, this journey of faith and tradition. I have been freezing and sunstruck, exhausted, hungry—all

194

"At last Compostela... most exalted of all the cities of Spain"

Codex Calixtinus

Journey's end brought shouts of "Mon Joie!" from pilgrims sighting Santiago's triple-towered cathedral. Weeping with joy, many prostrated themselves, then advanced on their knees. Riders dismounted to walk with bared heads.

Thronging the city on July 25, St. James's Day, today's pilgrims cheer gigantes and pipers, and wind through the streets with a procession bearing the saint's image (opposite). High Mass follows in the 12th-century cathedral, packed with pilgrims and alive with Romanesque sculpture. There the devout hope for "pardon and muche faire grace."

Not all pilgrims completed their journey. Some crossed the Pyrenees, bought bogus "diplomas," and headed home. Others perished. One told how nine companions died from tainted fruit and water—"the which I did ever refrain myself."

ALBERT MOLDVAY, NATIONAL GEOGRAPHIC STAFF. OPPOSITE: MICHAEL KUH

these extremes from which today we are protected. I have been given kindness and hospitality everywhere. For me these 29 days have been a march through history and brotherhood that I shall never forget. Ah, but forgive me, monsieur, I am preaching to you as if you were one of my parish."

Not surprisingly, Père Georges refuses my offer of a ride for the last few miles. After walking this far, he would hardly do otherwise. So I drive alone to the hill of San Marcos. And there, beneath me suddenly, it lies, the culmination: the balustraded spires of St. James's cathedral, swirling, airy, eminently worth all the miles and all the days. I am moved, of course, though I wish Père Georges had come along. His thrill would have trebled my own.

MAKING MY WINDING DESCENT into the old stone quarter of Santiago, passing the granite façades of churches and palaces embellished with saints and scallop shells, entering the great gray ensemble where few pieces are new, no addition askew, I forget Père Georges in the force of my admiration. Nor am I alone. Today's pilgrims throng the flagstoned streets to join the companions of Aymery Picaud, whom I've carried in my heart since Conques.

I pass the white spread of the Burgo de las Naciónes, which can house 4,000 pilgrims. But I want to sleep closer to my goal, the cathedral. So I push on, through the gorgeous old maze, emerging in the noblest square in Spain. On my left towers the rose-gold mountain of stone—the cathedral, at last! On my right stands the former royal hospital where I know at a glance I must stay: the matching rose-gold Hostal de los Reyes Católicos.

"I wonder if you'll understand?" I ask the man at the desk. "I'd like a room with the sound of cathedral bells."

"Of course, sir," he smiles, *muy simpático.* "You are not the first pilgrim."

As I unpack, with half an eye admiring the valerian rooted in the lichened wall across from my window, its violet flower catching the last of the sun, I'm delighted by a brazen boom: James's bells bounce from corner to corner around my canopied bed. Tonight the church mice shall not sleep much closer to St. James than I.

Bagpipes awaken me July 24, the day before the feast of the apostle. I jump to the window to see Galician pipers skirling in scarlet waistcoats up the stairs toward the cardinal's palace. To such squealing and droning, I fancy, even the great James might itch to jig the local *muñeira.* Children surround the palace, screaming in slightly frightened delight as papier-mâché giants twirl to the piping as fast as the men inside them can manage. His Eminence, the cardinal, peers out of his window like a Velázquez portrait.

SILVER-CAPED *Santiago receives the traditional embrace from behind as a pilgrim (opposite) climaxes a journey of faith. Precious stones stud the image; an altar of alabaster, jasper, and silver has encased it since 1672. Below lies the "fair vaulted sepulcher" where, said the Codex, "the air is kept sweet with divine odors."*

Candles cast a flickering blessing on an altar (above) to St. James as Matamoros (Moorslayer); in that ghostly guise the apostle led Christian armies against the Moors.

In medieval garb, a bewhiskered believer proudly wears the cockleshell badge (left), sign of a completed pilgrimage, calling to mind Sir Walter Raleigh's lines: "Give me my scallop shell of quiet . . . my gown of glory. . . ."

After following the pipers under many arcades—granite umbrellas for a city that has the heaviest rainfall in Spain—I detour to the market. Cautious housewives, shopping baskets on their heads, squeeze the flat gold cheeses. Fat silver sardines, fresh from the sea, attract long queues. But I prefer the *pimientos de Herbón,* grown near here. Thumb-size and green, they are fried and eaten whole. Delicious, but an occasional hot one explodes on your palate. Then only a chunk of bread and some Ribeiro wine—thick and red and taken from a white porcelain cup, Galician style—can douse the flame.

At a jet carver's shop I get a sudden whim to buy not a pilgrim's scallop shell but an infidel *higa.* Older than Christianity, these small jet hands with the thumb clasped between the first two fingers are worn as an amulet against the evil eye. Galicia and neighboring Asturias are Celtic-superstitious, and many's the *espíritu malo* that a higa has banished.

Fireworks at midnight turn the plaza into a noonday blaze. Through clouds of powder smoke, dazzles of catherine wheels, and the rainbow tracers of too many rockets, St. James's towers rise into the night—as close as medieval manpower could build them to heaven. It is now, by the clock, July 25.

I steal a few hours' sleep before morning bagpipes beckon me to the cattle market. Half the countryside has come to this once-upon-a-time fair, to combine trading with faith. Bruegel people, most dressed in black. But red is the wine that floats their transactions, and purplish-red the sucker-skinned octopus we gorge by wooden platefuls. Smoking hot from iron caldrons, snipped into disks of white flesh, doused in oil, and powdered with salt and scarlet pimiento, this *pulpo* tastes not unlike lobster. Here is the Galician trinity of farm, sea, and faith against the backdrop of James's church, from which fly the red-and-gold banners of Spain on this day of the national patron saint.

*T*HE BELLS TOLL DEEP in their great bronze throats. It is time for the solemn Mass that has brought us from all corners of the world to this medieval time capsule of Compostela. Inside the cathedral, on the high altar's fringe, I kneel. Thousands of pilgrims are with me in place, many millions more in time—all of them in the footsteps of medieval men who first received the cockleshell in a spirit not unlike that of the Crusaders who took up the cross.

While the fiesta fireworks pop outside, the *botafumeiro,* the man-size silver censer, swings dizzily from its ceiling pulley, higher and higher until it soars the length of the transepts. I am half hypnotized by its smoking arc. This surely is the very end of my journey.

And then at my elbow I hear fervent French. I recognize the voice and its weight of gratitude, remembering how it sounded that day at the last granite cross. It is the colleague of Aymery Picaud, the priest from Poitiers. How fine to find him again at this perfect moment!

Père Georges nods an abstracted smile to me through his devotions. *"Merci,"* he repeats several times quietly . . . *"merci, Saint Jacques."*

BURNING *like a pilgrim's fervor, incense sheds a fragrant benediction from the* botafumeiro, *silver censer that swings in awesome arcs from the cathedral's lofty vault. For centuries pilgrims have marveled at the sight, dazzling moment in an unforgettable odyssey.*

MICHAEL KUH

By T. S. R. Boase

The World of Richard the Lionheart

T HE HEAT OF JUNE and the hum of its busy flies closed in on the encampment sprawled on the plain outside the walls of Acre. Here on the coast of Palestine, European men-at-arms had suffered through a second winter of want and "rains that fell without ceasing." Now they sweltered in their tents and scanned the horizon for friendly sails.

They were Crusaders, many of them survivors of the Christian Kingdom of Jerusalem. A matchless Saracen leader, Saladin, had united Egypt, Damascus, and Aleppo against them. He overran their kingdom and seized the Holy City. When, in August 1189, the Christians sought to retake the vital port of Acre, Saladin deployed his forces in the hills behind, pinching the besiegers against the town's walls.

To add to their hardships, disastrous news reached the Crusader camp. The Holy Roman Emperor, Frederick Barbarossa, marching to their aid through Asia Minor, had drowned in a Cilician river. Only a remnant of his army made it south to Acre.

But in the spring of 1191, fresh troops arrived with Philip II of France, whom a chronicler would call Philip Augustus. At 25, he had already ruled France for a decade. Cold, shrewd, shock-haired, blind in one eye, he was no one's fool and a friend to few.

And now finally, in June, English galleys hove into sight and began

Lionized by a land he scarcely knew, crusading Coeur de Lion, of "lofty stature" with features that
"showed the ruler," spurs a Victorian bronze charger before London's Mother of Parliaments; Adam Woolfitt

landing men on the beaches. Their king, at 33, had reached the full power of manhood. Tall and handsome, fearless and tireless, he was quick to anger but naturally generous, a leader whom men understood. Already his troubadours were calling him Richard Coeur de Lion—the Lionheart.

For a century the knights of Europe had been inspired by the crusading spirit. The Crusades diverted the incessant baronial squabbling to more hallowed ends. Warriors sought salvation in wreaking revenge upon the infidels who persecuted Christ's followers and defiled His Holy City. New virtues of sacrifice and dedication came into uncouth society with a concept of knightly duty called chivalry.

The casual dubbing of a knight by his overlord gave way to a ritual bath of purification, an all-night vigil in a church, the donning of a white linen robe and scarlet mantle, and the taking of an oath to use his sword for Christ.

No one better personified the chivalric ideal of daring deeds in the service of the cross than Richard the Lionheart, hero of the Third Crusade.

THOUGH BORN IN ENGLAND, at Oxford, Richard was a son of Aquitaine, a vast territory of southwestern France between the Loire and the Pyrenees. His language was not English but the tongue of *chevalerie* and the *Chanson de Roland,* his heart's realm not the chill and misty north but a southern land of sunlight and romance where life was by turns impetuous and languid—where, an English chronicler observed of the people, "when they set themselves to tame the pride of their enemies, they do it in earnest; and when the labors of battle are over . . . they give themselves up wholly to pleasure."

"Peace delights me not!
War—be thou my lot!
Law—I do not know
save a right good blow!"

Song of troubadour Bertran de Born
echoes above the din of an age when
"Lord Richard laid siege to castles and
towns, and destroyed them, and took
lands and burnt and laid them waste. . . ."
Broadsword and ax cleave helmed
heads and chain-mail hauberks
with the clang of anvils as one
man at left strains at a trebuchet;
its counterweighted arm could heave
boulders, kegs of flammables, even
a dead horse over citadel walls.
   Scorning "a cow's death" abed,
knights thirsting for loot, laurels, and
land—or bored with castle humdrum—
raided neighbors at the drop of a
gauntlet. Few epic battles raged,
mostly skirmishes, hasty sieges,
ravaging of hapless peasants' crops.
A vassal owed his lord but 40 days'
soldiering a year; castle defenders need
not hold long to see foes melt away.
Richard stayed on by using mercenaries.
Wages came from scutage—cash paid
by tenants in lieu of knight service.
   The church's Truce of God banned
war on weekends; the Peace of God
sought to shield women, children, clergy.
Yet knights battled on. Sang Bertran:
"Come barons, haste ye, bringing
your vassals for the daring raid;
Risk all—and let the game be played!"

13TH-CENTURY ARTIST CLOAKED A BIBLICAL
BATTLE IN GARB OF HIS OWN DAY;
PIERPONT MORGAN LIBRARY, NEW YORK

203

"*If its walls were made of solid iron,*"
sneered France's king, "*yet would I take them.*"

"*By the throat of God!*" roared Richard. "*If its
walls were made of butter, yet would I hold them.*"

*Hearty oaths of royal rivals seem to ring yet from Château Gaillard, Lionheart stronghold
300 feet above the now-peaceful Seine. "How beautiful she is, my year-old daughter,"
exulted Richard in 1197 as the triple-moated wonder of his age began to take shape.
Though she emptied his purse, she balked Philip II's lust for Richard's Normandy.*

*Boon companions, mortal foes, crafty Capetian and headstrong Plantagenet played a
lifelong game on the feudal chessboard of France. Philip played Richard, son, against father;
younger brother John against Richard. When the Lionheart curbed Philip's raids with
"Saucy Castle" (Château Gaillard) and dubbed a sister citadel "Push Forward," Philip countered
with fortress "Swallow All." Checked by Richard, he wrested Normandy from feckless John in 1204.
Key to its defense, "impregnable" Château Gaillard fell by stealth—through the latrines!*

RICHARD'S ROOTS *ran deep in sun-warmed soil of southwest France. Here stretched Aquitaine, domain of his mother, gay, headstrong Eleanor. Her divorce from Louis VII had shorn the French king of the largest, richest region in his realm; her marriage to Henry II wedded it to England and triggered three centuries of strife.*

Henry of Anjou and Eleanor of Aquitaine (right) both towered above their time. As learned in discourse as he was bold in battle, Henry gave England laws, some stability, a measure of peace—though courtiers railed at his foul table manners, mercurial whims, volcanic energy, his day-long treks that stranded them in dark forests groping for a place to sleep.

Such ways irked Eleanor, polished daughter of a cultured court where her ladies debated plaints of the heartsore in "Courts of Love" while scribes recorded the verdicts. Though she bore Henry eight children—history marks Richard as her "eagle of the third nesting" and John as the king whose barons wrested freedoms in Magna Carta—the royal pair struck sparks. She poisoned Henry's mistress, some said; but he already had his queen locked up. When he ceded lands to his sons, Eleanor goaded them to revolt. Named by Caesar for its rivers, Aquitaine ran with blood as the Angevin "devil's brood" warred each other down. Now the region flows with cognac and claret to cheer the connoisseur.

GRAPE HARVEST AT COGNAC; GJON MILI. VINEYARDS NEAR BORDEAUX (RIGHT); PIERRE BELZEAUX, RAPHO GUILLUMETTE. CROWNED HEADS ON 12TH-CENTURY CAPITAL FROM LANGON IN THE CLOISTERS COLLECTION, METROPOLITAN MUSEUM OF ART, NEW YORK

206

Aquitaine's terrain changes from the coastal *landes* (sand barrens) and lush vineyards round Bordeaux to the uplands of the Limousin. Oak forests turn russet in autumn, reflecting in the many rivers. It is a land of churches—the eastern domes of Périgueux and Angoulême, the flat, wide vaults over the broad, aisleless churches of Poitou, Romanesque sculpture filling every niche of the façades. It is also a land of castles—towers and walls built by Henry II still greet the eyes at Niort, Loches, and Chinon. Young Richard had many opportunities to gain from his father's works his lifelong interest in fortification.

But throughout his career his mother was the dominant influence upon him. Eleanor, Duchess of Aquitaine and Queen both of France and England, lived into her eighties as one of the pivotal personalities of medieval times. Her taste, and Richard's, for the songs of troubadours came down from her grandfather, a Crusader who became a legend for his wild ways, his many mistresses, and his poems that wandering *jongleurs* sang at baronial feasts. Cynical, bawdy, irreverent, he composed songs about war and wenching and sometimes life's emptiness:

> I know not the star under which I was born,   Some sprite made me what I am
> I who am neither gay nor sad   One night on a mountain top.

Eleanor contributed in her way to the civilization of the day. While guiding Richard at Poitiers, she gathered around her a group of young people, all enthusiastic for the new poetry and the new freedom of talk. Her "Courts of Love" met in the great hall of the castle, where one wall still stands and where Eleanor's name remains fresh in the mind. Her eldest child Marie, "the joyous and gay countess" of Champagne, sometimes presided. The gallantry of the Courts of Love gave women a new standing and brought a note of elegance into the stark medieval picture. Now ladies were the subject of poems and presided at courtly debates—just as they presided over tourneys, another device to channel warlike passions, a game of combat rather than a fight to the death.

One day at a "court" the theme was whether love could survive in marriage, and they decided it could not. Indeed, feudal marriages had little room for it. Troubadours sang of love to ladies already wed or pledged (often in childhood) to others; and usually they were beyond illicit reach. Since landholdings were involved, noblewomen were closely watched.

Certainly love had little to do with Eleanor's first marriage at 15. When she had inherited Aquitaine three months earlier, after her father's death on a pilgrimage to Compostela, Louis, heir to the French throne, had hastened south with an imposing array of knights to secure this prize fief to the Capetian realm.

He married its heiress in St. André Cathedral in Bordeaux. Before the couple reached Paris, the old king died, and Eleanor's husband became Louis VII.

Friction was inevitable between the beautiful, spirited girl and the monastery-raised husband she called "more a monk than a king." Gossip even linked her with her uncle, Raymond of Poitiers, Prince of Antioch, when in 1147 she joined Louis on the Second Crusade. Eventually Louis, grieved that Eleanor bore him two daughters instead of the male heir he needed, agreed to the annulment of

SCOTLAND

IRELAND

WALES

ENGLAND

Shaded area denotes
the Angevin Empire
under King Richard

Cambridge
Oxford
London
Glastonbury
Winchester *Thames* Canterbury

Boulogne

*Henry II's knights slay Becket
in Canterbury Cathedral.*

KINGDOM
OF DENMARK

GERMANY

ENGLISH CHANNEL

FLANDERS

Meuse
Rhine
Aachen • Cologne
• Coblenz
← Marksburg
• Speyer

LORRAINE

HOLY

ROMAN

EMPIRE

Rouen
Château
Gaillard
• Paris

NORMANDY

BRITTANY

MAINE
Le Mans•

CHAMPAGNE

FRANCE

Seine

Clairvaux

*Holy Roman Emperor
Frederick I contests
with Pope Alexander
for control of Italy.*

ANJOU
Fontevrault
Chinon •Tours
POITOU •Loches
Niort •Poitiers
Taillebourg
Angoulême •Limoges
Châlus
•Périgueux
•Bordeaux

•Orléans

•Vézelay

Loire

Cluny

Clermont

ALPS

Padua •
Po
•Ver
Bologna
Genoa• •Portofino •Ravenna
San Marino•
LOMBARDY
Arezzo•
Tiber
•Asso

*Richard as duke of Aquitaine
pays homage to King Philip
of France near Le Mans.*

Garonne

AQUITAINE

Le Puy

Rhone

BURGUNDY

LEON

CASTILE

NAVARRE

PYRENEES

Toulouse

•Marseilles

CORSICA

STATES OF
THE CHURCH

•Ro

Ebro

ARAGON

Barcelona•

SARDINIA

Las Navas
de Tolosa
✕
*King Alfonso VIII of
Castile unites Christians
against Moors.*

GRANADA

MOORS

MEDITERRANEAN SEA

*Pope Alexander III
canonizes Becket.*

Palermo

MOORS

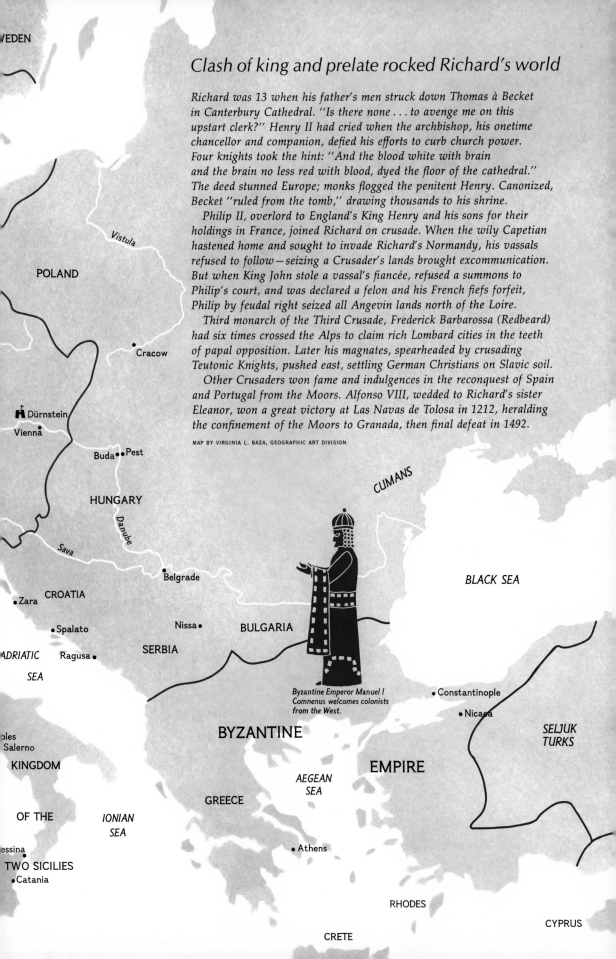

Clash of king and prelate rocked Richard's world

Richard was 13 when his father's men struck down Thomas à Becket in Canterbury Cathedral. "Is there none . . . to avenge me on this upstart clerk?" Henry II had cried when the archbishop, his onetime chancellor and companion, defied his efforts to curb church power. Four knights took the hint: "And the blood white with brain and the brain no less red with blood, dyed the floor of the cathedral." The deed stunned Europe; monks flogged the penitent Henry. Canonized, Becket "ruled from the tomb," drawing thousands to his shrine.

Philip II, overlord to England's King Henry and his sons for their holdings in France, joined Richard on crusade. When the wily Capetian hastened home and sought to invade Richard's Normandy, his vassals refused to follow—seizing a Crusader's lands brought excommunication. But when King John stole a vassal's fiancée, refused a summons to Philip's court, and was declared a felon and his French fiefs forfeit, Philip by feudal right seized all Angevin lands north of the Loire.

Third monarch of the Third Crusade, Frederick Barbarossa (Redbeard) had six times crossed the Alps to claim rich Lombard cities in the teeth of papal opposition. Later his magnates, spearheaded by crusading Teutonic Knights, pushed east, settling German Christians on Slavic soil.

Other Crusaders won fame and indulgences in the reconquest of Spain and Portugal from the Moors. Alfonso VIII, wedded to Richard's sister Eleanor, won a great victory at Las Navas de Tolosa in 1212, heralding the confinement of the Moors to Granada, then final defeat in 1492.

MAP BY VIRGINIA L. BAZA, GEOGRAPHIC ART DIVISION

Byzantine Emperor Manuel I Comnenus welcomes colonists from the West.

SWEDEN

POLAND

Vistula

Cracow

Dürnstein

Vienna

Buda Pest

HUNGARY

Danube

Sava

Belgrade

CROATIA

Zara

Spalato

Nissa

SERBIA

Ragusa

ADRIATIC SEA

CUMANS

BLACK SEA

BULGARIA

Constantinople

Nicaea

SELJUK TURKS

BYZANTINE

EMPIRE

AEGEAN SEA

GREECE

IONIAN SEA

Athens

Naples

Salerno

KINGDOM

OF THE

Messina

TWO SICILIES

Catania

RHODES

CYPRUS

CRETE

their marriage on the convenient grounds of consanguinity — too close a blood tie.

Less than two months later Eleanor startled the feudal world by marrying Henry of Anjou, some ten years her junior, the vigorous, determined duke of Normandy and heir to the English crown. She brought him Aquitaine; thus the Angevin empire comprising England and the greater part of France was founded. And to the increase of Louis' chagrin, Eleanor bore Henry II five sons and three daughters. Richard, born September 8, 1157, was the third son.

William, the first, died young. Henry, the second, was designated his father's heir. Richard was destined to succeed to his mother's Aquitaine; Geoffrey got Brittany; John was called "Lackland" because nothing was left for him.

Not yet 12, Richard did homage to Louis of France for the county of Poitou and the duchy of Aquitaine. Though fiercely independent, these Angevin dominions

still came under the suzerainty of the French crown. Three years later, clutching sacred lance and banner, Richard was solemnly installed as duke of Aquitaine in the church of St. Hilaire at Poitiers. One of the noblest Romanesque churches in France, it stands today drearily overlooking railroad yards and bus stops.

Aquitaine bridled when the Angevin Henry took it into his own hands and tried to exert his severe orderliness. Even Eleanor had close escapes from ambush. Once, defending her, the young knight William Marshal, unhorsed and outnumbered 60 to 1, fought "like a wild boar beset by hounds" and was wounded and captured. Eleanor paid his ransom and royally rewarded him.

Richard grew to manhood in the thick of such violence. At 21 he established his fame by his strategy and élan in taking Taillebourg. When the defenders, lured out by his ravaging of their lands, sallied against him, Richard drove them pell-mell back through the gateway into the town, which he burned. Within two days the citadel on the crag above surrendered. "Never before," noted a chronicler, "had a hostile force so much as looked upon the castle."

These had been years darkened by struggles of sons

THE ART OF COURTLY LOVE *plucked Eve from the pit and placed her on a pedestal. She became a rose in a garden of delight—a fantasy world walled off from feudal society where a woman's real state depended on her real estate. Queen Eleanor was to poets at Poitiers "what dawn is to birds." They sang for her of courts where lady is mistress and man the vassal, striving, yearning in her service.*

Knights would have broken lances over this golden-tressed maid of Arezzo (right), gowned for a joust.

*Men of steel in suits of iron
forged legends of valor
untarnished by time*

Richard warred in a hauberk of mail, as did his
noble gendarmes—men-at-arms—and his sergents,
or troopers. Such a tunic might comprise 40,000
hand-riveted links. Worn over a leather gambeson,
mail could ward off sword strokes. Then Richard
and Philip Augustus put the crossbow into the field.
Chroniclers decried the weapon as unchivalrous;
the church banned its use against any but infidels.
But as crossbows continued their deadly work, iron
plates began to shield knights from the heavy bolts.

ARMOR THROUGH THE AGES LINES JOHN WOODMAN HIGGINS ARMORY IN WORCESTER, MASSACHUSETTS; B. ANTHONY STEWART, NATIONAL GEOGRAPHIC STAFF

By the 1400's horsemen had become clanking tanks.

From cold iron lumps armorers pounded plates, then shaped and joined perhaps 200 into a shining "white harness" tailored even to its owner's fingers. Thin plates formed supple segments, sliding rivets letting joints flex; thick plates, shaped to deflect weapons in war or joust, lay where blows might fall. Some suits reached 120 pounds, took three years to make, a fortune to buy. Sun made them ovens. Unhorsed, a knight was at his foe's mercy. But for man and boy, horse and boar-hunting dog, armor marked the aristocracy; no one else could afford it.

While metal-plated lords spurred to the fray, levies of peasants in naught but gambesons fought with flails, boar spears, and clubs—to knights, mere rabble for butchering, not worth ransoming. But the infanterie (the infants) came of age with the Swiss pikemen at Laupen, the English longbowmen at Crécy. One harness in the armory above bears a breastplate holed by a musket ball, harbinger of armor's doom.

against father and brother against brother. Henry II gave his sons titles but never ceded his own control over their territories. He would indulge his princes, then interfere. His hot-blooded sons resented him more and more. His queen saw him less and less, and he found other women, particularly Rosamond Clifford. The fact that legend has been busy telling how Eleanor forced "Fair Rosamond" to poison herself is but evidence of the powerful impression of Eleanor's personality. To her enemies great crimes seemed appropriate to her.

Henry himself shocked Christendom when his long and bitter quarrel with Thomas à Becket ended in the archbishop's martyrdom. Their father discredited, their mother humiliated by him, the princes rose in rebellion. But Henry moved with masterful strokes and within a year brought them to terms. His sons, begging with tears for pardon, received it. Eleanor, seeking to join the princes during the revolt, was seized by Henry's knights near Chinon, dressed as a man. She surely offered neither tears nor pleas. For the next 15 years she would remain under guard in England, save for occasional Christmas family reunions.

In 1180 Louis of France died and his stern son Philip succeeded him. He was only 15, but never youthful. Three years later, England's young Henry died.

Richard, now the heir, faced another breach with his father, who claimed that since Richard would have Anjou, Normandy, and England, John should have Aquitaine. Richard's Aquitaine? His mother's Aquitaine? Never!

While the dispute raged, news broke in the autumn of 1187 of Saladin's capture of Jerusalem. Richard heard it one evening at Tours. Next morning, impetuously, he took the Crusader's cross. "You should by no means have undertaken so weighty a business without consulting me," roared his father. But the outrage against

MIGHTY MARKSBURG *speaks in stone of the castle world Richard knew. Raised above the Rhine in the 12th and enlarged in later centuries, it knew attack but never defeat, repair but never the "restoration" that dimmed the medieval aura of its surviving sisters.*

Spurred by Byzantine and Saracen example, crusading-era builders sited citadels atop crags, ringed them with walls and moats, created a complex of defenses within defenses. Towers, self-contained forts like Marksburg's polygon, bulged at corners to let bowmen cover the foot of the walls. Rising from the innermost court (right) the donjon, or keep, offered the ultimate refuge. Climbing in through a high entry, defenders drew up their ladders and braced for weeks of salt beef, bread, and ale. Last to bow was a lord's banner, purling from this highest tower until flung down to signal defeat.

An insult to Duke Leopold of Austria's banner at Acre led to Richard's capture and confinement above the Danube in Dürnstein, one of 10,000 castles to rise in German lands alone.

215

FACE OF A FEUDAL FORTRESS
ever ready for war frowns on Marksburg visitors. One grim chamber houses "morning stars" (spiked iron clubs), "cat's eyes" (spiked ball on chain), and an iron girdle to padlock a lady's chastity while her lord crusaded. Woe to a traitor: jailers fitted him with red-hot copper mask (right), cast him to rot in the dungeon (under the donjon), or had stallions pull him to pieces.

Tower stairway (below) turns right, as many did, to cramp sword arms of ascending foes. Dark turns often hid pitfalls. Kitchen fireplace (bottom) could roast a sheep for diners in the thick-walled Rittersaal, or Knights' Hall (opposite). Little but chests furnished castles; into them went clothes and valuables. The signal to pillage: "Break open the chests!"

216

Christ's name awakened a response even in Henry. He took the cross himself. So did the aged German emperor, Frederick Barbarossa, and the cautious Philip of France. Jerusalem's loss seemed to offer peace to Europe.

But not immediately. One more quarrel broke out, and when the old king fled from the flaming city of his birth, Le Mans, Richard was hard in pursuit. He might have captured his father, but William Marshal, faithful to his sovereign, barred the way and struck down Richard's horse. "I will not slay you," he snarled. "But I hope the devil may."

Henry died soon after at Chinon: Henry, the great ruler and lawgiver over northwestern Europe, the passionate, restless man, as maladroit in his personal relationships as he was skillful in the affairs of state.

ICHARD WAS KING OF ENGLAND. And now "Queen Eleanor," a chronicler tells us, "moved her royal court from city to city and from castle to castle... sending messages throughout England that all captives should be liberated for the good of the soul of Henry, her lord, for in her own person she had learned by experience that confinement is distasteful to mankind, and that it is a most welcome refreshment to the spirit to be liberated from it."

Richard himself was soon in England to organize his government for his absence and to raise money for his crusade. It seemed to some that "the king put up to

217

PHEASANT *fit for an ermined lady gladdens a 15th-century feast. Gone is the murky castle hall, littered with weapons, trophies, bedding of retainers who sprawled on benches as boarhounds cracked bones on the rush-strewn paving.*

Sleek greyhound patrols a tile floor inspired by Moorish Spain. Squires in puffed sleeves and pointed shoes serve to the sound of shawms, oboe ancestors that skirled the Saracens to battle.

Crusades of Richard's day woke the taste buds of Europe. Nobles once content with flat fare emptied purses for treats they had savored in the Levant: pepper, cloves, raisins, dates, a candy the infidel called sugar. Cellars in the 12th century cooled beer, mead, cider, nectar, and "clove-spiced wine for gluttons whose thirst is unquenchable." Physicians favored costly "water of gold" to prolong youth and cure sundry ills; we call it brandy.

Castle dwellers rose with the sun, broke fast with bread and wine. A heavy dinner could begin in the morning; supper might bring pastry, fruit, and wine.

From kitchens where turnspits did roasts "to a turn," varlets scurried with dishes that needed little chewing; in days of crude dentistry, few had teeth for it. Little that could be eaten was not. Clever chefs might stew chicken heads, feet, and innards in a delight called "garbage" — or sew half a pig to half a capon and serve a heraldic "cockatrice." Among 31 dishes of one feast: eels boiled inside out in wine, lark pasties, roast carp, larded milk. Few kinds of birds escaped the pot; knights ate crow with gusto, hailed peacock as "food for the brave."

Pairs of diners shared cup and trencher. Feasting over, all danced, gave ear to minstrels, or watched falcons chase songbirds freed from a huge pie. The seneschal counted the silverware, and peasants lined up outside for leftovers.

15TH-CENTURY FRENCH ILLUMINATION FROM "RENAUD DE MONTAUBAN"; BIBLIOTHÈQUE DE L'ARSENAL, PARIS

sale everything that he had." One report had him saying, "I would sell London itself if I could find a buyer."

Into that city—hailed by a chronicler as "among the noble and celebrated cities of the world"—rode Richard and Eleanor for the most lavish coronation hitherto recorded. It set a pattern for the centuries to follow.

But the feast in the great hall of Westminster that William Rufus, son of the Conqueror, had built, was marred by a tragic event. A deputation of the Jewish community came to offer gifts to the king. The crowd fell upon them. A general attack on the Jewish quarter followed, and many were killed. Other massacres occurred throughout England. Richard punished instigators, but the crusading spirit fostered bitterness against Jews.

"His blood be on us, and on our children"— the terrible cry of the mob at the Crucifixion

220

was not forgotten. Jews were also resented as wealthy traders, prospering on the usury forbidden to Christians.

In December 1189, after four months in his kingdom, Richard set out on his journey eastward. At Tours he received a pilgrim's staff, "and when he leaned upon it, it broke." A disturbing omen.

He embarked from Marseilles, and Roger of Hoveden, chronicling the ports Richard passed on the Italian coast, tells of the king landing at Ostia, of pirates' castles and Roman roads, of the island of Ponza "where Pilate was born"; of smoking Stromboli, of stays at Naples and at Salerno, where there was a famous medical school.

Richard's fleet now arrived from England, and he entered Messina harbor at the head of 114 ships. "So noble was the sound of the trumpets and clarions that the city quaked and was greatly astonished. . . ."

Sicilian culture, where Moorish and Byzantine influences ran strong, must have seemed strange to these visitors from the north. Yet England had many ties with Sicily, whose Norman dynasty had turned the Mediterranean from a Moslem into a Christian sea. These ties had been strengthened when Richard's youngest sister Joanna, bringing a rich dowry, had married William II of Sicily.

Richard found her widowed and without heir. The throne had been seized by Tancred of Lecce, illegitimate grandson of Roger II, creator of Norman power in Sicily. Tancred

PAST PEARLS *like Portofino (opposite) Richard in 1190 threaded down the Italian boot to a Norman kingdom that outshone his own. Here for generations had come the younger brothers of Norman nobility. Primogeniture left them landless; Norman blood made them ill content to remain so. Hiring as free lances to pope and pirate, carving for themselves a place in Italy's sun, these nobodies in Normandy became sovereigns in Sicily. They sacked Rome, defeated Byzantine emperors, seized African shores. By 1059 southern Italy bowed to onetime bandit Robert Guiscard, "the cunning." His brother Roger conquered Sicily; in 1130 his nephew Roger II ruled both domains as king.*

Like Crusaders to come, Normans in Sicily invaded Saracen soil. At most a few thousand, ruling a medley of Latins, Greeks, Moslems, and Jews, they kept local customs, promoted trade, sugar crops, the silk industry, and public baths little known in the north. Their use of seaborne cavalry lent techniques to William's conquest of England. Tax censuses of their douane (from the Arabic diwan) prefigured the Domesday Book. Their translators gave Europe works of Plato, Aristotle, Euclid, Ptolemy.

Richard's brother-in-law William graced Monreale, "royal mount," with a cathedral and fountained cloister (left) wedding styles of East and West. In the palace at Palermo— a capital richer in royal revenue than all England—Norman rulers kept harems and eunuchs, and awed guests to this "stupendous city . . . rising before one like a temptress."

Their line died with half-German Holy Roman Emperor Frederick II— stupor mundi, "wonder of the world," said admirers; a "baptized sultan," growled foes. Poet, philosopher, scientist, he kept a vast zoo, even took it on trips. He wrote a treatise, still a classic, on the art of falconry (center). Nobles alone rated a falcon. Richard seized an Italian peasant's bird—and nearly missed his crusade as irate villagers mobbed him!

had taken Joanna's dowry and imprisoned her at Palermo, while scheming against Richard with Philip, who had already arrived with the French Crusaders.

Here was a situation to arouse the Lionheart. He "took Messina more quickly than a priest could say his matins," and sister and dowry were handed over to him.

Eleanor now arrived at Messina, having crossed the Alps in winter. She brought Berengaria of Navarre, a princess known to have attracted Richard's notice; Eleanor felt it time Richard had an heir. He had long been betrothed to Alice, Philip's half sister, who had been brought up at the court in England. The marriage had been delayed time and again. Now, when Philip pressed for it, Richard bluntly told him that his sister had been seduced by Henry II, and, Richard said, he would not wed his father's mistress.

Berengaria sailed with Joanna for the Holy Land. A storm drove their ship to shelter at Limassol, on Cyprus, where Richard later joined them.

Cyprus was all that Richard would see of the Byzantine world, whose splendor his mother had experienced at the court in Constantinople. When he landed, he was opposed by Isaac Comnenus, a tyrant bent on plundering the fleet. Richard overran this island of castles, taking them one by one. Surrendering, Isaac begged not to be placed in iron fetters, and Richard had silver chains made for him—it was the kind of grim joke the king enjoyed. His booty included Isaac's magnificent horse Fauvel, which Richard rode throughout the Crusade.

Amid all this Richard married Berengaria. A chapel in the castle is sometimes shown as the place, but nothing of Richard's time remains in Limassol.

ACRE STANDS ON A SPIT of land that forms one of Palestine's few natural harbors. Richard's practiced eye scanned the port, barred from seaward with a great iron chain, from landward with mighty walls and ditch. Philip, who had arrived earlier, greeted him, and "the two kings conducted each other from the port and paid one another the most obsequious attention," records a chronicler. "Then King Richard retired to the tent . . . and entered into arrangements about the siege, for it was his most anxious care to find out by what means, artifice, and machines they could capture the city without loss of time."

An attack was planned, but camp fever, which had taken heavy toll during the two-year siege, prostrated both kings. Richard, already troubled by ague, recovered less quickly than Philip. But he had his men carry him, wrapped in silken coverings, to a shelter within range of the most formidable tower—the "Accursed Tower"—so he could join crossbowmen in shooting at the defenders.

"His sappers also carried a mine under the tower," continues the chronicler,

SPORT OF KNIGHTS *turned hearts and fortunes on the tip of a lance.*
As challengers in sleeveless coats of arms, bearing blazoned shields, entered the lists (enclosure), heralds called out names and honors. Paired in joust, teamed in melee, knights honed battle skills while damsels thronged galleries to "well and clearly see who jousted best for their Lady Love." To favorites they tossed scarves, hose, strips of skirt. Berengaria, Richard's queen, first caught his eye at a tournament in her father's kingdom of Navarre. Victors held crestfallen losers for ransom; a few made fortunes at it, notably William Marshal, who in an industrious career of homicide captured 500 knights.

CRESTED GERMAN KNIGHT WALTHER VON KLINGEN, SHATTERING A LANCE, UNSEATS AN ADVERSARY; FROM CODEX MANESSE, C. 1300, UNIVERSITÄTSBIBLIOTHEK HEIDELBERG; LOSSEN FOTO

"and having made a breach, they filled it with logs of wood and set them on fire; when, by the addition of frequent blows from the petraria [a stone-hurling catapult], the tower fell suddenly to the ground with a crash." Fierce fighting took place in the breach. The following day, July 12, 1191, Acre surrendered.

"And when the day came that the Turks, so renowned for their courage and valor . . . and famous for their magnificence, appeared on the walls ready to leave the city, the Christians went forth to look at them, and were struck with admiration when they remembered the deeds they had done."

In the meeting of East and West during the Crusades mutual respect grew. The Arabs admired the bravery of the Franks (as all Crusaders were called), their resoluteness in warfare. But they were shocked by the liberties Franks allowed their women and horrified by their crude medical practice. Franks who had settled in Syria in the First Crusade soon appreciated Arabic culture and some spoke Arabic. Christians and Moslems even became allies in local feudal struggles. Such tolerance shocked the Third Crusaders, arriving full of fervor.

Just as these Crusaders fought for the Sepulcher of Christ, so the Moslems now waged holy war—the jihad that their Koran taught. Indeed, Saladin had a deeper sense of sacred cause than Richard. Where Richard enjoyed the songs of troubadours and rough camp jests, Saladin was happier discoursing on theology with learned men. Courageous, thoughtful, capable of a wide grasp of affairs, Saladin was also high-strung, subject to fits of depression, and easily moved to tears. A brave or noble act, whether by friend or foe, won his esteem.

JOUST OF THE SARACEN *turns back Arezzo's clock. Quarters of the Italian city challenge one another by herald (page 6); each fields standard-bearers (below), buglers, bowmen, foot soldiers, and two knights tended by squires carrying crested helms (right). In the piazza (opposite) glowers Buratto the Saracen. Knights score if they lance the pivoted effigy's shield, but lose points, and gain welts, if hit by hardwood balls hung on its arm.*

Early tourneys knew few rules, much blood. Sixty died in one, a knight slew his son in another. Richard's own brother Geoffrey, jousting at Philip's court in Paris in 1186, was thrown from his horse, trampled, and killed.

Popes banned such sport. "Those who fall in tourneys," railed a monk, "will go to hell." Few heeded. To be ready for war, taught one text, "a knight . . . must have seen his own blood flow, have had his teeth crackle under the blow of his adversary."

Heavier armor, blunt weapons, rigid rules tamed later tourneys. And few died as knights leveled lances at rings on poles—whence came the brass rings of carousels.

JONATHAN S. BLAIR

He admired Richard's courage, and at one time there was strange talk of a peace based on the marriage of Richard's sister Joanna with Saladin's brother al-Adil. Richard is said to have knighted one of the latter's sons. Even in open warfare chivalrous courtesies could be exchanged. When Richard was sick before Acre, Saladin sent him fresh fruit and snow from the mountains.

Such chivalry now underwent a severe test. With Acre's capture, Philip declared his mission accomplished and departed homeward. Richard, with his many possessions in France, felt uneasy about Philip being there while he marched on Jerusalem. He was eager to get on with the Crusade.

But there were delays in carrying out the surrender terms. Saladin had not released all the prisoners, paid all the money, nor handed over the True Cross. Richard refused to wait any longer. He held 2,700 hostages from Acre. He could neither feed nor guard them on the march.

In the plain before the city, within sight of Saracen soldiers who tried to intervene, these rope-bound prisoners were slaughtered — the Christians "leaping forward eagerly, thankful with divine assent to take revenge upon those who

STREAKING *toward the Saracen, an Arezzo knight seeks to strike with lance-shattering impact, thus doubling his score. "Fairly broken!" was the cry when heroes split 14-foot shafts. A knight was as fond of his destrier (a war-horse led by the right, or dexter, hand) as he was of his sword. One hoped in heaven but "to see Blanchart, my old horse."*

JONATHAN S. BLAIR

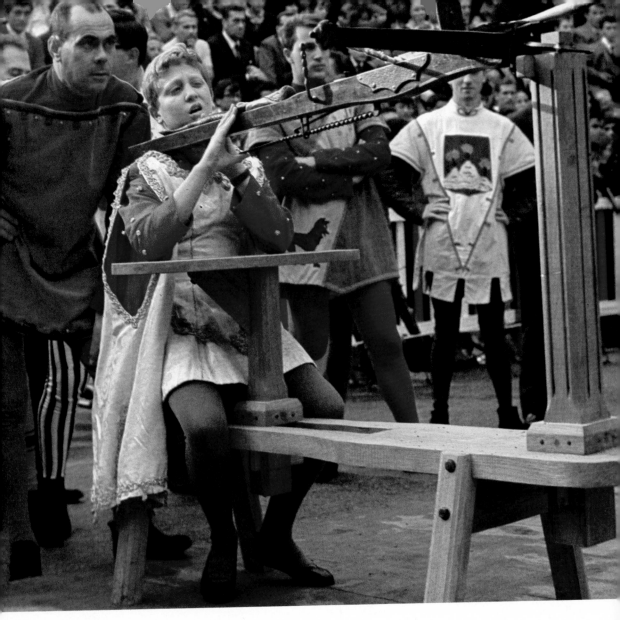

had destroyed so many Christians with bolts and arrows."

Massacres were not new to the Crusades. But this blood-bath at Acre stands out with particular repugnance, for Saladin had shown clemency many times. At Jerusalem he had even ransomed some Christian prisoners out of his own pocket. Hereafter little quarter was given.

The Crusaders marched south in the heat of August, past Mount Carmel, Caesarea, harried by Saladin's army that now outnumbered them three to one. At Arsuf, Richard, astride Fauvel, led a thundering charge that won the day for the Franks. He took Joppa and pressed inland. Fighting erupted such as he excelled in—slashing right and left "with arrows sticking out all over him like the bristles of

CROSSBOW'S TWANG *triggers scenes of chivalry as lads vie to make a brave showing at a San Marino fete. Medieval boys held: "Coward was he who was the first archer; he . . . dared not come close to his foe."*

Page at 7, squire at 14, a lad bent on knighthood trained for combat man-to-man. He learned to struggle into a hauberk (opposite), swing the fearsome flail, dodge the battle-ax that could cleave his helm, and wield the sword— also to swear oaths on holy relics in its knob. Knighted at 21, he donned spurs and rode to glory.

a hedgehog," or springing from his bed to repel a surprise attack, bare-legged on horseback.

In winter rains and hail his tattered force pushed through the Judaean hills to within a few miles of Jerusalem. But now it was stoutly held by Saladin, and a long siege impossible. A chronicler tells how Richard covered his eyes and exclaimed, "Fair Lord God, I pray Thee that Thou suffer me not to behold Thy Holy City since I cannot deliver it from the hands of Thine enemies."

That frustrated cry speaks volumes for the reverence with which rough, brutal warriors regarded their faith.

THE RETURN from Palestine brought unforeseen adventures. While Berengaria and Joanna landed safely at Marseilles, Richard twice was driven ashore by storm in the Adriatic. Assuming a disguise, he pushed on overland—a foolhardy stunt even for him. For he was traversing lands of Leopold of Austria, whom he had outraged at Acre by tearing down his ducal banner from a palace Richard claimed. Discovery was inevitable, and Leopold imprisoned him near Vienna in Dürnstein castle, still a romantic silhouette above the medieval town.

In England rumors flew: The king, hero of the Crusade, had disappeared. Two abbots went to the Empire to seek him through the ecclesiastical network—for news spread from monastery to monastery as travelers broke their journeys at them. Legend relates how the troubadour Blondel heard Richard singing in the castle at Dürnstein and answered with a song familiar to both. But Emperor Henry VI, Leopold's overlord and Richard's enemy, now had the Lionheart in custody in Germany.

Richard's mother worked for his release. She wrote the pope to enlist his help, signing herself "Eleanor, by the wrath of God, Queen of England." A ransom was finally fixed at a staggering 100,000 silver marks—more than a year's royal revenues from England and Normandy. When finally it was raised, Eleanor herself, now over 70 and "still indefatigable for every undertaking," journeyed with it up the Rhine to the emperor's court at Speyer, protecting the treasure with her prestige.

Richard returned to a hero's welcome in England, and to cope with the perfidy of his brother John, who had been scheming with Philip. He forgave him all too easily. In *Ivanhoe,* Sir Walter Scott drew on legend to have the

WEAPONS IN METROPOLITAN MUSEUM OF ART, NEW YORK.
TOP: PIERPONT MORGAN LIBRARY. OPPOSITE: TED H. FUNK

Lionheart meet Robin Hood's Merry Men in Sherwood Forest. Popular fancy, shrewder in some ways than history, noted the derring-do quality in both that made fitting such a meeting between Robin and Richard.

Characteristically, Richard introduced tourneys to England, where they had been prohibited under his father; and he charged a high fee for their license. Shortage of money plagued him the rest of his reign, as well as French threats to Normandy. He wished above all to capture Philip, thus gaining a large ransom and settling old scores. Daring forays and skirmishes failed. Once Philip, with Richard in pursuit, clattered across the bridge at Gisors, which gave way, plunging the French king into the river. "He swallowed some water," but escaped.

Philip was consolidating the Seine Valley route between Paris and the Norman capital, Rouen. Richard determined to block his way. High above a curve in the river, at Les Andelys, he built his remarkable Château Gaillard, utilizing all he had learned from his father's castles and those he had seen in Palestine. And here he hurled defiance at Philip.

The Lionheart's end came in a strangely trivial way. A peasant plowing near Châlus, in Aquitaine, turned up a golden "table," probably a Roman shield, and some gold coins. Feudal law gave the overlord rights to such a trove, but the lord of Châlus refused to hand it over and fled when Richard appeared.

Châlus, amid its oak-and-chestnut woods, has changed little. The narrow, winding Rue de Coeur-de-Lion leads to the castle, and villagers still point out the hillocks across the valley where Richard pitched his last camp. Reducing this small castle could only take a few days.

As Richard recklessly rode close to the walls without his full armor, a crossbowman, shielding himself, it was said, with a frying pan, discharged his bolt. The king paused to applaud the shot before raising his shield. The arrow struck his shoulder just below the neck. When Richard pulled, it broke, leaving the barb in the wound. Surgery caused a festering.

The castle was stormed, the defenders hanged—all except Bertran de Gourdon, who had drawn the mortal shaft. Brought before Richard, he gloried in his achievement: "You slew my father and my two brothers, now devise what torments you may for me." Richard, in a

"The good King Arthur of Britain, whose knighthood inspires us to be valiant and courteous, held a noble court....His name will live for all time"

Chrétien de Troyes, 12th century

King Arthur and his knights watch as Galahad vows
to seek the Holy Grail, chalice of the Last Supper.
Squires knighted in solemn ritual revered such
heroes as they rode forth to serve chivalry's ideals.

Formidable was the challenge—to serve at once
God, suzerain, and ladylove. For to the knightly
virtues of piety and valor, Eleanor's court had
added a third: the romantic quest wherein "dames
wax chaste and knights the nobler for their love."

Hymning this triple ideal, Chrétien de Troyes
extolled a hero who never was: King Arthur.
Historians glimpse him in Arturius, a 6th-century
warrior whose Britons slowed the Saxon tide. Celtic
myths clustered about his memory in Wales, even in
Brittany where some of his men fled when he fell.
By Richard's day troubadours sang of a chivalrous
Arthur, championed by 12 stalwarts who sat at a
Round Table lest any claim precedence. Slain by a

kinsman—his nephew Modred, who refused him
homage—Arthur would one day rise to rout oppressors.

By Merlin's magic, these 6th-century Britons
arrived at Eleanor's court in shining 12th-century
armor, courteous, just, loyal, compassionate,
munificent, invincible, eager to slay any dragon
in honor of the ladies they adored from afar.
Intimacy spelled trouble. When passion triumphed
over feudal loyalties, as with Tristram and Iseult,
and Lancelot and Guinevere, ruin and remorse
resulted. Whereas Galahad, who never tasted the
heady wine of womanlove, won the Grail.

To bask in Arthur's aura, Henry II hied to
Glastonbury and, true to legend, unearthed bones
some said were Arthur's, asleep with Excalibur,
his magic sword. His knights, paragons of chivalry,
stayed alive in prose and poetry to our time, when
modern troubadours produced the musical Camelot.

231

gesture that came so easily to him, pardoned the soldier and granted him 100 shillings.

On April 6, 1199, the king died in his mother's arms.

By his request, Richard was taken to Fontevrault Abbey, there to lie by his father. (His heart, "his unconquerable heart" as a chronicler calls it, he asked to be sent to Rouen.) Eleanor hoped now to find rest at her beloved abbey. But the years demanded all her statecraft to preserve Richard's realm for John, last of her sons. In 1204, three weeks after Philip seized Château Gaillard while John remained idle, she died at Fontevrault.

One by one they vanished, the great figures of the time. Eleanor outlived most. Richard's fame endured and grew: the intrepid Crusader riding Fauvel against the Saracens, the warrior whose name Arab mothers invoked to quiet their children, the royal prisoner who charmed his captors.

True, as ruler in Aquitaine Richard enforced order with brutality. As king of England he knew little of the country except as a source of money. But legend formed around the king who was a troubadour; the knight who challenged infidels—and the king of France—to personal combat and found no taker; the paragon of chivalry who forgave, even rewarded, the man who mortally wounded him.

No one embodied more the admired traits of his age, when for a century men had set their faces toward Jerusalem.

NOBLEST CALL of knighthood rallied Richard and thousands to a surging pageant of faith: the Crusades. "Had ye but seen the host when forth it came! The earth trembled," exulted a chronicler as men and monarchs marched to wrest sacred sites from Moslem hands. Fleets of Genoa, Pisa, Venice wafted them to the Holy Land and kept sea lanes open to Levant ports.

Richard's arrival in 1191 broke a two-year stalemate at Acre, where thousands of Crusaders died taking this meeting place of continents, its grandeur reminding one chronicler of Constantinople. In 1948 Zionists tunneling out of prison bared a noble Gothic hall (opposite). Here pilgrims and Knights Hospitalers of St. John dined and vaults rang with a battle hymn, "Wood of the Cross," that drove Christian soldiers onward.

Richard, helm sprigged with broom, the planta genista of a Plantagenet, rides sword in hand on his Second Great Seal (below). To raise funds to fight Philip, he scrapped his first in 1198; all who held charters sealed with it must pay anew. The Lionheart's second seal gave England her three heraldic lions.

Apter symbol for him might be the crossbow. He fostered it in France, fell to the bolt of a lowborn sniper; thus "the lion by the ant was slain." But his world lives on. Fair play and sportsmanship flowered in the tourneys, romantic love evolved from knighthood's code. Even our salute mimes knights raising visors in days when the Lionheart, "hurtling like a thunderbolt, poleaxed the paynim [heathen] beneath the walls of Acre."

ST. LOUIS OF FRANCE DEPARTS FROM AIGUES MORTES ON THE 7TH CRUSADE, 1248; 15TH-CENTURY ILLUMINATION FROM "VOYAGES D'OUTRE MER"; BIBLIOTHÈQUE NATIONALE, PARIS. RICHARD'S SEAL, COURTESY DEAN AND CHAPTER, CANTERBURY CATHEDRAL. OPPOSITE: THOMAS NEBBIA

*Starvation stalked them, Saracens slew them, greed tempted them —
but faith drove them on. From the heart of Europe to the walls of Jerusalem,
National Geographic's Franc Shor walks with history*

In the Footsteps
of the Crusaders

B ATTLE-WORN, plagued by hunger and thirst, warriors of the First Crusade drove baggage-laden camels and oxen and horses past the mosque of the prophet Samuel to the summit of the hill called Montjoie. Before them, bright in the pitiless Judaean sun, stood the goal toward which they had struggled for three years: Jerusalem, the Holy City, a prize sought by conquerors since the time of Nebuchadnezzar.

Confronting the Crusaders on this day in 1099 were fortress walls laid out during the second-century reign of the Roman emperor Hadrian, walls strengthened by succeeding defenders and now manned by an overwhelmingly superior force of well-trained Arab and Sudanese troops. Excitement swept the Crusader ranks. Could they take the city?

Their long march had claimed a fearful toll. "At the most we did not have

A barefoot Christian army circles besieged Jerusalem, goal of the Crusades; painting for National Geographic by Tom Lovell

more than twelve thousand able to bear arms," chronicled Raymond of Aguilers, a chaplain, "for there were many poor people and many sick." He estimated the Moslem strength as five times greater. Greed and suspicion rent the Crusader leadership. Faith alone sustained them: "Nothing, whether great or small," said Raymond, "which is undertaken in the name of the Lord can fail. . . ."

To a scornful Moslem the bedraggled host before the walls seemed "a canine breed." But thousands of miles back, in the heart of feudal Europe, knights and bishops had marched forth grandly with peasants and tradesmen; the sons of kings with serfs and freemen. Banners fluttered. Trumpets blared. And these *cruce signati*, or crossbearers, the sign of their Savior emblazoned on their tunics, headed east—the knights in chain mail, swords swinging from their belts.

The call to arms had come from Pope Urban II on a November day in 1095. To a hushed multitude outside the French village of Clermont (today's Clermont-Ferrand) he told of Turkish marauders profaning sacred shrines, persecuting pilgrims who sought the footsteps of Christ in the Holy City. Byzantium, guardian of Eastern Christendom, had pleaded for help. The chronicles give varying accounts of the pope's exact words, but the shouted reply of the thousands gathered there

is beyond doubt. *"Deus lo volt!"* they cried. *"God wills it!"*

The strange magnetism of a devout pontiff had stirred a response greater than even he could have prayed for. Men rushed to take the cross and risk the unknown in fulfillment of one of mankind's proudest dreams.

*T*HERE IS CONTAGION in such a dream. Reading of it nine centuries later, I found the old lure new once more and set out to follow the path of those First Crusaders, to see what they had seen. I left Clermont-Ferrand on an April morning when the blooms of the genet brushed the Auvergne countryside with a golden glow. Behind me stood a gaunt statue of Urban II, arm upraised, urging the faithful forward. Ahead stretched their long road.

Though many of the Crusaders blazed the trail on foot, I had neither the time nor the legs for that. Early morning hikes, however, gave me intimate glimpses of some of the most magnificent countryside in Europe as I made my way across the Loire, up the Rhine, and down the Danube.

At Cologne, great commercial center of the Rhineland then as now, I picked up the route of Peter the Hermit, that swarthy zealot in monk's robes who, mounted on a scrawny donkey, assembled an army of peasants with his magic oratory. The poor in those troubled times felt they had little to lose; they were among the first to set out.

The Crusaders drew blood long before they reached the Holy Land—first Jewish blood, then Christian. In the

"GOD WILLS IT!" *echoed the stones of Clermont as Urban II stirred folk weary of feudal war and bent their fervor to a sacred cause. There his image towers today, recalling the French city's proudest hour. Pigeons wheel like lost souls. Response to the golden-tongued pontiff far surpassed his hopes; warriors from all Europe took up shield and lance (right) to join the First Crusade. "Who ever heard," marveled a chronicler, "such a mixture of languages in one army?"*

Soft arms held others at home. "Newly married men may not take the cross," decreed Urban, "without their wives' consent."

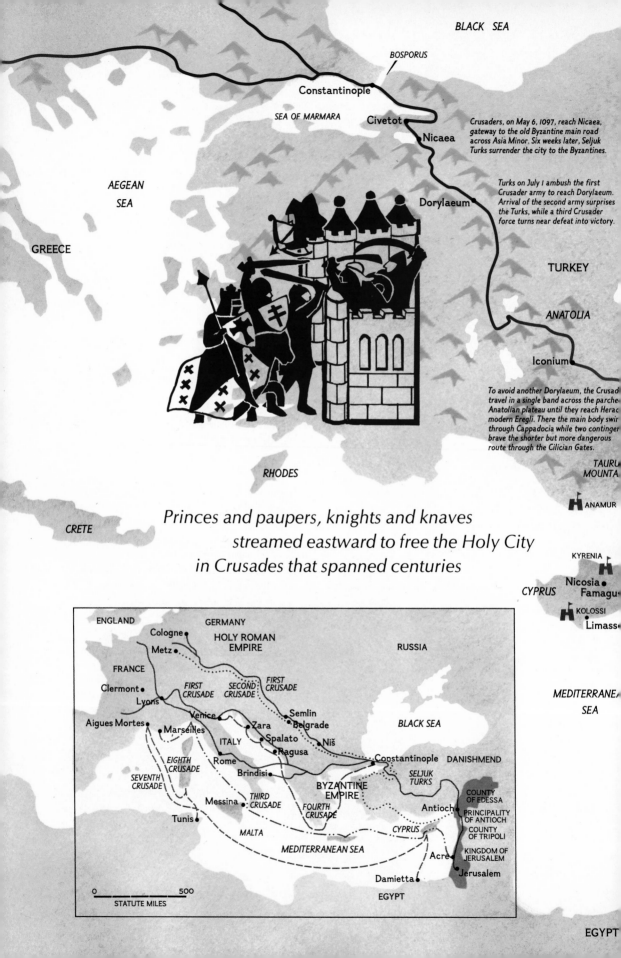

BLACK SEA

BOSPORUS

Constantinople

SEA OF MARMARA

Civetot

Nicaea

Crusaders, on May 6, 1097, reach Nicaea,
gateway to the old Byzantine main road
across Asia Minor. Six weeks later, Seljuk
Turks surrender the city to the Byzantines.

AEGEAN
SEA

Dorylaeum

Turks on July 1 ambush the first
Crusader army to reach Dorylaeum.
Arrival of the second army surprises
the Turks, while a third Crusader
force turns near defeat into victory.

GREECE

TURKEY

ANATOLIA

Iconium

To avoid another Dorylaeum, the Crusad[ers]
travel in a single band across the parche[d]
Anatolian plateau until they reach Herac[lea]
modern Eregli. There the main body swir[ls]
through Cappadocia while two continge[nts]
brave the shorter but more dangerous
route through the Cilician Gates.

RHODES

TAURU[S]
MOUNTA[INS]

ANAMUR

CRETE

KYRENIA

Princes and paupers, knights and knaves
streamed eastward to free the Holy City
in Crusades that spanned centuries

CYPRUS

Nicosia Famagu[sta]

KOLOSSI

Limass[ol]

MEDITERRANE[AN]
SEA

ENGLAND   GERMANY
      Cologne   HOLY ROMAN
    Metz   EMPIRE
FRANCE
                FIRST   SECOND   FIRST
Clermont   CRUSADE   CRUSADE   CRUSADE
  Lyons
        Venice   Semlin
Aigues Mortes   Zara   Belgrade
     Marseilles   Spalato
              ITALY   Ragusa   Niš
        EIGHTH   Rome
       CRUSADE   Brindisi
SEVENTH   BYZANTINE
CRUSADE   EMPIRE
         Messina   THIRD
                 CRUSADE   FOURTH
      Tunis   CRUSADE
            MALTA
              MEDITERRANEAN SEA

RUSSIA

BLACK SEA

Constantinople DANISHMEND

SELJUK
TURKS

COUNTY
OF EDESSA

Antioch   PRINCIPALITY
          OF ANTIOCH
CYPRUS   COUNTY
          OF TRIPOLI

Acre   KINGDOM
       OF JERUSALEM

Damietta   Jerusalem

EGYPT

0   500
STATUTE MILES

EGYPT

Crusader Castles

0   100

STATUTE MILES

MAP BY LEO B. ZEBARTH AND MUNRO KINSEY
GEOGRAPHIC ART DIVISION

ASIA MINOR

oreme•

Caesarea
Mazaca

CAPPADOCIA

Coxon

Tyana•

ANTI-TAURUS MOUNTAINS

Heraclea

CILICIAN
GATES ANAZARBUS

LAMPRON IIAN Marash

Tarsus TIL HAMDOUN

CAMARDESIUM

SYRIAN GATES

eucia

St. Simeon•
Antioch

Latakia SAONE Marra

MARGAT

ARWAD
KRAK DES CHEVALIERS Massiaf

Arca

Tripoli Orontes SYRIA

LE MOINESTRE

Beirut• LEBANON

Abayh•
Sidon• Damascus

Tyre• BELFORT

Acre• HORNS OF HATTIN
✕ SEA OF GALILEE

MT. CARMEL

CHASTEL PÈLERIN

rsuf• SAMARIA

•Joppa

MONTJOIE Jordan R.

Ascalon• JERUSALEM
•Bethlehem JORDAN

BLANCHE GARDE

DEAD SEA KERAK

ISRAEL

Euphrates

Edessa

•Aleppo

Crusaders crossing the Anti-Taurus Mountains find the road little more than a steep, twisting trail; October rains turn it into a muddy deathtrap.

Baldwin's forces quit the main army east of Heraclea and establish a Christian state in Edessa, February 1098.

Antioch's fortifications resist Crusaders, who receive supplies from Genoese ships at St. Simeon. On night of June 3, 1098, an Armenian betrays the Turks, letting knights in to occupy Antioch.

Knights lay siege to Jerusalem on June 7, 1099. After receiving desperately needed supplies from English and Genoese ships putting into Joppa, they assault the Holy City walls on July 13. By the evening of the 15th, Jerusalem—goal of the Crusade—is theirs.

First Crusade (1095-99) funneled through Constantinople, then fought its way across Asia Minor to Jerusalem and triumph in 1099. Conquering Christians carved out the Kingdom of Jerusalem, the states of Edessa, Antioch, and Tripoli, and girded them with castles whose stones still stand. A resurgent Islam, retaking Edessa in 1144, brought new waves of Crusaders pouring out of Europe (inset map). But none could match the glorious achievement of the first.

Inspired by Bernard of Clairvaux, led by Louis VII of France and Conrad III of Germany, the **Second Crusade** (1147-49) met defeat in Asia Minor and futilely besieged Damascus.

Alarmed by Saladin's reconquest of Jerusalem, Europe's mightiest monarchs—Richard the Lionheart of England, Philip Augustus of France, Frederick Barbarossa of the Holy Roman Empire—embarked on the **Third Crusade** (1189-92). Frederick drowned near Seleucia in Turkey; Richard and Philip regained Acre after an epic siege. Alone, the Lionheart won other coastal cities and treaty rights for pilgrimages to Jerusalem.

Christian slew Christian in the **Fourth Crusade** (1202-04). To pay for passage French knights agreed to help Venice conquer rival Zara on the Dalmatian coast. The Crusaders went on to sack Constantinople, mortally wounding the splendid Byzantine Empire. Venice gained a trading empire; the knights never reached the Holy Land.

In the disastrous **Children's Crusade** (1212), led by a visionary French lad, Stephen of Cloyes, thousands embarked at Marseilles—only to be sold into African slave marts by ship captains. German children marched overland; most perished from hunger and disease.

Warriors of the **Fifth Crusade** (1218-21) won Damietta in Egypt, planning to exchange it for Jerusalem. Nile floods forced a Christian retreat.

Frederick II, Holy Roman Emperor and King of Sicily, delayed starting on the **Sixth Crusade** (1228-29) so long that the pope excommunicated him. Undaunted, he regained Jerusalem through negotiation. But Frank and Saracen scorned peace. In 1244 Jerusalem fell to the Moslems.

Saintly Louis IX of France seized Damietta in the **Seventh Crusade** (1248-54), was captured and ransomed. In 1270, after embarking on the **Eighth Crusade**, he died in Tunisia. Armies continued to move east, but Crusader bastions fell one by one until in 1303 the Knights Templars yielded their last toehold in the Levant—Arwad off Syria. Knights Hospitalers held on at Rhodes until 1522, later moved to Malta. The crusading idea lived on, but its spirit and force were dead.

239

Rhine Valley, despite the pleas of bishops, some crossbearers killed and robbed Jews, whom they saw as ancient enemies of their faith and an easy source of plunder. In Croatia Peter's legions slew Byzantine allies. Hungry, fired by rumors of ill-treatment of an advance unit, his rabble killed 4,000 at Semlin (modern Zemun). Then, in most unchristian fashion, they set fire to nearby Belgrade. Southeast, at Niš, Byzantine troops beat the motley force so badly it never recovered. Peter escaped but lost his money chest and a fourth of his men.

*P*OPE URBAN had urged the Crusaders to assemble at Constantinople, the Byzantine capital. By early 1097 more than 60,000 of them had arrived there, to the consternation of Emperor Alexius Comnenus. True, he had asked the pope for help against the rampaging Seljuk Turks, but he had wanted mercenary troops. Entire armies were quite another thing. "He dreaded their arrival," wrote his daughter, Princess Anna, "for he knew their irresistible manner of attack . . . and he also knew they were always agape for money."

An uncharitable view, perhaps, but Anna had reason for skepticism. Unruly crossbearers had pillaged the outskirts of Constantinople, and one duke had actually led an attack against imperial forces. Part of the trouble stemmed from the fact that Urban had never appointed a combat commander. Adhemar of Monteil, the kindly but courageous bishop of Le Puy, represented the pope in religious matters. But constantly competing for military control were some of the proudest

240

"OH, WHAT A NOBLE *and beautiful city!" Wondrous Constantinople, rhapsodized by a Crusader scribe, lives on as Turkish Istanbul. Fabled Golden Horn, an arm of the Bosporus, divides the business quarter from the old city, where minarets rise round Hagia Sophia and the Blue Mosque (at left).*

In Europe's richest city, then the jewel of Christendom, Crusaders gaped at fine rugs on palace walls, panes of glass or alabaster, marts teeming with traders from Spain, Russia, central Asia. As the tide of crossbearers swelled at journey's midpoint, uneasy Byzantines exacted vows of fealty from their allies and prodded them promptly on to battle infidels. In their wake came fresh armies, many in high-prowed ships (right), to crowd the magic port.

241

princes of Europe: tall, blond Godfrey of Bouillon, Duke of Lower Lorraine, and his younger brother Baldwin of Boulogne—descendants of Charlemagne; Hugh, Count of Vermandois, arrogant younger son of King Henry I of France; Raymond of Toulouse, cantankerous Count of St. Gilles; Robert, Duke of Normandy, carousing eldest son of the Conqueror; and ambitious Bohemond of Taranto, who led the Normans of southern Italy with his nephew Tancred.

Alexius treated them with diplomacy, generosity, and, when necessary, with firmness. The Turks had overrun most of Asia Minor, and the once vast Byzantine Empire was reduced to little more than the Balkan Peninsula. Alexius wanted to make sure that these Crusaders did not retain control of areas they captured to the east and south. He gave them gold and jewels in return for their pledge to turn over to him any liberated Byzantine cities. All but Raymond of Toulouse took the oath, and he accepted a modified version. None of the Crusade leaders was encouraged to prolong his stay in Constantinople. Alexius provided guides and transported the armies across the Bosporus as rapidly as possible.

*T*HE MAN who hastened me on my way was the director general of Istanbul Customs. "Just how quickly can you get out of the country?" he asked. Then, noting the look on my face, he laughed: "Not that we don't want you in Turkey. But there is a limit on how long a vehicle technically in transit can remain in the country. Unless you want to pay duty on your car of about $1,500...."

JOSEPH J. SCHERSCHEL AND (LEFT AND OPPOSITE)
JAMES L. STANFIELD, BOTH NATIONAL GEOGRAPHIC PHOTOGRAPHERS

"Stop right there," I said. "How long may I have?" He wondered if I could get across the Syrian border within ten days. "It took the Crusaders two years," I chuckled, "but I've got the Turks on *my* side, so that should make the difference. Thank you. I can make it."

The road to Iznik, the Nicaea of ancient times, made me wonder if I had been overly optimistic. South from the Sea of Marmara the road turned into a narrow winding track over roller-coaster hills. And suddenly the modern Turkey of automobiles and Western-style shops and dress disappeared. Here was a different world: tiny farmhouses with mud walls and thatched roofs; small truck plots and little orchards; men in baggy pants guiding wooden plows behind oxen; women hanging tobacco on farmhouse walls to dry. Take away the tobacco, and the Crusaders might have seen identical sights when they plodded this way.

It was dusk when I came to the lake beside which Iznik dozes. Near here a Turkish army in October 1096 ambushed the remains of Peter the Hermit's force. His impatient men, disregarding instructions to wait for the crusading armies behind them, had set out to attack enemy-held Nicaea. A hail of arrows unhorsed the mounted leaders; cold steel completed the rout. The Turks pursued the broken

"God triumphing, the...city of Nicaea was surrendered"

Stephen of Blois

For six weeks in 1097 Crusaders besieged the Turkish capital, hacked apart a relief army, watched their own men slain. Fulcher of Chartres saw Turks atop walls (now moldering above) "let down iron hooks ... and seize the body of any of our men.... Having robbed the corpse, they threw the carcass outside." Desperate defenders surrendered secretly to Byzantine Emperor Alexius Comnenus and opened a lakeside gate to his men (left). Crusaders fumed at Alexius— "a fool as well as a knave."

Nicaea's voice still echoes in Christian ears. Here in 325 the first ecumenical council forged the Nicene Creed, which reaffirmed the divinity of Christ.

army back to Civetot, and there the People's Crusade perished in a bloody, nightlong massacre. Peter, in Constantinople at the time, waited to join the main Crusader forces.

THE EASY DESTRUCTION of Peter's rabble may have led the Seljuk sultan, Kilij Arslan, to pay too little attention when the organized armies of the First Crusade neared his capital, Nicaea, in May of 1097. Busy in the east subduing the rival Danishmend dynasty of what is now central Turkey, he had most of his army with him and had left his wife, children, and treasury within the walls of Nicaea.

By early June the entire crusading forces were arrayed before the Seljuk capital. Godfrey and Tancred, Bohemond, Robert of Normandy, and Stephen of Blois were there, and Raymond of Toulouse had arrived in time to blockade the southern wall before the first Turkish reinforcements appeared. Kilij Arslan had learned of his mistake, but too late.

The anonymous author of the *Gesta Francorum*, one of the great source books of the Crusade, describes Raymond's repulse of the Turkish relief attempt: "Armed on all sides with the sign of the cross, he rushed upon them violently and overcame them. They turned in flight, and most of them were killed. They came back again, reinforced by others, joyful.... As many as descended remained there with their

245

heads cut off at the hands of our men; moreover, our men hurled the heads...into the city." Crusader losses were heavy, but the knights turned eagerly to an attempt to undermine and burn the city's walls. When they discovered that the Turks were getting supplies at the lake gate, Emperor Alexius sent ships to blockade it.

Alexius feared his allies' "fickleness," as his daughter wrote, but the Byzantine court showed that it too was capable of fickleness—even of massive intrigue. Alexius had no wish to see Nicaea sacked. Most of its citizens were Christians, and, taken intact, the city would be a useful part of his empire. So he negotiated a secret surrender. On his orders Manuel Butumites, commander of the Byzantine lake flotilla, slipped into the city and offered the Turks immunity and rich gifts.

It was important that the Crusaders not know of the deception. The Byzantine agent in the Crusader camp, briefed by Butumites, urged an assault on the walls. The knights attacked at dawn, as arranged. But the first light of the sun showed the standard of Byzantium standing above the city. To make the Westerners believe the city had been taken by assault, Alexius' vessels at the lake gate showed many banners, with a great blowing of trumpets.

But the treachery was apparently not kept secret, and Raymond of Aguilers, historian as well as chaplain for Raymond of Toulouse, wrote that as long as Alexius lived "the people will curse him and proclaim him a traitor."

Heartened, nonetheless, by the victory in their first full-scale encounter with the Turks, the Crusaders set out along the road across Asia Minor. Crossing the plain of Dorylaeum, the army divided into two groups. Bohemond led the first and Raymond of Toulouse the second, which followed a day's march behind.

Kilij Arslan was not yet finished. Gathering support from Emir Hassan of Cappadocia as well as the Danishmend forces, he ambushed the Crusaders near Dorylaeum, today's Eskişehir. Bohemond's forces, encamped on the plain, bore the brunt of the first attack at dawn. Raymond of Aguilers says the Turkish forces numbered 150,000.

"We were all huddled together," recounts Fulcher of

ASSAILED BY HUNGER, *thirst, and the merciless sun, soldiers of Christ cast off arms and armor on the Asia Minor steppes. "We scarcely came out alive," records the* Gesta Francorum. *Christian hill folk eased their pangs, taught them to carry water in animal skins, guided them along the way. Heat, haze, and mirage remain; man and donkeys (lower) wade a phantom lake on a dusty Turkish road.*

246

THOMAS NEBBIA. UPPER: PAINTING FOR NATIONAL GEOGRAPHIC BY STANLEY MELTZOFF

Chartres, another chronicler—"indeed, like sheep shut in a pen, trembling and frightened, surrounded on all sides by enemies, so that we were unable to advance in any direction. It was clear to us that this befell us as a punishment for our sins."

For six hours the vanguard held out, through shower after shower of Turkish arrows. There was no place to run, and capture meant certain slavery. Then, near noon, the second Crusader army came up. The Turks, who thought they had trapped the whole Crusader force, fell back, and the combined Christian armies took the offensive. As the battle hung in the balance, the bishop of Le Puy, who had led a detachment over mountains to the Turkish rear, attacked.

Caught between the two lines, the Turks fled, leaving behind their tents along with the sultan's treasury and his two emirs. The Crusaders paid dearly in lives, but they had broken the back of Turkish resistance in Asia Minor.

"WE CONQUERED *for the Lord the whole of . . . Cappadocia," wrote Stephen of Blois. A route avoiding the hazardous Cilician Gates led Crusaders through this haunting land where wind and water whittled pinnacles from soft volcanic tuff. Here early Christians and Byzantine monks, seeking solitude and safety, chiseled hermits' cells, churches with arches and domes, multistoried monasteries in cliff and cone. Many still blaze with priceless frescoes. Some provide cozy shelter for Moslem farmers whose wives, like the woman of Van (below) and wives the world over, often find two hands barely enough.*

FARRELL GREHAN, PHOTO RESEARCHERS. RIGHT: HELEN AND FRANK SCHREIDER, NATIONAL GEOGRAPHIC STAFF

On the long trail to Antioch, however, the Christian armies discovered that nature was an enemy equally to be feared. Thirst tormented the Crusaders; many died of it. And the Turks had devastated the land. "There was absolutely nothing for us to eat," reported the writer of the *Gesta Francorum*, "except grain which we tore from the stalk and ground in our hands."

Yet the spirit of the army proved more important than hunger and thirst. When horses and oxen died of starvation, Crusaders loaded their tattered possessions on the backs of sheep, goats, dogs, even pigs. And in hardship they were drawn even closer together in spirit. "Who ever heard such a mixture of languages in one army?" asks Fulcher. "There were French, Flemings, Frisians, Gauls, Allobroges, Lotharingians, Germans, Bavarians, Normans, English, Scots, Aquitanians, Italians, Dacians, Apulians, Iberians, Bretons, Greeks and Armenians. . . ." But, adds

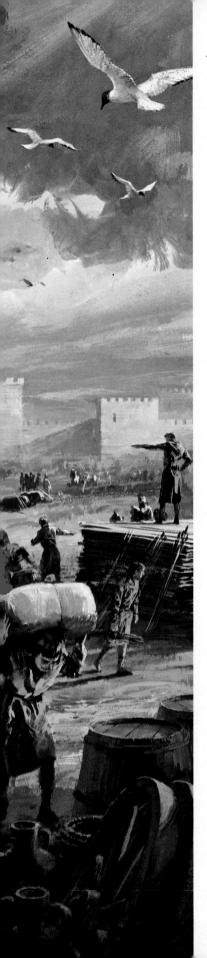

"We must mention those men who dared to sail the strange and vast Mediterranean... out of love of crusading" Raymond of Aguilers

Genoese ships, opening a sea lane from Europe and Cyprus, unload recruits and supplies at St. Simeon in November 1097 for the attack on Antioch. But rations ran short. A chronicler wrote: "Grain and all food began to be excessively dear before the birthday of the Lord." Antioch's fortress, with its 400 towers, held until June, then fell by intrigue. Soon after, Turkish troops trapped the Crusaders inside.

PAINTING FOR NATIONAL GEOGRAPHIC BY ROBERT ADDISON

the writer from Chartres, "we who were diverse in languages, nevertheless seemed . . . brothers in the love of God."

The Crusaders' plight was brought home to me one scorching day as I followed their path through Anatolia. My car broke down and I could not fix it. Heat waves tortured the horizon, and teasing mirages like pools of water spotted the parched road ahead. I put my hand on a fender—and snatched it back in pain. After two hours a Turk passed by riding a donkey. What I needed most at the moment was water. Fifteen kilometers—nine miles—ahead, he told me.

As I was mulling the prospect of a Crusader-like walk of three hours in that blazing sun, a huge truck pulled up in a cloud of dust. The driver, a lithe, hawk-nosed youth with a gleaming smile beneath his crescent mustache, leaped out. "Need some help?" he asked in English.

"If you're a mechanic, I sure do," I replied. "And do you have any water?" He handed me a canvas water bag and I took a long draught. "Every truck driver in Turkey has to be a mechanic," he laughed. "There aren't many repair shops in this part of the country." Half an hour later my car was purring smoothly. The truck driver would take no payment. We shook hands and resumed our journeys.

SIX WEEKS OF PRIVATION brought the Crusaders to Iconium, today's busy Konya, which had been abandoned by the Turks. Surrounded by lush valleys and rich orchards, it offered a haven to the weary Christians. They rested, then set out across Anatolia. This great expanse of Turkey which the Crusaders found so inhospitable is still dry, but far from forbidding. Wheat fields stretch from horizon to horizon, broken by occasional patches of sugar beets.

Beyond the Anatolian plain the Taurus and Anti-Taurus mountains loomed. Two Crusade leaders—Baldwin of Boulogne, with a group of Flemish and Lorrainers, and Tancred, with a troop of southern Normans—took the more direct

251

route, south and east through the towering, easily defended Cilician Gates. But the main body of the army, fearing ambush in that sharp defile, marched north through Cappadocia to Caesarea Mazaca (Kayseri), thence south to Coxon (today's Goksun). There they were welcomed with food and supplies by Armenians, whose nation in the third century had become first in the world to adopt Christianity.

Between Coxon and Marash the Crusaders encountered formidable passes. "We . . . entered a diabolical mountain," records the author of the *Gesta Francorum*, "which was so high and steep that none of us dared to step before another through the pass. . . . There horses fell headlong, and one pack animal pushed over another." Indeed, as Sir Steven Runciman observes in his *History of the Crusades*, the mountains "took more lives than ever the Turks had done." It was a tired, depleted army which stood at last before Antioch.

ONCE the third largest city of the Mediterranean world, Antioch in October of 1097 presented walls bristling with 400 towers. The city stretched three miles long and a mile wide, and a fortress crowned a hill rising a thousand feet above it. While Antioch remained in Turkish hands, that road to Jerusalem could not be traveled.

The besieging Crusaders intercepted a Turkish supply convoy and in November received additional help from a Genoese squadron which appeared at the nearby port of

"It was held in great veneration by all, and handled gloriously"

Fulcher of Chartres

Crusaders gasp as a humble youth, Peter Bartholomew, unearths a corroded lance head beneath Antioch's Church of St. Peter. A vision, he said, had revealed to him the hiding place of the lance which had pierced Christ's side at the Crucifixion. Weeping with joy, men kissed the relic; word raced through the army that God had sent a marvelous sign of His favor. Hopes rekindled, the knights made ready to break the Turkish siege.

Crusaders revered Antioch for its ties to early Christendom. In this brilliant provincial capital of the Roman Empire St. Peter founded his first bishopric, tradition says. Antioch, on the Orontes, survives as Turkish Antakya (below). Hikers on Mt. Silpius view a city one-fourth its medieval size.

JAMES P. BLAIR, NATIONAL GEOGRAPHIC PHOTOGRAPHER. OPPOSITE: PAINTING FOR NATIONAL GEOGRAPHIC BY BIRNEY LETTICK

St. Simeon. But they failed to conserve supplies. By Christmas provisions were low, and in January 1098, men driven by hunger began to desert. By March the Christian forces had smashed a Turkish relief attempt and a raiding party. Spring and new crops, plus supplies from Cyprus and Constantinople, eased the commissary problems.

Then, as summer came on, a new threat loomed — Kerbogha, the *atabeg,* or governor, of Mosul, marching to relieve Antioch with troops from Persia and Mesopotamia. And Stephen of Blois deserted with a French contingent.

Stephen left too soon. On the very night of his desertion, June 2, an enemy captain, probably an Armenian in Turkish service, betrayed the city. He let a group of Bohemond's troops scale the wall at the tower he held.

"Without delay," Fulcher of Chartres reports, "the gate was opened. . . . The Franks shouted: 'God wills it! God wills it!' For this was our signal cry. . . . When the Turks saw the Franks running through the streets with naked swords and wildly killing people . . . they began to flee. . . ."

The Turkish commander, Yaghi-Siyan, fled on horseback but fell from his mount and was beheaded by an Armenian. His son, Shams ad-Daula, managed to lead a small party up to the hilltop citadel, where he fought off Bohemond's attack. In the city below, Greek and Armenian inhabitants joined the Crusaders in massacring Turks.

"By nightfall on 3 June," Sir Steven Runciman writes, "there was no Turk left alive in Antioch. . . . You could not walk on the streets without treading on corpses. . . . But Antioch was Christian once more."

THEN SUDDENLY the besiegers became the besieged. Shams ad-Daula still held the citadel, and Kerbogha's forces invested the walls. The Christians grew desperate as the Turks tightened their grip. The *Gesta Francorum* recounts that many soldiers of the cross "died of hunger. . . . Horse and donkey flesh was sold and eaten."

While hunger was taking its toll, a peasant reported a series of visions which were to change the course of history. Peter Bartholomew, the servant of a Provençal pilgrim, came before the princes of the Crusade with an account of supernatural visitations from St. Andrew. The saint had told him

"IF ALL THE PAGAN WORLD *rushed against them, they would not budge,"*
warned a Turkish scout when Christians broke out of besieged Antioch
in 1098. Raymond of Aguilers holds high the Holy Lance as Turks
fire the grass. Inspired by their newfound relic, the knights drove
to victory. "The Lord labored surprisingly well," Raymond reported.

PAINTING FOR NATIONAL GEOGRAPHIC BY BIRNEY LETTICK

that the very lance which pierced Christ's side as He hung on the cross was buried beneath the Church of St. Peter in Antioch. The leaders divided over the veracity of the vision, but a search of the church was ordered.

"After we had dug from morning to evening," Raymond of Aguilers recounted, "the youth who had had the vision of the lance disrobed and, taking off his shoes, descended into the pit in his shirt. . . . At length, the Lord was minded to show us His Lance. And I, who have written this, kissed it when the point alone had appeared above the ground. What . . . exultation then filled the city I cannot describe."

Shortly thereafter Peter had another vision: St. Andrew urged the Christians to fast for five days, then attack. The

Mighty Krak — "a bone stuck in the very throat" of the Moslems

Legacy of faith-fired knights, Krak des Chevaliers — Castle of the Knights Hospitalers — rears massive towers near Massiaf, Syria. On a Moslem fort's site, Crusaders began the citadel in 1110. Enlarged a century later, it could hold 2,000 knights. Hospitalers,

fighting monks who chanted Latin Masses in the chapel, swapped yarns in French in the guardroom.

Castle cisterns held a five-year supply of water—and filled steamy Roman baths. A windmill ground grain, and a stable quartered 400 chargers behind a wall 80 feet thick that awestruck Moslems called "the Mountain."

In 1271 the Krak's proud garrison, shrunk to 200, lost the mighty pile in the twilight of the Crusades, duped by a sultan who forged an order to surrender.

THOMAS NEBBIA

fast was ordered and on the morning of June 28 the Christians marched out. Raymond of Aguilers was given the honor of carrying the Holy Lance.

The Crusaders fought as men possessed. Kerbogha's emirs deserted him. Suddenly the whole Turkish army fled in panic. For once, the Crusaders did not stay to loot but pursued the enemy, slaying great numbers. Then they returned to collect treasures abandoned by the Turks, many of whom had also left families behind. "When their women were found in the tents," Fulcher of Chartres reports with peculiar pride, "the Franks did nothing evil to them except pierce their bellies with their lances."

The citadel above the city surrendered, and the Crusade

leaders decided to rest until November, avoiding a summer march through the Syrian desert. In midsummer an epidemic swept Antioch, taking the life of Adhemar, Bishop of Le Puy. With his death the bitterness between the leaders came to the surface. Bohemond wanted the captured city. Raymond of Toulouse refused. The soldiers, according to Raymond of Aguilers, threatened to rebel. "Since the princes . . . are unwilling to lead us to Jerusalem," he reports them as saying, "let us choose some brave knight in serving whom loyally we can be safe, and, if it is the will of God, we will arrive in Jerusalem with this knight as leader. . . ."

The soldiers warned that if the dispute about Antioch continued, they would "tear down its walls." The potential mutiny inspired Raymond and Bohemond to make "discordant peace between themselves." In January of 1099, with Bohemond in possession of Antioch, Raymond marched the expeditionary forces south.

A siege of Arca, northeast of Tripoli, delayed the Crusaders. The siege was futile. It also brought about the death of Peter Bartholomew. He had announced another vision—this one calling for an immediate attack on Arca. When his advice was ignored, he demanded an ordeal by fire, and the ancient test was administered. With Holy Lance in hand, he ran through blazing logs; he died of his burns.

In June the Crusaders took Ramle, a few miles inland from today's thriving

"Shall we dillydally until all of us are liquidated?"

Raymond of Aguilers

Weary from their ordeal at Antioch, surviving Crusaders struck south through lands where Nebuchadnezzar and Alexander fought to conquer, apostles and prophets strode to save. When some Crusaders paused to plunder a town, comrades bristled: "Why should we alone fight the whole world? . . . Let us march to Jerusalem."

A Druse father and son of Abayh (opposite), near Beirut, descend from folk who watched the Christians pass. An offshoot of Islam, the Druse sect dates from those uneasy days.

Weathered stones of Lebanon speak of the Crusaders' passing. Their Castle of the Sea still sentinels Sidon (right), whence Phoenicians rowed to riches. At Tyre, crosses from Crusader graves recall a chronicler's cry: "Oh, how many thousands met a martyr's blessed death. . . !"

258

Israeli city of Tel Aviv. A night raid liberated Bethlehem. With the birthplace of Christ once again in Christian hands, the last and greatest task remained.

A N ECLIPSE OF THE MOON, regarded as an omen of good fortune, put new heart into the weary armies as, throughout the night of June 6, 1099, they slogged across the inhospitable Judaean hills toward Jerusalem. Each man, ambitious to occupy castles and villas, struggled to forge ahead of the next.

Morning found the Crusaders upon the summit of Montjoie. Beyond stood the Holy City, held by the Egyptian Fatimid dynasty, which had driven out the Turks the year before. "Rejoicing," writes the chronicler of the *Gesta Francorum*, "we ... began to besiege the city in a marvelous manner." But victory was not to come easily. Despite valiant efforts, the first assault failed.

Nine centuries later, as I stood on the crest of the road looking down at Jerusalem, it was easy to see why. Valleys offered natural defenses. To the southwest of the city was the forbidding Vale of Gehenna; the Valley of Kidron ran on to the east, between the city and the Mount of Olives. Another gully lay in front of me, along the western wall. Only to the south and along the northern bastion was the terrain favorable to an attacking army.

A bleak prospect faced the Crusaders; long weeks of horror lay ahead. The governor of Jerusalem, Iftikhar ad-Daula, had emptied the surrounding pastures of their herds, blocked the springs, and poisoned the wells. Since 637, when Moslems had captured Jerusalem, Christians had continued to live in the Holy City and

259

worship at their sacred shrines. Now the governor drove thousands of them outside the city walls, to compete with the Crusaders for scarce food and water. Within, the disciplined garrison had warehouses heavily stocked; cisterns held enough water for a long siege. And a drainage system dating from Roman times minimized the danger of disease.

Iftikhar's preparations were all too effective. The besiegers found only the Pool of Siloam unpoisoned—the site, Holy Writ declared, where a blind man was cured when Jesus sent him to wash in its waters. And the pool, which still courses today beneath the city's south wall, lay within range of the Moslems' arrows and stones.

The spring at the pool, says Raymond of Aguilers, flowed only every third day. The thirst-crazed Crusaders consumed the water "with such great crowding and haste that the

GALILEE, *round whose shores Christ preached, toils to a timeless tempo. Fishermen still seine its sea; reapers uproot its barley with dull sickles (left) little changed since Bible days.*

As the First Crusaders won the Holy Land, Tancred of Sicily possessed the lake region and dubbed himself Prince of Galilee. In 1187, by Galilean peaks called Horns of Hattin, Saladin crushed a Crusader army. Nobles were ransomed, knights beheaded. Foot soldiers shuffled into slavery; one was traded for a pair of shoes. The Christian Kingdom of Jerusalem never recovered.

men pushed one another into it, and many baggage animals and cattle perished in it. . . . The stronger, even at the price of death, forced their way to the very opening in the rocks through which the water flowed, while the weak got only the water which had already been contaminated."

WITH the First Crusade seemingly halted at the very threshold of the Holy City, a Christian fleet landed June 17 at the ancient port of Joppa, part of modern Tel Aviv. Despite a surprise attack from the sea, the sailors delivered vital cargoes of food and, even more important, rope, bolts, and other hardware. The seamen turned eagerly to help build siege machines and scaling towers.

Wood, however, was still in short supply. Robert of Flanders and Tancred solved that problem, leading raids 40 miles to the forests around Samaria and returning with timbers loaded on camels and the backs of Saracen prisoners. Now wooden towers on wheels, fitted with catapults, were readied to be pushed against the city walls. Knights could leap to the attack from bridges near their tops.

261

Then the dreaded sirocco came. The hot, dusty south wind blew for days, and men went mad. Bickering among the leaders over who should rule Jerusalem mounted with the summer heat. News came in early July that an Egyptian army of overwhelming size was on its way to relieve Iftikhar's beleaguered troops. The princes of the cross knew that their army could never stand against such a force.

Just when all seemed lost, a Crusader named Peter Desiderius told the leaders of a nocturnal visitation by the much-mourned Adhemar, Bishop of Le Puy. The vision, writes Raymond of Aguilers, bade Peter to pass on the following instructions: Each Crusader must "turn from his evil ways. Then with bare feet march around Jerusalem invoking God, and you must also fast. If you do this, and then make a great attack on the city on the ninth day, it will be captured."

A fast was immediately proclaimed. On Friday, July 8, the bishops and lesser clergy led the procession, bearing on high their crosses and sacred relics. Then came the knights and able-bodied men, marching to the call of trumpets and bear-

"Rejoicing and exulting, we reached the city of Jerusalem"

Gesta Francorum

Christian joy palled before the bristling walls of the sacred city. Born and razed in Bible times, rebuilt by the Roman emperor Hadrian as Aelia Capitolina in the second century, Jerusalem fell to the Arabs in the seventh. A frayed Crusader army faced the Egyptian caliph's seasoned troops braced behind walls that traced the bastions of Aelia.

Modern bridge (opposite) spans a chasm of time where diggers have bared remnants of gates reared by Crusaders, Byzantines, Romans, and Jews. Over them a parade of pedestrians—and a steel-sinewed porter hefting a refrigerator—pass through the majestic Damascus Gate, built during the 16th-century reign of the Turkish sultan Suleiman the Magnificent.

Under stone arcades that the Crusaders left in Old Jerusalem, a village woman (right) weighs tiny apples from her orchard. Through stormy millenniums Jews have clung to colonies in this hallowed hub of three faiths, today Israel's capital.

TED SPIEGEL, RAPHO GUILLUMETTE

263

ing their standards and arms. Barefoot, they made the circuit of the walls. Above, on the ramparts of Jerusalem, the Moslem defenders moved with them, shouting their ridicule. When the Crusaders reached the Mount of Olives, says Raymond, they were exhorted: "Now that we are on the very spot from which the Lord made His ascension and we can do nothing more to purify ourselves, let each one of us forgive his brother whom he has injured, that the Lord may forgive us."

WITH FEVERISH LABOR NOW, the Crusaders covered their siege towers with hides as protection from the flaming liquid called Greek fire. (Once a feared secret weapon of the Byzantine Empire, it was showered down the walls by defenders. The chronicle lists a variety of ingredients: naphtha, pitch, sulphur, and resin.) When the Saracens saw the great towers wheeled into position, they strengthened and heightened the walls opposite them.

Under cover of night, the Christians countered by moving the towers, explains Raymond, adding: "You who read this must not think that this was a light undertaking, for the machines were carried in parts almost a mile to the place where they were to be set up. When morning came and the Saracens saw that all the machinery and tents had been moved . . . they were amazed. Not only the Saracens . . . but our people as well, for they recognized that the hand of the Lord was with us."

The attack began the night of July 13, and the defenders let loose a hail of stones and rivers of Greek fire. By evening of July 14 Raymond of Toulouse had placed his tower against the south wall, but the defenders fought off every attempt to scale the ramparts. Next morning Godfrey's tower was wheeled against the north wall, near the present Herod's Gate. The battle hung in the balance during the morning hours of July 15. Archers shot blazing firebrands to drive the defenders from the walls, but the siege towers were battered and burned. Toward the end of morning, it appeared that the attack was doomed.

"However, when the hour approached on which our Lord Jesus Christ deigned to suffer on the cross for us," the *Gesta Francorum* exults, "our knights began to fight bravely in one of the towers—namely, the party with Duke Godfrey and his brother Count Eustace. One of our knights, named Lethold, clambered up the wall of the city, and no sooner had he ascended than the defenders fled from the walls and through the city."

Godfrey himself soon followed, and the pick of his army swarmed up scaling ladders and into the city. They opened the Gate of the Column (now excavated beneath the Damascus Gate), and the Crusaders' shock troops streamed through the streets. With the survivors of his bodyguard, Iftikhar took refuge in the Tower of David, whence he sent emissaries to Raymond of Toulouse offering a fabulous ransom for his life and the lives of his retainers. Raymond accepted, and Iftikhar and his bodyguard were escorted to safety outside the walls.

Few other defenders were so fortunate. Men, women, children perished by the sword or by fire. Nor were the Moslem defenders the only victims; the Jews of

"OH YE WHO BELIEVE! *When ye rise up for prayer, wash your faces . . . and your feet." Obeying the Koran, Moslems ring a pool for ritual cleansing before Friday worship. Golden Dome of the Rock for 13 centuries has sheltered the sacred slab where, Moslems say, Abraham prepared to sacrifice his son and Mohammed rose on horseback through Islam's seven heavens to his God. For such shrines Moslems fought to hold Jerusalem.*

TED SPIEGEL, RAPHO GUILLUMETTE

"All the hellish din of battle broke loose...stones flew... and arrows pelted like hail"

Thus Raymond of Aguilers recalled the scene as Crusaders stormed Jerusalem's north wall near the ungilded Dome of the Rock. Mangonels hurl boulders; when two Arab women try to hex a weapon, its stone hurtles "whistling through the air" and smashes "the lives out of the two witches." Some missiles thud against cushions of wet straw; archers aim flaming shafts at the mats. Soldiers swarm up a siege tower protected by hides, scorning Greek fire rained down by defenders. Gangs raise ladders while bowmen behind slotted fences cover them. Sensing defeat, Arabs break when Crusaders gain a foothold atop the wall. "No one," boasts the Gesta Francorum, "has ever seen . . . such a slaughter of pagans."

Jerusalem had sought refuge in their chief synagogue. They were accused of having aided the defenders, the synagogue was put to the torch, and no Jew is known to have survived. Daimbert of Pisa, who replaced Bishop Adhemar as religious leader, would report to the pope: "If you desire to know what was done with the enemy who were found there, know that [in the area of Solomon's Temple] our men rode in the blood of Saracens up to the knees of their horses."

And when the slaughter was over, reports the *Gesta*, the army "scattered throughout the city and took possession of the gold and silver, the horses and mules, and the houses filled with goods of all kinds."

Toward evening the leaders of the Crusade, who only a week before had filed barefoot around the seemingly impregnable walls of the city to the jeers of the Moslem defenders, walked in solemn state to the Church of the Holy Sepulcher. There they gave thanks to God. "It was well worth all our previous labors and hardships to see the devotion of the pilgrims," wrote Raymond of Aguilers.

ONCE AGAIN Christians could walk freely in the steps of Christ and worship at His tomb. Pope Urban's shining dream had come true. But the eloquent pontiff did not live to share the triumph. He who had summoned the faithful to the cross died in Rome two weeks after the capture of the Holy City, before word of it could reach him.

"How they rejoiced ... and sang a new song to the Lord!"
Raymond of Aguilers

Jerusalem theirs, exultant Christian warriors fall to their knees in the Church of the Holy Sepulcher. "Their hearts offered prayers of praise to God, victorious and triumphant," wrote Raymond of the supreme moment in the struggle to free the cradle of Christendom.

The joyous thanksgiving filled the church rebuilt by Byzantines in 1048 where, tradition held, the skull of Adam was buried and the cross of Christ rose. The Gospels call the site Golgotha; from the Latin came the name Calvary. Both signify "the place of the skull."

The faithful still flock to the holy places. Modern pilgrims (above) shoulder heavy beams on the Via Dolorosa, the Street of Sorrows, recalling Christ's agony on His way to the cross.

Though the Moslems regained Jerusalem within a century, Urban's vision lived on long after. For two hundred years Christians continued to take the cross, left home and worldly wealth behind, and streamed eastward, some to death, some to glory. Moslem power swelled. The Byzantine Empire and its magnificent civilization declined.

But European civilization leaped forward. Ships that carried grain and timber to the East returned with wares

JERUSALEM THE GOLDEN *has sheltered her shrines through centuries of history writ in blood. Though the faiths diverge, pilgrim paths entwine in a holy city of synagogues, churches, mosques. Each echoes the Book of Common Prayer's entreaty: "Pray for the peace of Jerusalem."*

that added elegance and luxury to Western life—jewelry, rugs, perfume, glass mirrors, spices, cane sugar. Romantic song and legend celebrated the Crusaders' deeds, renewing the ideals of Christian knighthood. Oppressive feudal ties dissolved as crusading nobles traded liberty to towns and individuals for money to finance the great venture. The exchange of ideas and techniques sharpened the skills of government, navigation, building with stone. All Europe's arts and sciences profited, and along with the driving faith of the crossbearers there grew a zeal for learning that turned men's eyes to new horizons.

AERIAL VIEW LOOKS EAST FROM JAFFA GATE OVER THE WALLED OLD CITY. BEYOND THE GLEAMING DOME OF THE ROCK AND THE WAILING WALL TO ITS RIGHT RISES THE SUN-SPLASHED MOUNT OF OLIVES. DOUBLE-DOMED CHURCH OF THE HOLY SEPULCHER LIES AT LEFT CENTER. TED SPIEGEL, RAPHO GUILLUMETTE

To Bologna, Paris, Oxford trekked young men like Chaucer's clerk
to "gladly learn and gladly teach" — and to riot, tipple, and wench.
Kenneth M. Setton visits the campus of past and present to record the

QUESTING LIFE OF
THE SCHOLAR

THE TROUBLE BEGAN as usual in a tavern, the Swyndlestock. Some Oxford students called for wine, which the vintner John of Croydon brought. The students said the wine was no good; John insisted it was. A quarrel ensued. "At length the vintner giving them stubborn and saucy language, they threw the wine and vessel at his head." He withdrew in a rage to summon relatives and friends. They rang the bell of St. Martin's, the town church, and bellicose burghers responded quickly, "some with bows and arrows, others with divers sorts of weapons."

Now the bell sounded in St. Mary's, the university church, rallying the excited students. For the remainder of the day—February 10, the feast of St. Scholastica, 1355—town and gown archers shot at each other. Fortunately, none had the skill of England's famed longbowmen, and no one

Bologna students harking to their law professor enliven his 14th-century tomb relief; Albert Moldvay, National Geographic Staff

was killed. But the next day townsmen fell on students at their recreation in Beaumont fields, killing several. Again the church bells pealed. Into town streamed rustics eager to settle old scores. Joining townsmen, they ransacked and burned student halls, killed and mutilated students—even broke into chapels to drag forth their quarry. Except for Merton College students, safe behind stout walls, most gownsmen fled Oxford.

Now church and crown intervened. The town was placed under an interdict, its citizens denied the sacraments. The university emerged triumphant from royal investigations. Henceforth its chancellor and other officials would govern the town over the mayor's head—setting the quality of ale, wine, and bread; checking weights and measures; controlling markets, fixing rents, seeing that streets were cleaned.

And for nearly five centuries, until 1825, the town did penance on St. Scholastica's day. At a special service in the university church, the mayor, bailiffs, and 60 burghers each would stride forward to give a penny at the high altar.

Thus did crown and church show solicitude for the youths who would staff the chanceries of both. Students were regarded as clerks (clerics) and supposed to wear clerical garb. But not all were tonsured or in the minor orders.

THE SWYNDLESTOCK TAVERN had stood at Carfax, where the *quatre voies* (four ways) still meet. Here I began a walking tour of Oxford colleges with my old friend Dr. T. S. R. Boase, for some 20 years the president of Magdalen, and a contributor to this book. We made leisurely visits to the old

Divinity School, the Bodleian Library, New College, Magdalen, St. Edmund Hall, Merton, and Christ Church.

I asked Tom Boase if the current vogue of rioting had disrupted academic life at Oxford. "Not very much," he said. But student attitudes intrigued him. Once he tried to set up a committee meeting of dons and undergraduates.

"I'm afraid that hour won't do, sir," a student objected. "I have a tutorial at three, and I am rioting at four."

Oxford I had known for years, but I was delighted to see it through the eyes of Magdalen's president. The next day I retraced our steps to the cathedral chapel of Christ Church. There in quiet reverie my mind went back over the extraordinary history of universities—like parliaments, common law, and cathedrals an enduring legacy of the Middle Ages.

There had been resorts of learning in antiquity such as Athens and Alexandria, but no universities with formal enrollment, faculties, examinations, and degrees. After

275

Search for knowledge, pursuit of pleasure filled a student's day. Up at dawn, he tidies his cell-like room (right). At morning classes the professor lectures ex cathedra (from the chair); some listen, others scan texts, one daydreams. Scholars honed memories or jotted notes on waxed slates; few could afford costly parchment. Boys of 12 or 13 could begin in liberal arts, while older collegians pursued law, medicine, theology.

Gaming table (opposite) lured students from afternoon studies, with ruinous results. At night, many flouted bans against female visitors (far right), learning arts that only experience teaches.

"Let's away with study,
Folly's sweet. Treasure all
the pleasure of our youth."
Anonymous 12th-century Latin lyric

Rome's decline, monasteries and cathedral schools preserved learning, but their curriculum was limited and much ancient knowledge lost in centuries of turmoil. In the mid-11th century Salerno could boast a famous medical school. But not until the 12th—when the growth of trade and revival of towns quickened Europe's pulse—did a recognizable university arise. This was at Bologna.

In the course of the Middle Ages about 80 universities would dot Europe, and famous names emerge to attest the brilliance of the age—Peter Abelard, Albertus Magnus, Thomas Aquinas, Robert Grosseteste, Roger Bacon. . . .

Young men flocked to the new centers of learning to plunge into philosophy and theology, feudal law and Roman jurisprudence, the sciences and medicine, the newly recovered texts of Aristotle as well as writings of the church fathers. Ambition, love of adventure, thirst for fame and fortune drove them no less than the Crusaders who followed Bohemond and Richard the Lionheart to the Holy Land. By way of the lecture room, the successful student could move from a manorial village or his father's shop to the highest positions in church and state.

To evoke those exciting days I journeyed from England over the Alps to Italy— a trip known to many a medieval English clerk.

I SHALL ALWAYS REMEMBER my visit to Bologna. The tall towers, the beautiful churches, the arcaded streets and fine restaurants put me in a mellow mood. Entering the central square, the Piazza Maggiore, I stepped back into the Middle Ages. My eyes wandered from the grim façade of the Basilica of San Petronio to the crenellated Palace of the Notaries and the majestic Palace of Accursio, built on land which had belonged to Accursius, a noted professor whose gloss, or commentary, on Roman law became standard in lecture rooms. I satisfied an ambition of years by visiting the College of Spain, endowed in the 1360's and still receiving students. And I made special obeisance to the tombs of the law professors—stately monuments—for Bologna was above all a law school.

The rebirth of Roman law was a prime feature of the "12th-century Renaissance." Although the tradition of Roman law had survived in Italy, no one for almost five centuries appears to have studied the full text of Justinian's Code (imperial legislation from the second century to the sixth) and Digest (more than 9,000 extracts from 39 imperial jurists). The growth of town governments and the increasing complexity of Italian politics created a demand for administrators

14TH-CENTURY MINIATURE: STAATLICHE MUSEEN, BERLIN. UPPER: 15TH-CENTURY MINIATURES FROM "RULEBOOK OF THE COLLEGE OF WISDOM"; UNIVERSITÄT FREIBURG IM BREISGAU. SCULPTURE DETAIL ON PAGES 272-3, MUSEO CIVICO, BOLOGNA

277

"**IN EVERYTHING** *live together as students. . . ." Medieval rules nurtured old school ties that still bind collegians to communal living. Undergraduates dine in the great hall of Oxford's Wadham College (opposite), founded in 1613 from the wealth of Nicholas Wadham, who "had a good estate and no children to leave it to." Hall, chapel, and living quarters form a harmonious complex round the traditional quadrangle.*

Colleges first arose in late 12th-century Paris. In 1257 Robert de Sorbon (his name lives as a synonym for the University of Paris) founded one with strict statutes whose breach brought a fine of two quarts of wine. Earliest university students lived on their own, often neither wisely nor well. Tavern brawls bred riots like one above, where Pallas Athene watches town and gown lay to with swords, sticks, stones. Now, as then, youthful mischief turns to strife; Paris students in 1968 (above right) seized buildings, battled police to force academic change and reform a "bourgeois society" that grew from medieval roots.

trained in Roman law. Hundreds of young men journeyed to Bologna to hear the famed Irnerius lecture—one of the first known "professors" of Roman law. As early as 1119 an anonymous poet refers to *docta Bononia,* "learned Bologna," and some 40 years later Emperor Frederick Barbarossa, delighted with the revival of a system of law that exalted imperial power, granted students in northern Italy a charter of rights and privileges.

To protect themselves from grasping townsmen, Bolognese students eventually combined into two student bodies —the Cismontane University for Italian students (divided into Roman, Tuscan, and Lombard "nations") and the Ultramontane University for those from over the Alps (French, Picard, Burgundian, English, and other "nations").

In medieval Latin, *universitas* meant a corporation or guild, whether of stonemasons or scholars. What we mean by a university was a *studium generale*—a place where students gathered to study, and which granted the doctorate and the *ius ubique docendi,* the right to teach anywhere. By the 15th century, universitas and studium generale were used interchangeably to denote a university.

Through collective bargaining, the Bologna student guilds fixed rents and living costs. To townsmen, students meant profits, so when disputes arose the students usually won by threatening to leave. Students migrated from Bologna to Padua in 1222; from Oxford to Cambridge in 1209; from Prague to Leipzig in 1408. All became famous universities.

The hard-bargaining students also brought professors to heel by threatening to boycott their classes. The students

279

MIRRORED SPIRES *of medieval St. Séverin and faces of today's University of Paris students merge in a montage on a window of a Left Bank cafe. In the Latin Quarter of the city of light "whereon Philosophy hath set her ancient seat," in the milieu of hot-blooded Abelard and lovelorn Heloise, the freshness of youth never fades. From the world over come students—brilliant, brash, inquiring, defiant—to imbibe the wisdom of ages and to savor, as nowhere else, the precious years of bloom.*

JONATHAN S. BLAIR

paid the professors, hence had them at their mercy. A professor had to swear obedience to the students' rector; he could not vote in the university congregation, yet was bound by its decisions. Thus, while a student had to attend only three lectures a week to preserve his "scholarity," a professor could not absent himself a single day without the students' permission. If he wanted to leave town, he had to deposit money to ensure his prompt return. He could not "create holidays at his pleasure."

Moreover, each day that he failed to draw at least five students for a morning or "ordinary" lecture, or three for the less formal afternoon or "extraordinary" lecture, he was fined as though absent. He could not skip a chapter, and if he fell behind in his commentary on the legal texts, a fine was deducted from the ten Bolognese pounds he had placed in escrow at the start of the year. Students called *denunciatores doctorum* (denouncers of the doctors) reported infractions. The most dreaded penalty, the *privatio,* banned the professor (and sometimes his descendants!) from lecturing, thereby depriving him of his livelihood. We can sympathize

with the professor who announced: "Next year I expect to give ordinary lectures well and lawfully as I always have, but no extraordinary lectures, for students are not good payers, wishing to learn but not to pay...."

According to an old saw, the Italians had the papacy, the Germans the empire, and the French—the University of Paris. If students dominated Bologna, the professors were first to form an effective guild at Paris, where the university arose from the cathedral school of Notre Dame in the late 12th century. In 1200 King Philip Augustus issued a charter exempting students from the jurisdiction of lay courts and protecting their property from seizure.

On the Left Bank of the Seine I haunted the Latin Quarter, named for the language of the students who dwelt there. Sloshing through rain along the Rue Galande, one of Paris's oldest streets, I searched for traces of the medieval university. I went first to the church of St. Julien le Pauvre in the shadow of Notre Dame. (Continued on page 289)

MERRY MOURNERS *"bury" a Bolognese medical graduate and wish him* pace—*peace—as he departs from university life to another world. A female student, a rare sight until the 19th century, crosses the courtyard of the Archiginnasio, built in the 16th century to house Europe's oldest university. Earlier, scholars met in rented halls in Bologna, whose towers (opposite) inspired Dante's first known rhymes.*

JONATHAN S. BLAIR

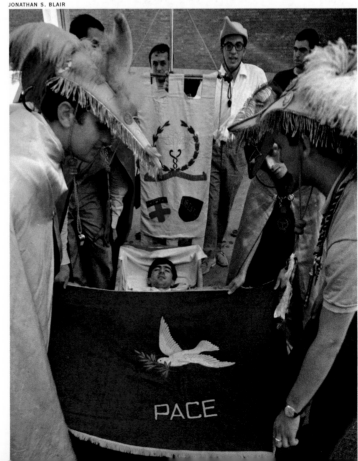

VOICES FROM THE MIDDLE AGES

"My lady looks so gentle and so pure...." Dante's elegant vision of love moves in a sphere far different from the misty, blood-drenched realm of the earlier *Beowulf*. And the solemn intoning of the *Dies Irae* makes a reverent contrast to the earthy portraits of Chaucer and the roguish ruminations of Villon. Through many voices medieval man speaks to us of love and hate, hope and fear.

DIVINE COMEDY
DANTE ALIGHIERI, 14TH CENTURY

Political activist as well as poet and scholar, Dante was banished from Florence and led an exile's life. His sonnets idealize his beloved Beatrice, wed to another. In his masterwork, the Divina Commedia, *he tours Hell, Purgatory, and Paradise, encompassing the medieval universe in one majestic view. Here he and his guide, the poet Virgil, enter the gates of Hell:*

Through me the way is to the City of Woe:
Through me the way into the eternal pain;
Through me the way among the lost below....
Relinquish all hope, ye who enter here.
These words, of a dim color, I espied
Written above the lintel of a door.
Whereat: "Master, the sense is hard," I cried.
And he, as one experienced in that lore:
"Here all misgiving must thy mind reject.
Here cowardice must die and be no more...."
Here lamentation, groans, and wailings deep
Reverberated through the starless air,
So that it made me at the beginning weep.
Uncouth tongues, horrible shriekings of despair,
Shrill and faint voices, cries of pain and rage,
And, with it all, smiting of hands, were there,
Making a tumult, nothing could assuage,
To swirl in the air that knows not day or night,
Like sand within the whirlwind's eddying cage.
And I, whose mind failed to discern aright,
Said: "Master, what is it that my ear affrays?
Who are these that seem so crushed beneath
    their plight?"
And he to me: "These miserable ways
The forlorn spirits endure of those who spent
Life without infamy and without praise.
They are mingled with that caitiff regiment
Of the angels, who rebelled not, yet avowed
To God no loyalty, on themselves intent.
Heaven chased them forth, lest their allegiance cloud
Its beauty, and the deep Hell refuses them,
For, beside such, the sinner would be proud."

SONNET
DANTE ALIGHIERI

Love reigns serenely in my lady's eyes,
    ennobling everything she looks upon;
    towards her, when she passes, all men turn,
    and he whom she salutes feels his heart fail;

so that, with drooping countenance, and pale,
    he then because of his shortcomings sighs:
    before her, pride retreats and anger flies:
    assist me, ladies, now to honor her.

All sweetness, all humility of thought
    stir in the heart of him who hears her speak;
    and he who sees her first is blest indeed.

And when she smiles her beauty is such as
    cannot be told, nor in the memory held,
    so fair, so new a miracle it is.

DIES IRAE
13TH CENTURY

Attributed to Thomas of Celano, disciple of St. Francis of Assisi, the poem vividly portrays the reality of Judgment Day in the medieval mind. Its somber cadences — Dies irae, dies illa/ Solvet saeclum in favilla,/ Teste David cum Sibylla — echo today in Masses for the dead:

Dreaded day, that day of ire,
When the world shall melt in fire,
Told by Sybil and David's lyre.

Fright men's hearts shall rudely shift,
As the judge through gleaming rift
Comes each soul to closely sift.

Then the trumpet's shrill refrain,
Piercing tombs by hill and plain,
Souls to judgment shall arraign....

When the judge his seat shall gain,
All that's hidden shall be plain,
Nothing shall unjudged remain.

Dante, crowned with poet's laurel, opens his Divine Comedy *as souls struggle heavenward through Purgatory. Florence glows golden in this 15th-century fresco by Domenico di Michelino in the city's cathedral; Scala*

Chaucer rides a pilgrim's trail on the Ellesmere manuscript of Canterbury Tales, *c. 1410, the Huntington Library, San Marino, California*

BEOWULF

8TH CENTURY

This oldest English epic, probably by an Anglo-Saxon bard from Northumbria, draws on Norse mythology as it portrays the warrior's quest for glory. Here the hero beheads the mother of the water dragon Grendel and the monster himself, using a weapon recalling Arthur's Excalibur:

Then he saw, hanging on the wall, a heavy
Sword, hammered by giants, strong
And blessed with their magic, the best of all
  weapons
But so massive that no ordinary man could lift
Its carved and decorated length. He drew it
From its scabbard, broke the chain on its hilt,
And then, savage, now, angry
And desperate, lifted it high over his head
And struck with all the strength he had left,
Caught her in the neck and cut it through,
Broke bones and all. Her body fell
To the floor, lifeless, the sword was wet
With her blood, and Beowulf rejoiced at the sight. . . .
He . . . went walking, his hands tight on the sword,
His heart still angry. He . . . took his weapon with him
For final revenge against Grendel's vicious
Attacks, his nighttime raids, over
And over, coming to Heorot when Hrothgar's
Men slept, killing them in their beds,
Eating some on the spot, fifteen
Or more, and running to his loathsome moor
With another such sickening meal waiting

In his pouch. But Beowulf repaid him . . . struck off
His head with a single swift blow. The body
Jerked for the last time, then lay still. . . .
     all that Beowulf took
Was Grendel's head and the hilt of the giants'
Jeweled sword; the rest of that ring-marked
Blade had dissolved in Grendel's steaming
Blood, boiling even after his death.
And then the battle's only survivor
Swam up and away from those silent corpses. . . .

SONG OF ROLAND

11TH CENTURY

First among French epics, this chanson de geste (song of lofty deeds) celebrates a feudal world prizing prowess, loyalty, and honor. Below, the brave Roland, aware at last that his party is being cut to pieces, sounds his horn—too late. Charlemagne, persuaded by the traitor Ganelon that Roland is only hunting, delays turning back:

And now Count Roland, in anguish and in pain,
With all his strength sounds the great horn again.
Bright drops of blood are springing from his mouth,
Veins in his forehead are cracking with the strain.
That mighty voice cries out a second time;
Charlemagne hears it, high on the mountain pass,
Duke Naimon listens, and so do all the Franks.
Then says the king, "That is Count Roland's horn!
He'd never sound it, except for an attack."
Ganelon says, "What battle can there be?
You have grown old, your hair is streaked with white;
The words you speak could well befit a child.
You ought to know how great is Roland's pride—
The wonder is God suffers it so long.
He captured Noples, and not by your command,
And then flushed out the Saracens inside;
He fought them all, Roland, your loyal man,
And then took water and washed the field of blood,
Hoping that you would not detect the fight.
Just for a rabbit he'll blow his horn all day!
Now he is playing some game to please his peers.
Who in the world would dare make war on him!
Ride on, I tell you! What are we waiting for?
We've far to go to see our lands once more."

The peasant knew Piers the Plowman's fate: to "sweat and toil as long as I live." 13th-century illumination, Bibliothèque Royale, Brussels

ROMANCE OF THE ROSE

**WILLIAM OF LORRIS, JOHN OF MEUN
13TH CENTURY**

*Twenty thousand lines, a work spanning forty
years, the* Romance *enjoyed immense popular-
ity. In the first part William devised an allegory
of courtly love peopled by Mirth, Fair-Welcome,
Danger, and such. In the second part the bourgeois, sometimes cynical John often digresses to
display his encyclopedic mind or to offer advice:*

> Woman should gather roses ere
> Time's ceaseless foot o'ertaketh her,
> For if too long she make delay,
> Her chance of love may pass away,
> And well it is she seek it while
> Health, strength, and youth around her smile.
> To pluck the fruits of love in youth
> Is each wise woman's rule forsooth,
> For when age creepeth o'er us, hence
> Go also the sweet joys of sense,
> And ill doth she her days employ
> Who lets life pass without love's joy.
> And if my counsel she despise,
> Not knowing how 'tis just and wise,
> Too late, alas! will she repent
> When age is come, and beauty spent.

*Mummers dancing to drums, bells, cymbals celebrate a winter feast;
14th-century French miniature in the Bibliothèque Nationale, Paris*

> They have woe in winter time, and wake at midnight
> To rise and to rock the cradle at the bedside,
> To card and to comb, to darn clouts and to wash them,
> To rub and to reel and to put rushes on the paving.
> The woe of these women who dwell in hovels
> Is too sad to speak of or to say in rhyme.
> And many other men have much to suffer
> From hunger and from thirst; they turn the fair
>   side outward,
> For they are abashed to beg, lest it should be
>   acknowledged
> At their neighbors what they need at noon and even.

PIERS THE PLOWMAN

WILLIAM LANGLAND, 14TH CENTURY

*Welling up from the peasantry comes a cry of
suffering—an allegorical poem attributed to a
cleric who may have known poverty in London
with wife and child. It extols the simple life,
warns the heartless rich of retribution in hell:*

> The needy are our neighbors, if we note rightly;
> As prisoners in cells, or poor folk in hovels,
> Charged with children and overcharged by landlords.
> What they may spare in spinning they spend on rental,
> On milk, or on meal to make porridge
> To still the sobbing of the children at mealtime.
> Also they themselves suffer much hunger.

CANTERBURY TALES

GEOFFREY CHAUCER, 14TH CENTURY

*Vintner's son, veteran of French campaigns, dip-
lomat, civil servant, member of Parliament—
Chaucer knew all levels of English society and
portrayed them with earthy humor and vigor.
The tales are told by pilgrims bound for Becket's
shrine. We meet the friar, "a very festive man":*

> A friar there was, a wanton and a merry....
> He heard confession gently, it was said,
> Gently absolved too, leaving naught of dread.
> He was an easy man to give penance
> When knowing he should gain a good pittance....
> His tippet was stuck always full of knives
> And pins, to give to young and pleasing wives.
> And certainly he kept a merry note:
> Well could he sing and play upon the rote.
> At balladry he bore the prize away.
> His throat was white as lily of the May;
> Yet strong he was as ever champion.
> In towns he knew the taverns, every one,
> And every good host and each barmaid too—
> Better than begging lepers, these he knew ...
> He lisped a little, out of wantonness,
> To make his English soft upon his tongue;
> And in his harping, after he had sung,
> His two eyes twinkled in his head as bright
> As do the stars within the frosty night.

THE DECAMERON

GIOVANNI BOCCACCIO, 14TH CENTURY

Natural son of a Tuscan merchant and a Parisian woman, Boccaccio won fame at Florence as a poet and diplomat. His prose classic, a collection of tales told by gentlefolk who have fled to a country estate to escape the Black Death, aims only to entertain. Many of the 100 stories, like the sampling below, dwell on affairs of the heart:

There were once two noble knights of Provence, one of whom was named Messer Guglielmo Rossiglione and the other Messer Guglielmo Guardastagno. Both were valiant men-at-arms and therefore loved each other. It happened that Messer Guglielmo Guardastagno fell deeply in love with Messer Guglielmo Rossiglione's beautiful and charming wife. She fell in love with him too, and they often came together.

The husband found it out. He was so much enraged that his old love for Guardastagno changed to mortal hatred. He armed, and laid an ambush in a wood through which he knew Guardastagno had to pass. When he came up, Rossiglione rushed at him furiously, lance in hand, shouting: "You are a dead man," and so saying thrust his lance through the knight's chest. Rossiglione cut open Guardastagno's breast with a dagger, tore

Jester and girl embrace on title page of a Villon collection, including his major work, The Testament, *and other poems, published c. 1505. Bibliothèque Nationale, Paris*

out his heart with his own hands, and then remounted his horse and returned to his castle.

Rossiglione dismounted and called for the cook, to whom he said: "Take this boar's heart and make the best and most delicious dish of it you can." The cook sent him the dressed heart and he had it set before his wife. The lady had a good appetite, tasted the dish and thought it good; and therefore ate it all up.

"What you have eaten," said the knight, "is verily the heart of Messer Guglielmo Guardastagno, whom you loved so dearly. And you may be certain it is he, because I tore the heart from his breast with these hands."

No need to ask whether the lady was in anguish. After a little time she said: "You have acted like a base and treacherous knight. But, please God, no other food shall ever follow a food so noble." And jumping to her feet she ran to a window and threw herself out of it. This window was high above the ground so that the lady was not only killed by her fall but smashed to pieces.

THE BALLAD
OF DEAD LADIES

FRANÇOIS VILLON, 15TH CENTURY

Born the year Joan of Arc was burned at the stake, Villon studied at the University of Paris — then turned to a life of crime, haunting alleys, taverns, brothels. He wrote of the degradation of life and the cruelty of death, themes appropriate to his time, when chivalry itself was dying:

> Tell me where, in what country,
> Is Flora the beautiful Roman,
> Archipiada or Thaïs
> Who was first cousin to her once,
> Echo who speaks when there's a sound
> On a pond or a river
> Whose beauty was more than human?
> But where are the snows of yesteryear?
>
> Where is the learned Heloise
> For whom they castrated Pierre Abelard
> And made him a monk at Saint-Denis,
> For his love he took this pain,
> Likewise where is the queen
> Who commanded that Buridan
> Be thrown in a sack into the Seine?
> But where are the snows of yesteryear?
>
> The queen white as a lily
> Who sang with a siren's voice,
> Big-footed Bertha, Beatrice, Alice,
> Haremburgis who held Maine
> And Jeanne the good maid of Lorraine
> Whom the English burnt at Rouen, where,
> Where are they, sovereign Virgin?
> But where are the snows of yesteryear?

DEAN CONGER, NATIONAL GEOGRAPHIC STAFF

FESTIVE FINGERS OF FIRE *seem to trace a willow weeping over the Arno at Florence,*
where Dante wept for his divine Beatrice, enshrining his love in fiery lines that sparkle yet.
In a city where bankers sought culture as well as coin, the university established
the first chair of poetry in 1373. The professor: Boccaccio. His subject: Dante.

Here Dante and Petrarch worshiped; here Villon and Rabelais sought forgiveness
for their sins; here were held colorful university assemblies in the 13th and 14th
centuries. I let imagination carry me back to the 12th century....

Some of my colleagues still harbor the idea that blondes and books do not mix.
Certainly the handsome Peter Abelard found this to be true. His subtle mind, bold
rationalism, deep learning, and animated personality attracted students wherever
he lectured, at Melun, Corbeil, Paris—so many, he modestly informs us, that the
inns could not hold them nor the earth feed them. Although he preceded the
university by half a century, it was he who made Paris the center of all Europe
for the study of theology, philosophy, and the liberal arts.

If Abelard sometimes lost his head in the bitterness of learned controversy, he
also lost his heart, at the age of 38, to the lovely Heloise. He arranged to be taken
into her home as tutor: "We opened our books, but more words of love than of
lesson asserted themselves." After Heloise's uncle learned she was with child,
he had Abelard mutilated. The lovers were separated, each taking monastic vows.
Years later, when Heloise was an abbess, she wrote Abelard recalling how no
woman could resist the charm of his voice as he sang his love sonnets. "My
Abelard, you well know how much I lost in losing you...."

Despite the scandal and the condemnation of his teachings by two church councils, Abelard still regarded himself as the only competent philosopher in the world —*me solum in mundo superesse philosophum.* In his famous work *Sic et Non* (Yes and No) he set off the opinions of one authority against another, revealing that they often disagreed. Though he died disgraced, "in silence and in solitude," his method became the technique of university lecture halls, and from among his students time brought forth 50 bishops, 20 cardinals, and a pope.

His approach served the Bolognese monk Gratian, whose *Decretum* harmonized canon, or church, law; and Peter Lombard, whose *Sentences* became the major textbook of theology. It also influenced Thomas Aquinas, whose works have made a profound impress upon Christian society from the 13th century to today.

Aquinas was a big man, friendly, robust, endowed with a prodigious memory and remarkable powers of concentration. Scion of a noble family accustomed to facing danger on the battlefield, he did not quail before the task of building in his *Summa Theologiae* a complete structure of Christian theology based on the twin sources of knowledge, divine revelation and human reason. For revelation he turned to the Bible and church tradition; in the use of reason he was guided by the logic of Aristotle. He was confident the two could not contradict, for God was the source of both. Thus theology and philosophy, faith and science were ultimately reconcilable, he taught, and the students of Europe listened.

A YOUNG SCHOLAR in the 13th century might be enjoying his first meal at an inn when a professor or one of his students appeared, trying to drum up trade. Universities touted their wares too. Toulouse proclaimed that the cardinal legate in France had promised its students and masters a plenary indulgence for all their sins, and there they used books banned in Paris.

The incoming freshman—a *bejaunus,* yellow bill—often received a merciless hazing. Especially in German universities, he was regarded as a stinking beast to be dehorned in a ceremony of mock solemnity. Afterward he had to give his tormentors a dinner which might leave him financially strapped for weeks.

Students wrote home, begging for money, "for the city is expensive and makes many demands." Professors helped them phrase the letters and provided models of proven efficacy. Bewildered and angry fathers replied: "I have recently discovered that you live dissolutely and slothfully . . . strumming a guitar while the others are at their studies, whence it happens that you have read but one volume of law while your more industrious companions have read several."

Student life *was* rough and turbulent. Picture if you will scholars making their boisterous way from tavern to tavern in the Latin Quarter, reeling from the Two Swords across the Petit Pont to the cathedral of Notre Dame—not scrupling, on one occasion, to play dice on the altar—and rolling back to wrangle and fight in the crooked little streets of the Left Bank. They "quarrel among themselves over dogs, women, or what-not, slashing off one another's fingers with their swords, or,

TENSE TYROS *once ringed Padua's anatomy amphitheater, oldest extant in Europe. William Harvey, who discovered how blood circulates, studied here soon after the hall opened in 1594. A half-century earlier Andreas Vesalius had fathered modern anatomy at Padua. Dissecting cadavers gathered from gallows and graveyards, he cut through misty medieval theory and gave man a clearer look at the structure of his body.*

JONATHAN S. BLAIR

290

"When you saw or cut a man, dip a rag in this and put it to his nostrils"

So Michael Scot in the 13th century held out the promise of painless surgery with the spongia soporifera—sleep sponge. Soaked in henbane, opium, and mandragora, it gave weak but welcome relief—like much of medieval medicine.

Scot was trained at Salerno, where medical study in the West had revived in the 11th century. As translations became available, students read works of Hippocrates and Galen and mined the lore of Jewish doctors and the Arab Avicenna, 11th-century court physician in Persia whose Canon of Medicine remained a text for 600 years. Skilled Arabs listed 130 diseases of the eye, described six operations for cataract, including removal by suction and by a gold needle.

Roger of Salerno in the 12th century reset poorly knit fractures and treated hemorrhages with styptics and ligatures. Roland of Parma practiced trepanning— perforating the skull to relieve pressure from liquids or swelling (right). The brothers Borgognoni cleansed wounds with wine, bound them with stitches. By the 15th century the doctors Branca restored noses and ears with tissue grafted from the patient's arms. Tools (lower) included the devaricator for prying wounds open, forceps,

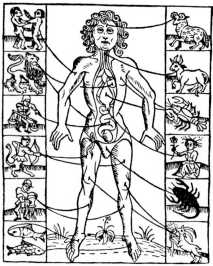

BLEEDING CHART, THE TRENTON FREE LIBRARY. 15TH-CENTURY SURGEON'S TOOLS, ISTITUTO RIZZOLI, BOLOGNA. 14TH-CENTURY DRAWING OF TREPANNING AND PALPATING, MUSÉE CONDÉ, CHANTILLY. APOTHECARY SHOP, FROM 14TH-CENTURY TRANSLATION OF AVICENNA'S "CANON," BIBLIOTECA UNIVERSITARIA, BOLOGNA; SCALA

surgical saw, and bloodletting knives.

Many believed disease stemmed from an imbalance in four body fluids, or humors—blood, phlegm, black bile, and yellow bile—and sought to restore the balance through bleeding. Zodiac charts (opposite) revealed the best times to bleed various parts of the body. As the church forbade its clerks to shed blood, bleeding was often relegated to itinerant barbers, "leeches," who also cut for the stone and hernia. Bloody rags, wrapped on rails to dry, gave us the barber pole.

Physicians checked pulse and urine and palpated—examined by touch (left). But diagnosis outdistanced a therapy tinged by magic. Drugs varied; along with useful ones such as castor oil, alum, and niter, the corner apothecary (above) stocked nostrums like powdered emerald, dried lizard, oil of snake, tincture of toad.

The medieval healer left a proud legacy of hospital care, public health services, false teeth, gold fillings, spectacles—and a prescription for practitioners to come: "Boldly adjust the fee to a man's position . . . never ask too little."

293

with only knives in their hands and nothing to protect their tonsured pates, rush into conflicts from which armed knights would hold back." Whole nations of students joined the frays, French against Germans, English against Picards. Called to trial, they pleaded "benefit of clergy" and sought judgment in the more lenient church courts.

But as today, most students worked hard and learned much. The Rue du Fouarre (Street of Straw, named, the story goes, for the straw dropped by students as they carried it to class to sit on) and the Rue St. Jacques felt the measured footfalls of a score of protégés of St. Nicholas, patron of scholars, to every drunken rascal's lurch.

As THE PURPOSE of a university was to learn, not to play, statutes forbade most games. William of Wykeham, Bishop of Winchester and founder of New College at Oxford, forbade chess, labeling it "noxious, inordinate, and unhonest." Dancing was usually prohibited, although at Basel officials ordered students not to attend dances unless invited—gate-crashing is nothing new. Even so, some preferred learning to the ladies. Called home from Siena to marry, a youth demurred, "for one may always get a wife, but science once lost can never be recovered."

Students, supposed to sit "as quiet as girls," were often unruly, stamping their feet and banging books against benches to express disapproval of the lecture. In 1215, statutes of the guild of masters at Paris prescribed that while lecturing, masters should wear a "round black cope reaching to the heels at least when new." The cope or *cappa* was the secular clergy's outdoor garb. Later, academic plumage brightened. Oxford professors wore green, blue, and blood-red robes, the last symbolic of Christ's passion.

Student and master rose before dawn to use every hour of nature's light; candles were costly. Winter's cold accompanied the student's every meal, enveloped him in its fold as he slept at night, and in the morning pursued him into the lecture room. No fire burned as cold hands tried to take notes in the shelter of long-sleeved copes.

In four to five years a student could get a bachelor of arts degree, and in three to four more years a master of arts or doctor of philosophy. Statutes forbade him to bring wine into the examination room, or to lie in wait with a dagger for the examiner who failed him. The successful candidate received his doctorate with a cap, a ring—symbol of his espousal of science—a kiss of peace, and a benediction. Sometimes he had to feast his professors and provide gifts for university officials. Then he wrote home: "Sing

unto the Lord ... your son has héld a glorious disputation. ... He answered all questions without a mistake. ... And he has duly begun to give lectures.''

As I strolled the Left Bank I thought of a genius known to us only as the Archpoet. He was a 12th-century Villon, a bitter wit, a proud beggar who would rather ride than walk, loved good food, good wine, and preferred a wench to solitude. Chided by his patron, an archbishop, for too much love of living, he turned on the prelate with the impudent confession of a Goliard, a vagabond poet:

> *In the public house to die*　　*That will make the angels cry,*
> 　*Is my resolution;*　　　　　*With glad elocution,*
> *Let wine to my lips be nigh*　"*Grant this toper, God on high,*
> 　*At life's dissolution;*　　　　*Grace and absolution!*"

This fresh and irreverent spirit caught the tempo of student life, and of an age that saw towns across Europe swell and burst their walls, offering to bold and eager men a new route to riches, power, and fame.

TWILIGHT VEILS *old Heidelberg on the Neckar, a vista revered by generations of scholars strolling the* Philosophenweg— *Philosophers' Way. Seeking a "handmaid of Paris," the Palatine Elector Rupert I founded Germany's first university here in 1386. Statutes banned fencing, blasphemy, catching burghers' pigeons; miscreants might land in the* studentenkarzer, *university jail (below). Old ways survive in illegal, surreptitious dueling and in drinking— "jesting eternally, quaffing infernally" at the Red Ox Inn (lower).*

By Paul Murray Kendall

THE WORLD OF JACQUES COEUR

OY FILLED the city of Rouen. French armies had invaded Normandy, forced the English to yield Rouen, and sent them scurrying in retreat to the Channel ports. Now, on November 10, 1449, Charles VII of France entered the city in triumph with a resplendent train. In shining armor the strange little king rode a charger caparisoned in azure velvet sewn with gold fleurs-de-lis. Next in honor came a quartet of dignitaries brilliantly arrayed in red velvet. Led by the count of Dunois, paladin of France, the group included "Sire Jacques Coeur," steward of the royal household, master of the mint, friend of the pope, owner of a merchant fleet renowned from the North Sea to the Levant.

Chroniclers celebrated the moment in poetry and prose, and especially noted the presence of a merchant in the world of lordly beings:

Jacques Coeur indeed was there, the man of pounds and pence,
Who had, with heartfelt care, showed utter diligence.

How different the scene from that day, 27 years earlier, when Charles, his throne disputed, his very person in peril, led his ragged court to safety behind the walls of Bourges, a cathedral town in the heart of France. Jacques Coeur's presence then went unremarked. For he was but a young townsman, the son of a fur merchant, starting his own family, dreaming who knows what dreams.

It was a poor time indeed for an entrepreneur to nurse ambitious thoughts. Strife and misery swept the land as the Hundred Years' War ground toward its closing decades. Up in Paris, where the infant Henry VI of England had been proclaimed king of France, thousands died of famine. In one terrible winter people scrabbled in the gutters for rotten apples that pigs disdained; by summer wolves had grown so ravenous that they dug up bodies in the cemeteries.

French nobles made separate truces with the invading English, thus giving themselves leisure to engage in plunder, while the passive little knock-kneed King Charles wept in his chambers. Often his threadbare household (such furs as it had, supplied on credit perhaps by Jacques Coeur?) could not pay the butcher or the baker; the royal doublets were patched. While councillors of the "King of Bourges," as Charles's foes derisively called him, pillaged the treasury to line their pockets, his unpaid starveling bands of soldiery pillaged the countryside.

Ruined and desperate men, accompanied by their trulls in the baggage wagons, roamed the provinces, roasting peasants over slow fires to make them reveal hidden valuables. A husband was thrust into a rabbit hutch atop which the brigands took turns assaulting his wife. When these fearsome *écorcheurs* (flayers) spotted a string of laden packhorses, the usual means of transporting goods, the carriers were lucky to escape alive. France was stripped to the bone.

Villages stood deserted; arable land returned to thickets of bramble. Men dared cultivate crops only near a walled town or fortified place, their ears tuned for the

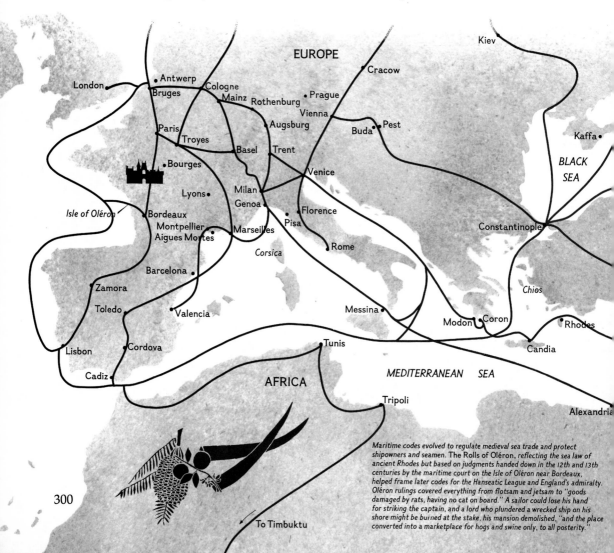

Maritime codes evolved to regulate medieval sea trade and protect shipowners and seamen. The Rolls of Oléron, *reflecting the sea law of ancient Rhodes but based on judgments handed down in the 12th and 13th centuries by the maritime court on the Isle of Oléron near Bordeaux, helped frame later codes for the Hanseatic League and England's admiralty. Oléron rulings covered everything from flotsam and jetsam to "goods damaged by rats, having no cat on board." A sailor could lose his hand for striking the captain, and a lord who plundered a wrecked ship on his shore might be burned at the stake, his mansion demolished, "and the place converted into a marketplace for hogs and swine only, to all posterity."*

watcher's horn signaling danger. Trade shrank to local exchange; industry, to supplying neighborhoods—when there was anything to supply.

SUCH WAS THE WORLD of Jacques Coeur's young manhood. He grew up in Bourges, a hodgepodge of crooked streets dominated by more than 40 church spires and the soaring cathedral of St. Étienne. The son of the fur dealer Pierre Coeur no doubt attended a good school, spending most of his time on Latin, devotional works, and lives of the saints.

In the family house-and-shop, not far from the castle of the hard-fisted duke of Berry, Jacques would also have learned the Latin of accounting; books often were kept in that language. In 1422 he married Macée, the girl next door. Soon after, upon the death of his father it would seem, Jacques inherited the business.

SIREN SONG of "grand commerce" lured shopkeeper Coeur from Bourges to Montpellier, thence to motley Levantine marts where Europeans walked with fear to fetch exotics Europe craved—and paid for dearly.
He studded France with warehouses, wove a web of partnerships, mined salt, silver, lead, and copper, trafficked at the ports of Spain, England, Flanders. Cargoes of metals and woolens he shipped across the Mediterranean in beamy vessels like one that sails a glassy sea in a window from his mansion at Bourges (below).

With diligence and diplomacy he eased Rome's ban on Christian trade with Islam, wrung port privileges from Egypt's wary sultan, gathered "every sort of merchandise that the brain of man could imagine." From caravan towns where continents met came spices and silks; from Barbary, and Timbuktu beyond the Sahara, ivory tusks, dates, oranges. King and nobles bought, competitors marveled, and, noted a chronicler, Jacques Coeur "gained alone, every year, more than all the other merchants in the kingdom."

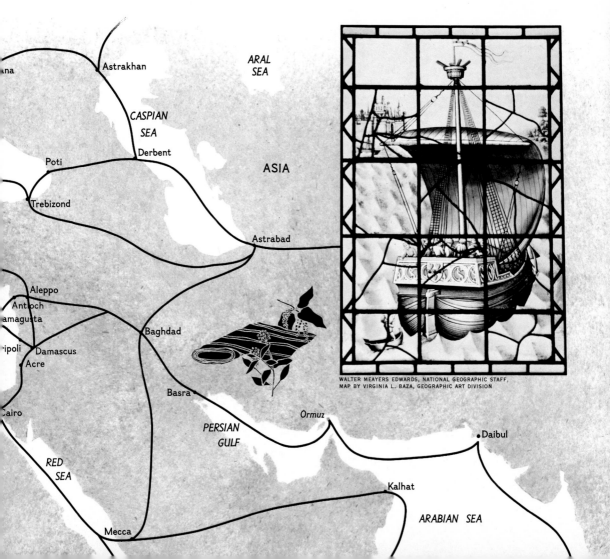

WALTER MEAYERS EDWARDS, NATIONAL GEOGRAPHIC STAFF, MAP BY VIRGINIA L. BAZA, GEOGRAPHIC ART DIVISION

BRIDE OF THE SEA, *Venice rides her fleet of islands in arcaded splendor. As strife sapped the mainland, Venice prospered on Eastern trade. Each year she wed her Adriatic anew as the doge cast a gold ring from the state galley. Jacques Coeur struggled to breach her maritime domain, in time made France a power in Levantine commerce.*

From Egypt in 828, merchants of Venice stole the body of St. Mark. The city acclaimed the apostle its patron and enshrined his remains in St. Mark's Basilica (opposite). Above its portal prance four bronze horses looted from Constantinople in the Fourth Crusade.

From Venice in 1271 (right) sailed Marco Polo, his father, and uncle for fabled Cathay. The traders returned after 25 years laden with gems and an immortal tale of the wondrous Orient.

Surely the rising young merchant saw Joan of Arc when she came to Bourges in 1429—that marvelous year when this inspired peasant girl lifted the despairing Charles from his lethargy and touched off the miracle of French resurgence.

But the nation remained an entrepreneur's prison, and Jacques Coeur decided to break out of it. For a time he joined in managing the mint of Bourges; then, in 1430, he and his associates formed a company to deal "in every class of merchandise, including that required by the king . . . in which they can make a profit." For the next two decades his enterprises accelerated dizzyingly until he became the prince of French merchants, the apparent equal of the greatest lords.

History but hints at how he did it. He must have accumulated capital by winning the confidence of men. To build his organization he found able associates and let their diligence make money for themselves and for him. And he moved his headquarters to the Mediterranean port of Montpellier. For he knew that only by fighting for a share of the lucrative traffic of the Levant, only by "grand commerce," could he hope to revive the moribund trade of ravaged France. Bold management and good luck could win enormous profits—1,000 percent on a single voyage!

Hazards loomed as enormous as the profits—storm and pirates, the uncertain temper of the sultan of Egypt, papal strictures on trade with the infidel, French laws against the export of coin, the fierce competition of Venetian and Genoese traders who monopolized the Black Sea and the whole Aegean region.

Jacques' first daring stride into this perilous world gained him nothing but experience. In 1432 we find him with four other merchants landing in a galley at Beirut. Each had rented space for his share of the cargo of woolens, honey, and metal wares. Their goods loaded on asses and horses, the traders set out on the two-day journey to the caravan center of Damascus, the greatest metropolis, after Cairo, in the sultan's domain. At the gate of every town, the Frenchmen, like

303

NIMBLE *jesters cutting a caper liven a guild festival at Ulm in Germany. Their medieval prototypes cavorted at fairs that grew from holy days when vendors hawked wares among pilgrim crowds. Folk far from home made easy marks, they found; soon pitchmen, bawds, bards, and backpacking peddlers (right) hied to every fete.*

Sellers' stalls ring the bishop of Paris (opposite) as he blesses the famed Lendit Fair—named for an annual assembly (l'endit), gathered to view a holy relic. Clerics chafed as revel eclipsed rite: "Men busy themselves more with merchandise and feasting than with Masses...the Kirk must wait at the Kitchen's heels."

all Christians, were forced by order of the sultan to dismount and walk within. Finally, they wound down a narrow valley, rushing waters on one side, orchards on the other, to shining Damascus, perfumed by the rose water and candied fruits for which it was famous. Each night the merchants were locked in their dwelling places. Christians, generally hated in the Moslem world, were viewed with suspicion.

On the return voyage Jacques' vessel sprang a leak off Corsica. He and his companions managed to reach shore, but robbers stripped them of all but their shirts and let them make their way back to France as best they could.

Undaunted by this failure, Jacques persisted, building his network of trade until he had some 300 agents "distributed in many and divers places both on land and sea." He developed skilled sea captains, men who remained closest to his heart. Jean de Village, captain-general of the fleet, would prove his fidelity in a time of catastrophe. All had to be tough as well as resourceful, for a galley usually carried but three officers, and most of the rowers and other crewmen were vagabonds or shady characters provided by the press gang.

Europe yearned for spices and luxuries from the East; Jacques gathered them—along the Barbary Coast, at Damascus, at Famagusta on Cyprus, overflowing with precious stuffs; at hostile Alexandria, where the sultan's men removed the rudders and sails of arriving Christian ships; at polyglot Cairo, so packed with humanity that it was believed 100,000 people slept in the open air for lack of lodging—ports with masts rising thick against the Mediterranean sky, cities with glittering shops and caravans of balky, spitting camels.

The very names of the wares echo the romance of the grand commerce— belladonna and dates, ostrich feathers, apes and ivory; pepper, cloves, ginger, cane sugar (prized as medicine), musk, essence of violets; costly dyes like

cinnabar, cochineal, indigo, saffron, henna; exotic medicinals like camphor, cubebs, aloes, Bezoar stones (taken from the stomachs of goats and gazelles and worn in fancy lockets as a cure-all); Indian pearls, silks, brocades. . . .

EVEN AFTER HE HAD SURMOUNTED the thronging obstacles of sea trade and was landing his costly cargoes at Montpellier, Jacques Coeur had still to face perhaps his thorniest problem — the lamentable condition of trade in France herself. Impoverished nobles multiplied the already numerous tolls that roadblocked the realm. At every bridge, every ford, every border of seignorial lands, a convoy was forced to pay a fee. To move Eastern goods northward and acquire cargoes for his outbound galleys, Jacques set up warehouses and agencies, and

305

formed new commercial alliances—all effectively interlocked. In Rouen he formed a company for the sale of wool and velvet; in Limoges, for trade in spices, furs, and cloth; in English-held Bordeaux, for the supply of wheat and salt to that city; in Bourges, for dealing in armor, an especially profitable venture. He engaged in the salt trade along the Loire, Rhone, and Seine rivers, held interests in a paper mill and lead and copper mines around Lyons, transacted business with Italian financiers in the papal territory of Avignon. In 1437, with the French now in possession of Paris, he was appointed to reorganize the mint there.

From the beginning Jacques had aimed at the greatest market of all for his precious imports—the court. By 1439 he had achieved his goal; he had become the king's *argentier,* in effect the treasurer-steward of the royal household. It was a lucrative though somewhat perilous arrangement, for as treasurer Jacques paid for the goods which, as steward, he kept for sale.

His wonderful warehouse of pungent, glittering stuff at Tours provided spices for the king's table, drugs for his indisposition. Did the queen desire a gem-crusted golden saltcellar, the dauphin's wife yearn for a gown lined with sable, a great lord require rubies to adorn his sword-hilt? Jacques Coeur supplied them. And a word in the king's ear about the mercantile needs and opportunities of France—Jacques supplied that too. Numerous decrees in the 1440's suppressing tolls and regulating finances can probably be traced to the shrewd argentier.

With the backing of his master, Jacques dispatched Jean de Village to negotiate with the sultan of Egypt. Graciously received, Jean brought back to Charles a gift of curative balm, a leopard, and—best of all—the sultan's agreement to welcome French merchants at his ports and pilgrims to Jerusalem.

BY THE LATE 1440's Jacques Coeur had won ennoblement from the king and owned vast estates. His son Jean had been elected archbishop of Bourges before the age of 23; his daughter Perrette had married a nobleman. As the crown and symbol of his success Jacques built in his native town a dwelling which remains today a memorial of his opulence and his personality. A contemporary called it "so magnificent that neither princes of the blood nor the king himself had any residence comparable to it."

Though its walls no longer blaze with tapestries, the three-story mansion, with its thrusting roofs and chimneys and its galleried courtyard, maintains its impact

PRINCE, PRELATE, AND PROLETARIAN *alike envied the house that Jacques built at Bourges (far right). Here he basked amid sculptured whimsies like the stone servant surveying the street scene (upper), and knew the comfort of a well-heeled burgher (lower), reclining near the fire while his wife cooks. Coeur finished his mansion in 1450, enjoyed it but a year before his fall.*

ROMAN, VISIGOTH, AND FRANK *girdled French Carcassonne in stone. To such a stronghold—Anglo-Saxon* burh, *German* Burg, *French* bourg—*came merchants seeking markets and safety, adding shops and houses to churches and battlements. When the "borough" filled up, burgesses, burghers, and bourgeois clustered outside the town walls in a* faubourg. *And that's how suburbs began to sprawl.*

OVERLEAF: JONATHAN S. BLAIR

yet. Visiting it, I was struck by the mingling of grandeur and intimacy, the flaunting of idiosyncracy within a noble frame, the airy spaciousness tempered by comfort —comfort, that bourgeois concept of living developed by wealthy burghers in the 15th century.

Above the street entry two carved servants peer down from recesses on either side, searching for their master or merely enjoying the passing scene. Over the entry stands a jewel of a chapel, so tiny that the master and mistress had to squeeze into niches on each side of the altar. Above them a vaulted ceiling shone with white-robed angels and golden stars on an azure background.

Scenes over entryways tell the purpose of a room: The kitchen is signaled by a chef mixing spices, a woman washing a basin, a boy turning a spit. The mansion abounds with carvings. Like any good burgher Jacques Coeur wanted his money's worth; like the man of imagination he was, he breathed the warmth of life into his stone dwelling, made it the theater of his memory, his fancy, his humor. Everywhere he flaunted his merchant's maxims *(En bouche close n'entre mouche*—Between closed lips no fly slips), his rebus-like coat of arms with its red hearts *(coeurs)*, and his intrepid motto:

A VAILLANS CO RIENS IMPOSSIBLE

—To valiant hearts nothing is impossible. A challenge to the fates delivered with the grin of a pun.

Post-Gothic yet pre-Renaissance, monumental but charming, Coeur's mansion is a bourgeois fantasy, a townsman's success story in the Age of Chivalry.

Towns and trade generally had begun as intruders upon the feudal world, alien newcomers who only after a struggle achieved their freedom, their own organization, their special rule of law. In the dark centuries before the year 1000, merchants and town life as we conceive it hardly existed. Under the pounding

SHOPPING CENTER *of a medieval town proffers its wares on a rare paved street. Tailors snip and stitch, furriers array pelts, a barber shaves a customer as basins swing above his stall—utensils of a trade that included bloodletting and tooth pulling. Pastries scent a grocer's stall; his sign touts "good Hippocras," a spiced wine. Officials guarded buyers' rights, fined butchers who cut beef on boards last used for fish. Towns forbade work at night or in private; what a man might buy, he could see being made.*

15TH-CENTURY ILLUMINATION, BIBLIOTHÈQUE DE L'ARSENAL, PARIS

311

of the barbarians, Roman Europe fell back to an agrarian society. A submerged mass of peasants tilled the land, supporting the lords who ruled and fought, and the priests who prayed and taught.

By the turn of the millennium, time had tempered the ferocity of barbarian attacks, and the people of Western Europe were gaining resources and mobility. Long-distance traders, bands of hardy nomads, turned winter shelters into towns and crisscrossed the Continent, buying cheap in regions of plenty to sell dear in regions of scarcity.

In growing towns traders gained capital and strength. Along with the guilds of artisans and workers that supplied them, they succeeded—often against the bitter opposition of lords spiritual and temporal—in establishing a new order of society, the bourgeoisie.

From the ports and river mouths trade thrust inland. Southeastward from London and Bruges, southwestward from Lübeck and Stavanger, northward from Marseilles and Barcelona, the routes converged on the famous fairgrounds of Champagne. There in the 12th and 13th centuries, in

GUILD COMPLEX *ruled many a town as merchants, then craftsmen, formed unions in profusion and seated leaders on town councils. Dyers (opposite upper), elite goldsmiths like the Bruges artisan assembling a chalice (lower), glassworkers (below), road menders, bell ringers, even prostitutes formed guilds; Paris listed 101. Cabinetmakers joined one, chest makers another. Harness makers had their guild, saddlers theirs. Members met to air complaints, dined by rigid rules: "Look that thine hands be clean. . . . Hold thy tongue and spend thy sight." On holy days they paraded under heraldic arms like those of tailor, cooper, and miller at far right.*

Apprentice as young as 10, journeyman about 20, a man made master and set up his own shop when his guild approved a sample of his skill—his "masterpiece."

15TH-CENTURY BOHEMIAN AND (OPPOSITE) FLEMISH MINIATURES; BRITISH MUSEUM. ARMS OF MEDIEVAL GUILDS OF GHENT FROM THE CITY'S ARCHIVES. GOLDSMITH OF BRUGES; WALTER MEAYERS EDWARDS, NATIONAL GEOGRAPHIC STAFF

Tailors

Coopers

Millers

the towns of Bar sur Aube, Lagny, Provins, and Troyes, flourished the greatest marts in Europe. Italians brought luxuries of the East to trade for English wool, Baltic potash and rope, and Flemish and French cloth. The fairs had their own justice, their moneychangers, the most advanced accounting system of the time—and their swarm of jugglers, balladeers, quacks, and loose ladies.

As business methods improved, merchants shook off their last ties to peddler days, directed operations from their home cities, and let agents handle their wares. At the same time craft and trading guilds developed swiftly, and it was the guilds that provided the typical medieval texture of town life, town work, town politics.

Whatever the patron saint they prayed to, whatever the garb they wore, whatever they were called ("mysteries" in England, *métier* or *jurande* in France, *arte* in Italy, *Handwerk* in Germany), guilds had one essential purpose: protection against competition. Minute regulations, strictly enforced, laid down hours of work, prices, standards of quality, the number of apprentices and journeymen that a master might employ.

In the crafts the door to business success could only be opened by apprenticeship, which took from four to ten years. When an apprentice completed his term, he was admitted to the guild as a journeyman and went to work for wages by the day (*journée*) until he could set himself up in business as a master. His private life as well as his business practice was closely watched.

A young London textile dealer of humble standing in the mercers' guild found himself, upon announcing his engagement to the rich widow of a vintner, promoted to "the livery," the highest rank; but a lovelorn tailor's apprentice, dragged before the guild by his master, was scolded because he kept "the company of a woman which was to his great loss and hindering for . . . he was so affectionate and resorted daily unto her."

By the 13th century the townsman had thrust himself between knight and cleric to play a powerful role in the feudal world. Paris, giant of the

Medieval life ticked to a quickened tempo when men mechanized time

Tracking sun and moon, marking month and day, parading Biblical and symbolic figures, the great Orloj, or "time teller" (opposite), dominates the Old Town Square of Prague. Thousands thronged Bohemia's capital in 1480 to watch Master Hanus set his marvel going; legend says burghers blinded him lest he build a better one elsewhere.

As clocks blossomed in town after town, men fell in step to the clanking pulse of technology's first precision instrument, mentioned earliest in the 13th century. Monastic ideals stressed a measured pace of life, and monks had long used marked candles, water clocks, sundials. But candles blew out, water froze, clouds hid the sun; what then? To a weight hung on a reel, someone linked the ingenious "escapement." Its rocking bar harnessed the rig to a stop-go rhythm that put the tick in clocks. But heat swelled iron parts, cold shrank them. Friction dragged an unsteady foot. Some clocks lost half an hour a day.

Though they erred, they awed; many people thought them sired of Satan. Clock towers soon rivaled church towers, with figures called "jacks o' the clock" to chime hours and hustle students to school and burghers to business. Clocksmiths rose to lofty status; one works in finery above.

The clock—from *cloche*, or bell—retained the ring of days when, handless and faceless, it tolled monks to Mass. Now its tolling mourned the passage of quarter hours lost beyond recall. Meted out in miserly ticks, God's good time had become a commodity.

JAMES P. BLAIR, NATIONAL GEOGRAPHIC PHOTOGRAPHER
ABOVE: 15TH-CENTURY MINIATURE FROM "THE BOOK OF
THE CLOCK OF WISDOM"; BIBLIOTHÈQUE NATIONALE, PARIS

West, numbered some 200,000 people, Venice about half as many, London perhaps 50,000. The rich cities of Flanders provided the credit, and sometimes forcibly disputed the policy, of their rulers. Milan, Florence, Pisa became independent states; in Germany stood "free imperial towns" like Strasbourg and Mainz.

And the lesser fry of the chivalric world had begun to envy the townsfolk: "To be a free burgher . . . is to be in the best estate of all; they live in a noble manner, wearing lordly garments, having falcons . . . fine palfreys. . . . When the vassals are obliged to join the [feudal] host, the burghers rest in their beds; when the vassals go to be massacred in battle, the burghers go to picnic by the river."

Yet trouble was brewing within the town walls, and in the 14th century it foamed up in savage revolt. The rough sort of democracy of earlier days had given way to municipal oligarchies drawn from a select circle of rich guilds like the mercers, drapers, goldsmiths, and grocers. Inequalities in wealth and opportunity widened; a growing working class, the "blue nails" as their betters called

them, enjoyed no privilege but the hope of daily labor for a pittance. Smoldering hatred erupted; streets suddenly became a hell of knives and clubs. Eventually the risings were suppressed, sometimes with the aid of princes. Except in France, torn by the Hundred Years' War, the towns resumed their accustomed life.

Despite the turmoil and the oppressive regulations of the guilds, there were always great merchants with the adroitness to survive, to achieve renown that would reach the ears of posterity—such men as Marco Polo of Venice, the Medici, Bardi, and Peruzzi families of Florence. Dick Whittington, "the son of marchandy," thrice mayor of London, soared into legend with his cat. In France, however, no such figure as Jacques Coeur had ever appeared.

Though he walked in the world of princes, the argentier of Charles VII remained, in taste and outlook, an entrepreneur, a bourgeois immersed in those towns where he prospered. And it is there, in the daily rounds of the town, that we must seek him to catch the savor of his life.

how many times had Jacques Coeur, riding the roads of France, enjoyed the sight of a forest of spires, enclosed by white walls and towers, rising abruptly from the countryside. Nearing the battlemented gate, he would spy the busy town sergeants directing a leper—

SHADOW OF DEATH *darkened the medieval mind. Townsmen flocked to see the two-handed "glaive of justice" descend; fire, gibbet, and boiling oil also sped miscreants to their reward. But all paled before the hideous toll of the Black Death in the 1340's. From Asia rat-borne fleas spread bubonic plague along the trade routes to Europe. Shops emptied, crops rotted as men fled in terror, caroused, flogged one another in penitence. About one in three died, so many that the "living were scarcely able to bury the dead" (right).*

14TH-CENTURY ILLUMINATION FROM "THE PLAGUE AT TOURNAI"; BIBLIOTHÈQUE ROYALE, BRUSSELS
LEFT: 15TH-CENTURY ILLUMINATION FROM FROISSART'S "CHRONICLES"; BRITISH MUSEUM

announced by his rattle or bell — to the lazar house nearby, exacting a toll from outsiders come to sell in the market, keeping a wary eye for despised "forestallers" sent by other cities to buy up food supplies.

Once through the gates, Jacques was plunged into a noisy, reeking world of tortuous streets darkened by upper stories leaning toward one another. Houses of wood and plaster huddled against the ramparts or at the bases of churches — a crazy quilt of gables and chimney pots.

As he threaded his way past shop stalls, avoiding a flock of sheep or a gaggle of geese or the clutching fingers of a tradesman urging a bargain, Jacques could see tailors, cobblers, ironmongers at work. Some peered longingly at a nearby church clock, for hours of work stretched from dawn to dusk. But Saturday afternoon and Sunday were free, and some 35 church holidays lightened the year.

At day's end the apprentices, along with the master and his family, crowded into a few small chambers above the shop, twilight filtering gloomily through oiled parchment. Only the wealthy could afford glass windows.

The swirling life of the town coagulated about the municipal hall, the chief church, the market. The hall might resound with youngsters batting a tennis ball, in defiance of the mayor's ban. Through the marketplace, officials shouldered their way, watching for fraudulent weights, inferior wares, illegal buying and selling.

Smells hung in the air. Scavenger birds and the channel in the middle of the street (a sewer when it rained) could not cope with accumulating filth — rubbish swept from houses, worse dumped from upper windows, steaming deposits of horses and cattle.

Sounds struck upon the senses: "Wood for sale!" "Strawberries ripe!" "Hot sheep's feet!" "Rushes fair and green!" The town crier's trumpet heralding a new proclamation. And the bells of church and clock tower, always going. They boomed and sang above the tumult, for work, feast, weal and woe; sounded the hours of the day, tolled for the dead, broke into peals to celebrate a new pope or the entry of a great prince, clanged when riot erupted.

Sights thrust upon the nerves as vividly as smells and sounds. Joining a funeral, the mayor and aldermen issued from guildhall all in scarlet and fur and beaver hats and silver chains. Life was lived out of doors, passionately, at high pitch. Everything was exposed to public view. Crime

DAVID F. CUPP

PORTRAIT *of the Middle Ages framed in a Gothic arch, Rothenburg in Bavaria shows the proud face of an imperial town, beholden only to the crown. Time-mellowed walls guard its tall-gabled houses; only dress styles and a motor scooter mar its medieval aura, reminder of an era when burghers like Jacques Coeur grew great in urban bastions and men cried, "City air means freedom!"*

sat in the stocks, pelted with filth and jeered. Beggary showed its sores, Poverty its rags. Wealth and Power flaunted their splendor.

A traitor paid the supreme penalty in public. While thousands watched, he was cut down from the gallows alive, then disemboweled and quartered. The hangman's knife drove into the loins of one sufferer, who gasped, "Jesus, yet more trouble." In one town a thief had his ear nailed to a plank and was handed a knife; when he summoned the desperation to cut himself free, he was banished.

But townsmen shared happier spectacles—a troupe of players offering a knockabout farce on a stage of planks, or craft guilds unfolding the Biblical story with their miracle or "mystery" (guild) plays. The goldsmiths made splendid the Three

Kings from the East; the vintners enacted the Miracle of the Wine at Cana. At dawn on May Day citizens trooped to the fields to gather greenery and "bring in the May." Everybody, from Jacques Coeur to humble artisan, crept to the cross on Good Friday, carried candles around the church on Candlemas Day (February 2), listened to the bells all night long on Halloween, eve of All Saints' Day.

AMID THIS WORLD towered the famed merchant of Bourges. While his fleet— based at Marseilles after Montpellier silted up—furrowed the Mediter- ranean, Jacques sat with the royal council, undertook diplomatic missions to Genoa, helped heal a dangerous schism in Rome, earning thereby the gratitude of Nicholas V, first of the great humanist popes. When war with England flared anew in 1449, King Charles's treasury, as usual, was depleted. Jacques said simply, "Sire, all that I have is yours." French arms triumphed, and with the joyous entry into Rouen Jacques had his day. But he paid for it dearly.

With frightening suddenness he learned what it was to be both an outsider and a creditor of princes and magnates. Some resented him as an upstart; others chafed at his power. Even Charles, who owed him most, came to envy him.

In 1451 the king accused his argentier of poisoning the beautiful royal mistress, Agnes Sorel. Though this absurd charge was dropped, others were piled on— misuse of royal funds, illegal acts in trading with Islam. Jacques defended himself staunchly, but when he was stripped and haled to the torture chamber in 1453, his resistance collapsed. The court levied huge fines, confiscated all his property, ordered him banished from the realm after imprisonment "at the king's pleasure." Only the pope's intervention saved his life.

When all else was lost, his friends remained firm. In 1454 Jacques escaped from prison and took refuge in a Franciscan friary on the Rhone. The king's men sur- rounded the sanctuary, but faithful Jean de Village broke through and got his master safely out. Jacques reached Rome, where Pope Nicholas publicly honored him. When a new pope, Calixtus III, assembled a fleet in 1456 to fight the Turkish conquerors of Constantinople, Coeur commanded it. But in November of that year he fell ill and died on the Aegean isle of Chios.

He remitted his bones to a friary there, his fame to the chroniclers, and, in a moving plea, his innocence to the conscience of Charles VII. His plea would not go unheard. In time the land which had condemned him would do justice to his memory, even as it would honor, in greater measure, the martyred Maid of Orléans.

Seeking a saint, Edwards Park encounters an
"impudent little ghost" who fought like a man,
wept like a girl, died like a martyr. In shrine and statue
France hails its heroine of the age, remembering the

Miracle of St. Joan

Rose window crowns the Maid with a halo of glory. Statue by P. d'Epinay, 1901, in Reims Cathedral; Jonathan S. Blair

*H*er statue appears all over France. Sometimes discreetly gowned, long hair streaming and banner flying, she strides forward on a pedestal. But this is not Joan. Or in prayerful pose she turns a beautiful face heavenward. Neither is this Joan. But when she rides her charger, helmeted head cocked jauntily, or leans upon her sword hilt, tranquil and triumphant, I recognize my Joan of Arc—*la Pucelle,* the Maid, small, rather homely, but with a certain insouciance. And very, very brave. How, I wonder, would she have looked to an English soldier besieging Orléans in that spring of 1429?

He himself is easy to picture: a veteran bowman of the Hundred Years' War, in cap and jerkin of boiled leather, six-foot longbow slung across broad shoulders. He is no serf but a free yeoman who volunteered. He is proud of having learned, as Bishop Latimer later wrote, "to lay my body in my bow, and not to draw with strength of arms as divers other nations do." Such a soldier cared little about English claims to French lands. Enough for him that the lands lay open to plunder, and perhaps that his own great grandsire had fought at Crécy in this selfsame war.

All English lads were told of Crécy— of the French chivalry charging Edward III's little force, only to fall under a storm of English arrows. Again, a decade later in 1356, a French charge had been shattered at Poitiers by the yeomanry of Edward's son, the Black Prince. Generations passed, and a great French army moved to cut off Henry V's "band of brothers" at Agincourt, a dozen miles from Crécy, in 1415. Again, slaughter.

So a yeoman archer at Orléans in 1429 knew more of the habit of victory than of any exalted cause. He served the duke of Bedford, protector of England's boy king, Henry VI, and ally of the duke of Burgundy, master of much of France north of the Loire, including Paris. Their enemies to the south served a spineless princeling, his legitimacy so suspect that even his mother scorned him as the "so-called dauphin." Yet the French fought on, clinging to Orléans, key to the Loire Valley. Now rumors flew that they had been inspired by a virgin—a lass from Domrémy, where the Vosges foothills rise above the Meuse.

At Crécy, Poitiers, and Agincourt,

English longbows shattered the flower and pride of France

In Domrémy's green fields, saintly voices beckoned Joan to paths of glory

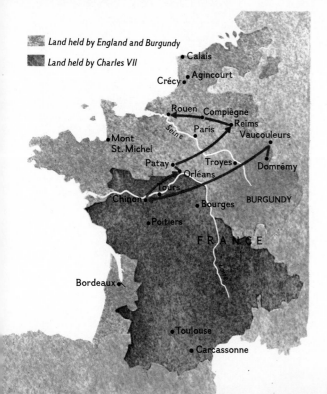

Land held by England and Burgundy

Land held by Charles VII

Calais
Crécy • Agincourt
Rouen • Compiègne
Seine • Paris • Reims
Mont St. Michel • Vaucouleurs
Patay • Troyes • Domrémy
Orléans
Tours
Chinon • Bourges • BURGUNDY
Poitiers
FRANCE
Bordeaux
Toulouse
Carcassonne

Joan's village and the countryside she knew have changed little in 500 years, although she would be astonished and probably amused to see shops named for her and tourists flocking to her restored house. It is larger than I expected; obviously Jacques d'Arc was a farmer of some standing. In the church next door Joan was baptized. Burgundians razed it, but it has been rebuilt. Prayer panels line the inside: *Merci à Jeanne d'Arc*. One recalls a later war: *Reconnaissance pour l'arrêt des Allemands en Lorraine. 12 Septembre, 1914.*

Beside her gentle hills Joan heard her voices—St. Catherine's, St. Margaret's, and St. Michael's—telling her to save Orléans and bring about the coronation of Charles VII, the scorned dauphin, at Reims. Joan's visitations were not unique. In their isolation and simplicity, medieval country folk turned

SUNRISE NEAR DOMRÉMY, JONATHAN S. BLAIR. ST. MICHAEL AND JOAN ON SILVER PLAQUE, THE AMERICAN NUMISMATIC SOCIETY. JOAN'S TRAVELS, GEOGRAPHIC ART DIVISION

unselfconsciously to God and His saints as though to a window in the mind which opened on new and wondrous vistas. Voices and visitations came to many people. Joan, with intelligence and perseverance, heeded hers and so changed history.

She ranks as probably the most persuasive teen-ager in all history. Consider: She got permission to visit an older man, a cousin by marriage. She talked him into taking her to a royal official at Vaucouleurs, 12 miles from Domrémy. After a rebuff (the official jested that she might be given to his soldiers for their pleasure), she won her way, donned men's clothing, and acquired a horse from the duke of Lorraine (an unlikely helper, allied with the Burgundians and English).

With arms and an escort she set out for Chinon, some 300 miles away, where Charles held court. "I felt such respect for her that I would never have dared to make her an unseemly proposal," attested one of the companions-in-arms who traveled with her, sleeping beside her night after night. She made her soldiers mind their language, telling one old captain to swear by his walking stick instead of turning the air blue around him.

As she entered the chateau of Chinon, Charles sought to trick her by changing places with a courtier. But Joan ignored the false monarch on the throne and walked straight to the dauphin, half-hidden among the crowd, and curtseyed. "Gentle dauphin, I am called Jeanne la Pucelle. The King of Heaven sends me to you with the message that you shall be anointed and crowned in the city of Reims, and that you shall be the lieutenant of the King of Heaven, who is the King of France...."

325

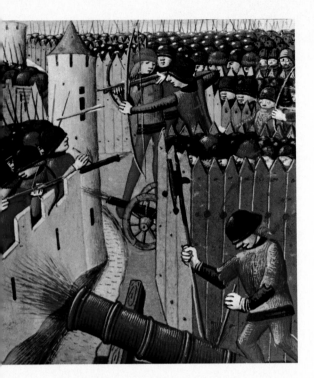

Cracking the English siege,
Joan entered Orléans triumphantly,
then saw her king crowned at Reims

When Joan appeared beneath the strongest
of the English bastions at Orléans, the
twin bridge towers called *les Tourelles,*
the English looked down in astonishment
on a boyish figure in plain armor, astride a
charger, who shouted up in a girlish voice
and demanded they surrender at once.
They replied she was a harlot and a cowgirl
and they would burn her if they caught her.
She yelled back they were a pack of liars.

A vestige of the twin towers stands yet
across the Loire from Orléans. On a rainy day
I stood beside it and tried to picture the
scene: Townsfolk swarm to the attack across
a now-vanished bridge, while Joan and her
men assault from where I stood. I imagined
the roar of culverins hurling great stone balls;
the grunts of men straining to put ladders
against the battlements; the yells and curses,
the clangs of sword against helm. And in the
middle of it, Joan, pestering her friend
Dunois, the Bastard of Orléans, to tell her
where the thickest fighting raged, screaming

at the English to yield, bursting into floods
of tears when they deride her as a harlot.

Just before the final battle Joan was offered
a fish for breakfast. No, she said, save it for
supper "when we have recrossed the bridge
and brought back a *god-don* who will eat his
share." God-don was the closest her tongue
could come to the favorite English profanity.
Standing where she fought, I was well aware
of her impudent little ghost.

Les Tourelles fell after a day-long battle;
the siege was lifted. La Pucelle became the
Maid of Orléans, and men thronged to her.
They pursued the English north, after wresting
from them pleasant towns beside the Loire,
until at Patay Joan won a great victory—and
wept as she held an English soldier's head
in her lap and heard his dying confession.

Winning battles came almost easier than
getting her reluctant dauphin to Reims.
At last Charles set out, and towns along the
way submitted to him and the young girl in
dented armor at his side. In July 1429,
he was crowned in the great cathedral,
while Joan stood by still clutching her banner.
"It has been through the pain," she explained.
"Reason enough for it to have the honor."

In the marketplace of Rouen, condemned as witch and sorceress, the Maid met a martyr's fate

It was a mystery that Joan could have gained the ear of the king; another that she could have lost it so swiftly after the coronation. Newly crowned Charles VII seemed embarrassed to owe such a debt to such a person; yet he would not permit her to return to her family as she wished. Instead, he let her lead ill-supported attacks on more English garrisons. Outside Compiègne Joan was captured by the Burgundians, who sold her to the English. Her fate was sealed.

England's only hope of salvaging the wreckage of its French claims lay in destroying Joan; it agreed to a trial for witchcraft. A church court then accused the "woman . . . called Jeanne la Pucelle" of being "a witch, enchantress, false prophet . . . thinking evil in our Catholic faith . . . inciting to war, cruelly thirsting for human blood . . . having utterly and shamelessly abandoned the modesty befitting her sex, and indecently put on the ill-fitting dress . . . of men of arms."

Throughout the trial Joan remained honest and direct, but she refused to answer some questions. What, she was asked, had she told Charles in private to make him accept her? "You will not drag it from my mouth."

CATHEDRAL SPIRE PIERCES A DARKLING SKY ABOVE ROUEN AND THE SEINE; GEORGE F. MOBLEY,

The judges quizzed her endlessly about the saints. "How did St. Michael look when he appeared to you? Was he naked?"

"Do you think that God has nothing to clothe him in?" replied Joan.

Did St. Margaret speak to her in English?

"Why should she speak English? She is not on the English side."

After five months of questioning, threats of torture, and being chained in the castle of Rouen with hated English soldiers as wardens, she was condemned to the stake, and was burned in the marketplace on May 30, 1431. She was 19. Her heart would not burn. Along with her ashes, it was thrown into the Seine so that it could not become a sacred relic.

Oddly, even the simple folk of France who had so adored her seemed willing then to forget her. The king had not lifted a finger in her defense. But 25 years after her burning a wave of remembrance swept France. The verdict against her was reversed. She was declared a heroine, a symbol of nationhood.

In time the English were driven from France, as she had foreseen, yielding even their last foothold, the port of Calais. Yet they too honored Joan sincerely. They had begun to do so even as the flames licked at her. She had cried out for a cross, and an English soldier bent and fashioned one of two sticks from the piled faggots and handed it to her.

As I stood at the site, gazing at her statue, I knew that if I had been that god-don, I would have done the same.

A bold German brotherhood dared icy seas and the wrath of kings to grip the medieval world with tentacles of trade. National Geographic's Tom Allen sails with the Hansa into a

Golden Realm of Merchant Princes

*I*N THE GRAY DAWN *Kind Wind* seems borne on ghostly wings that flutter, green and red, in the aura of her running lights. Suddenly, booms dip and the wings vanish into the North Sea. I feel *Kind Wind* tug against the plummeting nets as she goes to work, dragging the bottom for prawns.

The nets rise with the sun and spill out a wriggling catch. Karl, the mate, sorting the prawns on deck, shouts and swoops up a glittering speck. He hands me a gift older than that shallow sea: a drop of resin from a primeval pine. His ancestors called such a find a stone of the sun. We call it amber.

I left *Kind Wind* at her home port on Germany's northernmost coast and, like an amber hunter of old, carried my treasure along the amber roads that became northern Europe's first trade routes. For I sought the trail of the great traders of the Middle Ages, the strange, secretive brotherhood of the

Norway's mountain-girt port of Bergen was ruled by Hansa merchants; George F. Mobley, National Geographic photographer

Hanseatic League. On such well-worn paths to the sea the league was born. Here bands of German merchants joined together when robbery and murder stalked the trader who walked alone. United first for protection, then for profit, the Hansards built an empire out of marketplaces. From the 13th to the 15th centuries this merchants' realm would rival the realms of kings.

Hanseatic cities rimmed the Baltic and ruled the Rhine. In Hamburg, Bremen, Lübeck, Cologne, and in scores of other strongholds of commerce, a new class shouldered aside duke and count, and the old order lamented: "It is shameful that merchants should rule over high-born and noble men."

Even beyond their fatherland, they sought to rule trade—on the docks of London and Bergen, in the towns of Flanders, in the heartland of Russia. For the Hansa controlled the goods that sustained medieval body and soul. Amber, once bartered as Bronze Age jewelry, they sold for the rosaries of an age of faith. And in that age, when every altar in Europe glowed by the light of hallowed tapers, the Hansa sold the candle wax. When Christendom lived by a calendar of meatless days, the faithful ate Hansa fish, salted with Hansa salt, shipped on Hansa ships—and washed down by Hansa beer. When all northern Europe "was clothed in English wool," the Hansa strove to master fleece and looms.

SWEET SMELL OF PROFIT *rose from Norse nets to tempt Hansa merchants northward. Where modern Norwegians clean cod for freezing (above left), Hansards founded fortunes on dried fish for Europe's tables. Some hastened their enrichment by using two sets of scales, one for buying, one for selling. Today honest hands on Bergen's waterfront heft a balance (above) scarcely changed since then.*

Sawtooth gables serrate Bergen's skyline where houses in Hansa style (left) jam-pack choice dockside lots. Dogs and sentries patrolled the quay to keep townsmen out, secrets in. Hansards' prime northern outpost lives as Norway's second port.

333

We recall few of the Hansards by name. Members of the brotherhood usually hid in the shadows of the history they made. When they ventured to distant trading outposts, their passion for secrecy drove them behind the walls of their *kontors*. Literally "countinghouses," actually communes, the kontors evolved into Hansa islands surrounded by hostile, locked-out townspeople.

*I*N BERGEN, Norway's gate to the North Sea, I trespassed in a kontor. But I was greeted by archeologists, the inheritors of the *Tyskebryggen,* the German Quay. They had unearthed the haunts of the Hansa after fires swept centuries of clutter from the kontor site. From the foundation outlines of the cramped buildings, etched in the swampy soil, I could envision the walled-in life of those mercantile monks, cloistered here with their goods and gold.

In a nearby wharfside house, preserved as the Hanseatic Museum, I explored the rooms where Hansa masters and their apprentices lived and worked. A master hunched over his ledgers and ate his meals in privacy. His apprentices, packed eight or more in a room unheated and unlighted from fear of fire, slept on seaweed mattresses in bed boxes built along the walls. Sliding doors closed them in, two to a box hardly big enough for one.

I hefted a master's ox-tail whip that hung on the wall and mused on the brutal, monastic life these young men had chosen—to gain not paradise but prosperity. Like monks they vowed celibacy, obedience, and, until they became masters, poverty. Even for the masters the kontor was, officially, a womanless world. But bawdy tales—and a secret staircase in one master's suite—suggest that many a ranking Hansard was an amorous bachelor rather than a practicing celibate.

Hansa merchants in foreign cities lived with their goods; a house was a warehouse, not a home. They feasted in the kontor's communal hall, built far from warehouses so men could enjoy the light and warmth of oil lamps and hearths. But to lads seeking entry into the Hansa, the hall evoked the terror of initiations.

I can imagine a lad we know as Hufanus—literally Yardsman—hauled up the chimney over a stinking fire piled high with refuse. Unlike some, he survives the trial by smoke, endures dunking in wine tuns full of icy water—and then a final ordeal: To the beat of clashing cymbals, the strongest men of the kontor flog Hufanus until they tire. If he can rise from the "altar of sacrifice" and remain conscious through this long night of beatings and drinking, he can enter the Hansa. We are told that Hufanus sent to his mother back in Germany proof of his success: his bloodied shirt. His ten-year apprenticeship had begun.

Before Hufanus's apprenticeship ended, he probably knew more about the operations of the Hansa than scholars do today. Even the meaning of its name eludes us. *Hansa* once could have meant a military company, a fraternal sect, perhaps a mystic blood-brother cult. But by the early 13th century the Hansa clearly had changed from a league of merchants to a confederation of cities. Two of them,

SEALS OF HER SISTERS *spangle a 15th-century pact preserved at Lübeck, key city of the Hanseatic League. Here, usually around Whitsuntide, when spring made road travel easiest, members' delegates convened in conclaves called Diets to fix prices and tolls, punish cities which dared to breach league rules. Iron-bound oaken chests, or "testaments," like the one at top served as safe-deposit boxes for Hansa records.*

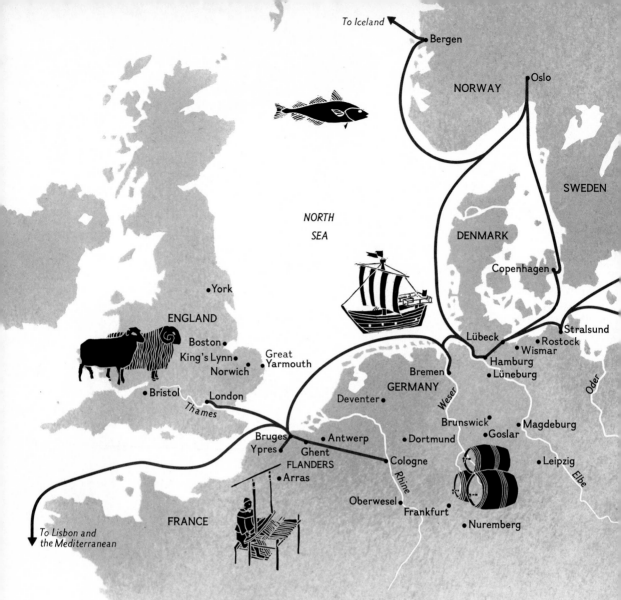

Hamburg and Lübeck, formed a trading alliance in 1210. By 1360 the Hansa—now named in documents as the Hanseatic League—numbered some 50 cities. Within another decade it grew strong enough to wage war and humble a Danish king.

Though the Hanseatic League never had an official capital, Lübeck long reigned as "Queen of the Hansa." Lübeck's location—on the sloping banks of the Trave River 14 miles from the sea—gave the Hansa an easily defended port on the western Baltic. Her independent status—an elected town council, her own mint—freed the merchants from allegiances to anyone except the emperor. They laid out Lübeck as neatly as a chessboard, with squares for the bishop, the knightly nobles, and, along the river wharves, the merchant kings.

The twin turrets of Holsten Gate still guard the grid of the old city, an island ringed by river, canal, and 20th century. Through the gate a medieval city beckons. Swans glide past the stepped-gable silhouettes of lofts that line the Trave. Here the canal boats unloaded salt borne from the mines of Lüneburg along Germany's first major canal. The Hansa monopolized the trade. In Lübeck, too, docked the

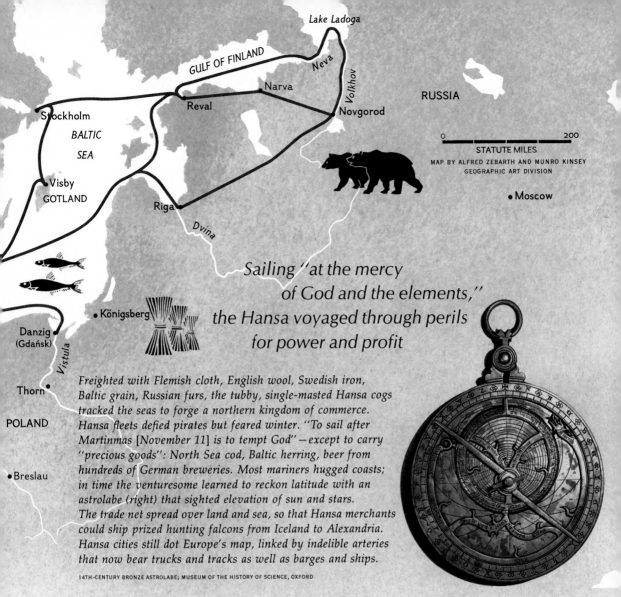

Sailing "at the mercy
of God and the elements,"
the Hansa voyaged through perils
for power and profit

Freighted with Flemish cloth, English wool, Swedish iron,
Baltic grain, Russian furs, the tubby, single-masted Hansa cogs
tracked the seas to forge a northern kingdom of commerce.
Hansa fleets defied pirates but feared winter. "To sail after
Martinmas [November 11] is to tempt God"—except to carry
"precious goods": North Sea cod, Baltic herring, beer from
hundreds of German breweries. Most mariners hugged coasts;
in time the venturesome learned to reckon latitude with an
astrolabe (right) that sighted elevation of sun and stars.
The trade net spread over land and sea, so that Hansa merchants
could ship prized hunting falcons from Iceland to Alexandria.
Hansa cities still dot Europe's map, linked by indelible arteries
that now bear trucks and tracks as well as barges and ships.

14TH-CENTURY BRONZE ASTROLABE; MUSEUM OF THE HISTORY OF SCIENCE, OXFORD

beamy Hansa cogs, deep hulls laden with the dried cod of Bergen, the herring of the Baltic, the copper and iron of Sweden, the furs of Russia. A merchant in the Estonian commercial center of Reval (now Tallinn, a Soviet port on the Gulf of Finland) fervently described his city's union with Lübeck: "The two towns belong together like the arms of Christ crucified."

Through the Queen City passed goods that would travel along a network that eventually linked the rivers and roads of southern Germany to Hansa agents as far away as Lisbon and Venice. Some raw materials went no farther than Lübeck's artisans' quarter. I wandered streets and alleys whose names recalled old trades: Bell Founder's Street, Spinning Wheel Maker's Alley, Tanner's Alley.

The medieval version of low-cost housing sprang up in a labyrinth of alleys hidden behind the city's rows of grand houses. "It is a maze you can get lost in," a Lübecker remarked as we threaded the alleys. "Perhaps that is why the old law forbade parents to let their children go out alone until they took this test: You offered your child an apple and a penny. If he took the apple, he stayed home, for he was too young to know what the world was all about."

337

Without benefit of test, I walked up the steep *Engelsgrube,* which roughly translates as "going down to the English." Ships from the London kontor docked at one end of the street; at the other I found the House of the Shippers' Guild, once home for "the common seafaring man." Inhibited from brawling by Biblical murals, shipmates ate together, sitting on high-backed benches that still bear the carved seals of Hanseatic ports. I sat at a ship's table of roughhewn oak and loaded aboard what the Hansa called a "cargo precious in value": fish and beer. Over my bench was the cross-topped seal of Riga, a Latvian port in the Baltic. A Soviet city today, Riga has replaced the cross of its old seal with a red star.

*T*WO HANSA PORTS, Bremen and Hamburg, ruled over trade in the North Sea as imperiously as Lübeck did in the Baltic. But the Danes controlled the peninsula that thrust from German land like a cupped hand. And within grasp of that hand was The Sound, the three-mile-wide strait that cogs had to transit on voyages between the two seas. If the Danish hand snatched The Sound it would wrest away a key Hansa monopoly, the Baltic herring industry.

Conflict with the Danes, which eventually flared into war, united Lübeck, Bremen, and Hamburg, the enduring triumvirate of the Hansa. Even in the 19th century, 300 years after the League had foundered, the three cities were still recognized in land deeds as the "Hanseatic" owners of London real estate. All three still proudly call themselves Hanseatic cities. And, as states of the Federal Republic of Germany, Bremen and Hamburg retain their free-city heritage.

As I wandered Bremen's old quarter, a merry-go-round swirled in the market square. Balloons soared and popped. Children pursued music grinders. And near the Gothic town hall, balanced in bronze, their fairy-tale journey ended, stood the Bremen Town Musicians—a rooster on a cat on a dog on a donkey, remember?

"Lübeck, most beautiful of all cities, yours is the crown of great glory"

Double diadem on a flower-decked brow, famed Holsten Gate dreams of days when walls spread from its flanks to girdle the city celebrated in the accolade above. Hansards hailed her as "Unser aller Haupt—Head of us all." Once guns poked from niches to menace visitors; now a museum inside bids them welcome to the Baltic's onetime queen.

Touring its exhibits, schoolboys (left) loom over a lilliputian Lübeck; Marienkirche's reconstructed spires still stand, and streets converge on the marketplace. Battlements and the River Trave guarded this city, laid out by Hansa burghers. Ships nestled against walls manned by eagle-eyed inspectors who controlled comings and goings of outsiders; tolls and tariffs curbed the inflow of their goods and kept the city coffers filled.

MODEL OF LÜBECK, 1650. JAMES P. BLAIR, NATIONAL GEOGRAPHIC PHOTOGRAPHER

"Is Bremen always this way?" I asked my companion.

"It's *Freimarkt*!" he exclaimed. "We work hard 50 weeks—and then *Freimarkt*!" Every year for more than 1,000 years Bremen has celebrated its freedom with the free market—once a customs-free trade fair, now an October harvest of fun. But, as in Hanseatic times, Bremen never really stops working. I crossed over gardens in the moat that had girded the old city. Across the bridge pulsed modern Bremen and its production prodigies—from a brewery that can fill 2,400,000 bottles a day to a shipyard with a 250,000-ton supertanker on the ways.

In the shipyard on the Weser River, I walked through a clanging land of giants. Out of factory doors five stories high came 70-ton prefabricated tanker sections later welded into components weighing 250 to 700 tons. A crane more than 200 feet high lowered a segment of steel hull. "That crane will lift 780 tons without straining," a hard-hatted engineer told me as a house-size compartment swung overhead. "We fit her together like a puzzle. It's really quite easy."

Not far from the yard, archeologists were putting together another maritime puzzle: 3,000 pieces of a Hanseatic cog built around 1380. The first cog ever found, she lay hidden until a Bremen harbor dredge uncovered her in 1962. Scientists dismantled the hulk and placed its oak ribs and planks in a preservative bath until they could be reassembled for exhibition. Before her discovery historians could only speculate on cog design from the single-masted, bluff-bowed ships on

the seals of Hanseatic cities. The clinker-built Bremen cog, steered by a great stern rudder, looks much like them. Seventy feet from stubby bowsprit to stern, 21 feet across the beam, the cog could bear a few hundred tons in fairly heavy seas. She apparently ran aground in a storm. Captain and crew would have stuck with her, obeying the stern Hansa law: "In case of shipwreck, the sailors ... must aid the merchant's agent to save the cargo."

I thought of the harsh ways of the Hansa as I voyaged on ageless sea lanes in another harbor of the league: Hamburg. Risen from World War II rubble, the city has regained its Hanseatic eminence as Germany's premier port. The flags of 50 nations fly where Hansa avengers condemned 150 foreigners for piracy and by the league's own law beheaded them all.

In Hamburg's harbor, a marine metropolis sprawling over 38 square miles, Hansards traded

JAMES P. BLAIR, NATIONAL GEOGRAPHIC PHOTOGRAPHER (ALSO OVERLEAF)

HAVEN FOR HANSARDS *in bygone days, Bremen bustles amid her mementos. In the old town hall, where ships of yore still sail (left), merchant-aldermen gathered, then adjourned to the* Ratskeller *(opposite) to tap Rhine* Wein *from carven vats. When townsmen defied a prelate in 1336, his men burned their wooden statue of legendary Roland. Soon Bremen built a bigger one in stone (above), a statue of liberty that guards the storied hall today.*

HARBOR OF HAMBURG *throbs round the clock, handling the cargoes of ships that sail from ports unknown to Hansards. But they'd recognize the wealth. "Of all rules," scoffed a visitor, "they are only acquainted with those of arithmetic." Her seamen brought Hamburg a tasty idea: raw beef shredded with a dull knife. Now hamburgers rival sausages that medieval cities like Frankfurt and Bologna made a specialty.*

341

Hamburg beer for Oriental spices and sweetmeats. The East still trades here: Among the freighters I spotted one from the People's Republic of China.

The Elbe River, which offers Hamburg an 80-mile highway to the North Sea, once bore the trade of Hanseatic cities hundreds of miles farther inland. Today it sunders Germany. Beyond the Elbe lie the lands of a modern league: East Germany, Poland, the Soviet Union. Germans call the Elbe a river of tears.

S NARLING DOGS and gun-toting guards prowled the barren scar of land that etched the frontier checkpoint east of Lübeck. Passengers' faces and visas scrutinized, baggage and compartments searched, the train started up again and crossed into East Germany. At Rostock, East Germany's showplace port on the Baltic, I stepped off the train and into the hands of an East Berlin official who became my constant companion. From Rostock to Novgorod in the Soviet Union I would be firmly ushered through Hanseatic cities.

Rostock, on the Warnow River eight miles from the sea, prospered as a Hansa port. But merchants feared the rise of an old town on the river mouth itself. To thwart the diversion of Rostock-bound business, they simply bought the entire town and decreed that no tradesmen could live there. Today Warnemünde, "mouth of the Warnow," still belongs to Rostock. I walked Warnemünde's seawall on a stormy day, drenched by the curiously unsalty spray of the Baltic. (The bottlenecked Baltic, more lake than sea, barely touches saltier ocean water.)

JAMES P. BLAIR, NATIONAL GEOGRAPHIC PHOTOGRAPHER.
BELOW: 15TH-CENTURY MINIATURE OF BRUGES; BAYERISCHE STAATSBIBLIOTHEK, MUNICH

At Danzig "they bought the gifts of Ceres with those of Bacchus"

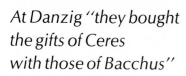

Oft rebuilt from fire and war, the Great Crane of Danzig (opposite) looks much the way it did to a French diarist in days when skippers traded wine for "Pomeranian gold"—grain. A low pulley hefted cargo, a high one stepped masts. Crews trod wheels for each, as in another Hansa harbor (right).

Prized Baltic port of the Hansa when Teutonic Knights ruled it, Danzig later belonged to Poland, to Prussia, at times to no one. Hitler's claim to the free city of Danzig triggered World War II. Reborn from rubble, the Polish port fills a lad's spyglass with views of flour mills and shipyards.

345

East of Rostock, the Hansa faced a hostile world: the Slavic realms of Pomerania and Poland, the Baltic lands of Lithuania, Latvia, and Estonia. Hansa outposts—Riga in Latvia, Visby on the mid-Baltic island of Gotland—lay open to attack. So the Hansa thrust eastward behind the shields of the Brothers of the Sword and the Teutonic Knights. The knights, black crosses emblazoned on their white surcoats, had served as Hospitalers in the Third Crusade. Financed by merchants of Lübeck and Bremen, they became merchants themselves, a land-hungry army that swept across eastern Europe, planting German towns.

The brothers, marshaled to show cross and sword to the pagans of the Baltic, fanned out from Riga. Knights and brothers became *Raubritter*—robber knights—who ignored the code of chivalry. Once, disguised as revelers, a band of knights attacked a fair in Gdańsk, a Polish port on the Vistula.

MIDWAY *in the Baltic rose Visby on the isle of Gotland, a bastion of the Hansa guarded by 44 towers and two miles of walls (above). The town ramparts rank among northern Europe's best preserved.*

Merchants from east and west enriched this wondrous haven in the unmarked sea. Roses scented its air; "window frames of silver" and women spinning "with distaffs of gold" entranced balladeers. But kings coveted Visby, pirates infested it, ships grew big enough to bypass it. Now the Swedish city greets visitors with medieval charm and a legacy even older: forest ponies bred since 3000 B.C. on this island of the Goths.

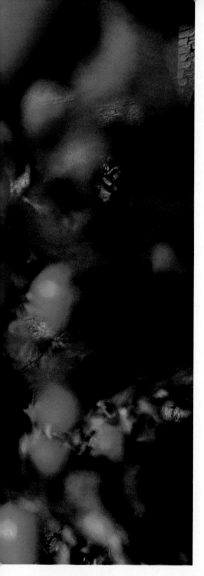

Screams drowned out hawkers' spiels. Blood stained their wares. By nightfall, thousands lay dead and the city was German. Poland had lost her gateway to the sea.

"Gdańsk! Gdańsk! Gdańsk!" a Polish architect shouted at me when I called his city Danzig. "It is Polish! It is Gdańsk!" His Polish passion welled from the 20th century, not the 14th. Some of the first shots of World War II were fired at Danzig by a German warship. Left in ruins by the conflict, the old harbor area has been carefully restored.

For decades, the harvests of Poland poured through Danzig into Hansa cogs. Amber, "Baltic gold," sailed to Hansa artisans in Lübeck. Poles who hid amber were killed by the knights. The alliance between Raubritter and merchants reflected the growing ruthlessness of the league. "Let us negotiate," a Lübeck merchant-mayor had cried in less militant days. "For it is easy to tie the pennant to the pole, but hard to take it down again." But now the old peaceful ways had passed.

In 1361 King Valdemar Atterdag of Denmark stormed Visby, the fabulously wealthy island city that gave the Hansa control of the Baltic. The Hansa lofted the pennant of war.

Since the 11th century, German merchants had been trading in Visby, crossroads for goods from East and West. A German warehouse, a seven-story medieval skyscraper, still stands, as does "the German church," St. Mary's. High on its outside wall I saw a sign of the Hansa: a projecting bar to bear tackle for hoisting goods to safe upper-story rooms. Into St. Mary's lofts the merchants also hauled their money chest, sealed by four locks. Keyholders from four cities had to be summoned to open it—in distrustful unison.

An inscription in a Gotland church limns Valdemar's invasion: "The farms are burned, defeated fall the people, wailing under the sword." In Visby's museum I saw riven skulls of some of the 1,800 islanders who fell defending the city. "The bones are those of old men, boys, even women," I was told. "We suspect the merchants stayed behind the wall, perhaps hoping to make a deal with Valdemar."

But he stripped the town and, seeking to drive the Hansa from the Baltic, attacked their ships. Now imperiled on the sea they called their own, the league declared war. Every Hansa city had to pay a war tax on all goods. Tax dodgers would be "un-Hansed"—the supreme penalty, a trade boycott of a city that could last 30 bankrupting years.

The burgomaster of Lübeck was given command of the war fleet the Hansa cities mobilized. In a bungled battle, he lost his ships—and then, in his own marketplace, his head. But the Hansa had more ships and more merchant-admirals to press the war. Year after year, Hansa fleets pillaged Danish ships and gutted Danish towns. In 1369 Valdemar, his realm virtually destroyed, finally pleaded for peace.

The Hansa dictated one of the most humiliating treaties ever signed by a king. The Germans won two-thirds of all revenue from the herring ports, free passage through The Sound, and the right to choose Danish kings for 15 years.

As the hanseatic empire spread its mercantile sway round the rim of the Baltic, it branched eastward into the land "of honey and wax and divers sorts of rich and costly skins"—Russia.

The Hansa merchants of Russia, called Easterlings, founded a kontor in Novgorod, hub of a "water road" network that spanned steppe and forest, Black Sea and Caspian. Beeswax for sacred candles, tallow for lesser lights, honey for mead, all came from backwoods farms. Hinterland fur traders of the north, adorned with long, braided beards, boated and portaged piles of pelts to Novgorod. And on perilous journeys through Mongol domains came the silks of China, damasks of the Levant, wines of Byzantium, spices of Turkistan.

Around their own church, St. Peter's, the Easterlings built

SQUAT TURRETS *of Die Pfalz have kept watch on the Rhine for 600 years. Freighters of the world's busiest river no longer pause to pay ruinous tolls, but they warily thread the vineyard-clad Rhine Gorge, lair of the Lorelei, legendary siren who lured rivermen to shipwreck. Rocks and robber barons made the gorge a gauntlet, menacing merchants on medieval Europe's greatest highway of trade. When victims joined the Hansa in self-defense, cities of the league lined the Rhine from Basel in the Alps to Dordrecht at the river's North Sea Delta.*

BRUCE DALE, NATIONAL GEOGRAPHIC PHOTOGRAPHER

349

a citadel. When they left it, they risked their goods and their lives. For, though treaties with Novgorod's princes officially protected them, they lived amid a people emboldened by a heritage of freedom.

In the 11th century powerful local merchants created a crude republic in the principality of Novgorod. The town leaders met in a marketplace *veche*, or assembly, during which they elected—and often fired—princes.

"The veche bell, which summoned the people, hung here," my Intourist guide told me. We stood near the east bank of the Volkhov, since medieval days the commercial side of the city. Through the arched remnants of riverside merchants' stalls I could see on the other bank the clustered cupolas of St. Sophia Cathedral. They loomed like helmets over the walls that girded the princely and holy half of the city. At medieval Masses in the cathedral, where 6,000 icons gleamed, the nobles sat, the peasants stood. But when neighboring town or invading Mongol threatened, all rallied there with the cry: "To stand and die for St. Sophia!"

The Hansa had its own catchphrase: "Who can prevail against God and the great Novgorod?" By skillful diplomacy, the Easterlings won from greedy princes a virtual monopoly. But Russian merchants railed against Hansa tricks, such as setting per-barrel prices on big barrels, then delivering goods in smaller ones. The Hansards were dealing with astute merchants, literate men in an illiterate age. I saw some of their 11th-century correspondence in a Novgorod museum: birchbark manuscripts, which bore Cyrillic marks made by bone or stone styluses.

BANQUET OF AHASUERUS, DETAIL FROM A 15TH-CENTURY ALTARPIECE IN ST. ANNEN MUSEUM, LÜBECK. OPPOSITE: BRUCE DALE, NATIONAL GEOGRAPHIC PHOTOGRAPHER

"How fine the manners are in this barbaric country, how beautiful the view of the city"

Cologne's splendor enthralled Petrarch, as did the city's women—"what figures, what faces, what bearing!" When the Italian sonneteer toured Germany in 1333, Cologne's cathedral stood "incredibly beautiful though unfinished." Begun in 1248, completed in 1880, the Gothic anthem rises beside the Rhine. River-borne wealth built it and made the city a magnet for the Hansa. Law prohibited foreign merchants from settling in Cologne.

Hansards spent their riches on patrician homes for their wives, Italian universities for their sons. Merchant patrons sponsored paintings that mirrored medieval manners, even in Biblical scenes (left). Linen cloth and gold dishes adorn the banquet table. Enameled knives—guests brought their own— slice dainty apples. Silks and velvets drape the ladies; frock of Italian brocade cloaks a bearded man of distinction. Stag socials of Hansa clubs were less elegant; rules banned barefoot merrymakers, rolling in mud, filching food, throwing knives or crockery.

WEALTH FLOWED into the Hansa homeland. A vast bureaucracy watched over the league's far-flung affairs—the Bergen kontor alone was big enough to house 3,000 men. In time only the young or adventurous Hansards toiled in such hardship outposts as Novgorod. Rich merchants could get richer staying at home. And no place in Germany could offer more luxury or profits than Cologne. Founded by Romans, embellished since Charlemagne's day, the cosmopolitan city on the Rhine had, by the 14th century, become a palace for merchant kings.

Triumphant over church and nobility, they ruled the city that called itself the "Rome of the North" and trumpeted to all Christendom the miracles of its stellar relic, the bones of the Three Magi. Adoration of the Magi lured kings and pilgrims, then patrons and artisans to create another magnet—Cologne's magnificent cathedral.

Goldsmiths, jewelers, and master craftsmen settled in the city to serve the nouveaux riches. Wives of roughhewn traders demanded the trappings of culture. Hastily contrived coats of arms appeared. In elegant new merchant homes, horny hands grappled dainty silver spoons. Greedy old men, brooding on death and hell, enhanced churches and consciences with golden bequests. Hansa leaders emerged

Goslar's anthem: "the hollow thudding …of bursting rock"

From mines that fascinated Goethe, Goslar has hauled 20 million tons of Harz Mountains ore in more than 1,000 years of gophering into the world-famed Rammelsberg. Silver, bright as the baritones of Goslar's Miners' Band (above), turned the town into a treasury and a favored resort of emperors, then into a source of coin for Hansa commerce. Miner's hammer and chisel adorn bandsmen's garb, black as the innards of the mountain that still yields ore.

In Goslar's plaza medieval merchants measured cloth on a bronze ell (opposite) that extends some 26 inches; poorer towns set up shorter ells. Day's end sent traders home to Bürgerhäuser (far right) that make old Goslar such a delight to the eye.

from their countinghouses. We begin to see them: One, named Tiedemann, who had worked in the London kontor, moved to Cologne, where he built a *Patrizierhaus* (patrician house), prospered as a wine wholesaler, and served as a pillar of the church. His ostentatious gifts—a 70-pound silver cross, a stunning gold reliquary—earned him a 20-line epitaph when, "wrapped in balsam and aromatic spices," he was buried in his splendid tomb in 1386.

Long, low, laden barges churned the Rhine below me as I stood on a bridge at Cologne. The barges passed at the edge of vision, for the slender spires of the cathedral beckoned eye and spirit. An evocation of eternity in the Middle Ages, the majestic shrine promised at least a tomorrow when it towered over devastation in 1945. The mighty Rhine, flanked by castles elsewhere in its course, flows humbly here, mirroring a cathedral's glory.

Cologne stamped high-quality goods with its seal, a medieval brand name. The city set prices and currency standards by the "Cologne mark," a silver measure. Much of the silver came from Goslar, nestled in the witch-haunted Harz Mountains.

The miners, defying underground demons, began digging silver from the humpbacked Rammelsberg in 968, during the reign of Otto the Great, ruler of what later would be called the Holy Roman Empire. The mountain became Otto's coffer and Goslar flourished as an imperial city. But as the empire faded in a Germany of warring princely states, Goslar joined another empire, the Hansa.

I followed a miner down a shaft that sloped 1,000 feet into the Rammelsberg. We crouched in a tunnel barely shoulder-wide. "Men were smaller then, you

know," the miner said, showing me even narrower niches where men had hacked out iron, copper, lead, and silver. "They came down here with oil lamps. When the lamps began going out, they knew they had to crawl to better air or die."

Water, tapped from a high lake, once had gushed through this shaft, spinning great wooden wheels that powered ore-hoisting machinery. When the water spilled out of the mines it kept working, flowing through the town in a stone-walled channel strung with 27 grain mills. One of the mill wheels still turns today near Goslar's 12th-century market square. Here, in Hansa days, justice was dispensed, for the law ordered that verdicts be proclaimed "under the sky." (On blustery days the judge could proclaim in the town hall where a chamber—still intact—provided an ersatz sky: a blue, star-embossed ceiling.) Any merchant adjudged bankrupt stood nude all day in the marketplace, proving poverty with nakedness. At night, still naked, he was driven from the town.

From the mines of Germany came more than ore. To convert the metals, an evolving science developed techniques that sent new sounds, new ideas echoing

DETAIL FROM A 16TH-CENTURY ALTARPIECE AT ANNABERG IN SAXONY. OPPOSITE: DAVID F. CUPP

BUSY AS TROLLS, *miners (left) work a slope for silver and lead, copper and gold. Tools of wood and iron in skilled German hands sank shafts so far into Saxony and Bohemia that a contemporary gasped: "What an enormous depth! Have you reached the Inferno?"*

Georgius Agricola's landmark treatise on mining in the 1500's (translated from the Latin into English by mining engineer, later President, Herbert Hoover and his wife) fits the scene well. Ore rides up by windlass; if it "is not metal-bearing, they pour out the earth and rock . . . thus . . . a hillock rises around the shed of the windlass." Good ore they "crush and wash," then haul to smelters in a medieval brainchild, the wheelbarrow.

Worries haunt a robed foreman, for if men "break their arms or fall into the sumps and are drowned the negligence of the foreman is to blame." Demons may hex a pit, but elfin helpers called trulli *ease mining toil.*

The depth of shafts, Agricola noted, "forced us to invent hauling machines suitable for them." Water wheels lifted ore, drained mines, vented "noxious air." One in the Rammelsberg (opposite) creaked into the 1800's.

through the land. Water-powered bellows stoked smelters to fiercer heat, producing stronger iron. To fuel the smelters, forests went up in charcoal smoke. Water-powered trip-hammers pounded out the better iron for nails and needles, nuts and bolts. German bell founders advertised a grim new trade: cannon-making. From Spain and Sweden came iron of unequal quality; Hansa experts learned to grade it for a variety of products, from anchors to fishhooks. Skilled German operators even worked the silver and lead mines of England.

IN THE 14TH CENTURY Hansa goods and Hansa money flowed to an England that desperately needed both. Edward III, his treasury drained by a war with France that would last a century, borrowed heavily from Hanseatic merchants, pawning the royal jewels, the crown of his queen—and his own crown. The Hansa also held

the scepter of English trade, reigning from their kontor on the Thames near London Bridge. The English called the kontor the Steelyard, possibly mistranslating *Stalhof*—"sample yard," a place where merchants displayed wares. The Steelyard, a walled complex that dominated the London waterfront, had grown with the Hansa's influence.

King Henry II had welcomed the Germans in 1157 in a treaty with Emperor Frederick Barbarossa, pledging "safe trade of marchandize." By the time of Edward III the Germans had the power to manipulate and even throttle England's economy. Shipwrights turned to the Hansa for pitch, hemp, tar, flax; the best timber for ships came from the

The Thames: gilded highway of the Hansa

Granted "friendly traffike" in 1157 by Henry II, German traders streamed upriver to London. By the 14th century Hansards were hoarding profits in a riverside redoubt, the Steelyard. Enraged at favored foreigners, mobs once hunted Germans, killing any who could not pronounce "bread and cheese."

THAMES MEANDERS PAST THE TILBURY DOCKS
BELOW LONDON; TED SPIEGEL, RAPHO GUILLUMETTE

Hansa monopoly in the Baltic. English soldiers in France ate stockfish (salted cod) bought from the Hansa. English archers bent "wood suitable for bows" imported from Danzig. And much of the money for the army came from Hansa loans to Edward. He paid for them with privileges.

Exempted from most tolls and taxes, landlords of one of the very gates of London, the Hansards ultimately won from Edward an incredible trade monopoly: "thence forth no stranger shall sell by retail in the City and suburbs . . . or be a broker, saveing always to the merchants of the Hanse of Almaine [Germany]."

The privileges were not reciprocal. English seamen were seized in the Hansa's continental ports, "cast into lothsom prisons, drenched in myre and water up to ye neck." Englishmen complained that foreigners "suck the thrifte away out of our hand as the wasp sucketh honie fro the bee."

But the Hansa wasps sought wool, not honey, and few in the English wool business got stung. More than half of England's landed wealth grew on the backs of sheep. Wool merchants raised great houses and magnificent churches in the sheep towns of the Cotswolds and East Anglia. "I thank God and ever shall," wool men proverbially prayed. "It was the sheep that payed for all."

For others, the price was high. In an age of dawning industry, sheep-raising kept capital in the pasture and held back the growth of towns. The Hansa wove fortunes from English wool by shuttling the golden fleece to Flanders — then back to England for sale as cloth. Hansa depots appeared in York and Bristol and in Norwich, Great Yarmouth, Boston, and King's Lynn on the shores of East Anglia.

Near the Hanseatic warehouse that stands in King's Lynn, I talked with a young archeologist engaged in a search for

"TRUE GOLDEN FLEECE" dapples a
Devonshire field; power shears
harvest it. In days when eight
million fleeces left England
yearly and wool was worth "half
the wealth of the whole land,"
merchants dotted their towns
with churches. Norwich (left),
a Hansa depot in wool-rich
East Anglia, wove worsted and
prospered to become second city
to London in the Tudor realm.
English wool men left us names
like Weaver, Fuller, Webster,
and Tucker, and a weapon that
workers still wield—the strike.

the port's medieval wharves. The River Ouse, which
meanders into The Wash and the North Sea, still links
King's Lynn with Hamburg and other European ports. But
the modern quays lie blocks from the Ouse's old and vanished course. "Our most interesting find yet," he told me,
"are timbers used to shore up the harbor bank. They're pine
and not local. We're fairly sure they're from the Baltic."

In 1751, when the Hansa lingered only as a memory, a
King's Lynn merchant purchased the Hanseatic warehouse.
In the town museum I saw the bill of sale. From it dangled
the seals of Lübeck, Bremen, and Hamburg.

Signs of the Hansa are that small in England—rotting
timbers, fading seals. In London, wars, fires, and progress
have long since obliterated the Steelyard. The Cannon

TED SPIEGEL, RAPHO GUILLUMETTE. OPPOSITE: WINFIELD PARKS, NATIONAL GEOGRAPHIC PHOTOGRAPHER

Street Railway Station, its land bought from the three surviving Hanseatic cities in 1853, stands on the Steelyard site. But around it still throbs the commercial heart of London: the City.

To find the last sign of the Hansa in London I left the bowler-hatted ranks of Stock Exchange brokers, walked past the stern Bank of England, and entered the hush of a small church, St. Margaret Lothbury. Merchants still worship in this jewel built by Christopher Wren. In the deep shadows I saw a richly carved screen that ran the width of the nave. An eagle, symbol of the Hansa then, of Germany now, surmounted it. The screen commemorates its German donors, one of whom had watched in anguish as the Great Fire of 1666 licked at the Steelyard.

THE MEN of the London kontor lived austerely in the early days. They slept in monastic cells from which they barred even charwomen. But in time the Steelyard mellowed. In its garden a tavern appeared, and the smart people of London —even common folk like Shakespeare's company of actors—dropped in for a tankard of Rhenish wine or a taste of caviar. Frescoes and carvings graced the walls of the Steelyard's great hall. Masters ate from silver plate. The dour men of the Steelyard had discovered the splendors of Flanders.

The wool of England long had entangled kings and merchants in the complex politics of Flanders. In the Hundred Years' War, when the count of Flanders sided with the king of France, the cloth-weaving city of Ghent proclaimed England's

"O wool, noble dame, thou art the goddess of merchants"

Poet John Gower eulogized wool ("O fair, O white") in 14th-century England, when Hansards bagged much of the isle's fleece. Tradition says the lord chancellor's seat in the House of Lords—a large stuffed woolsack (right)—dates from the reign of Edward III, whose costly wars made him heavily dependent on wool revenues and Hansa lenders. Later monarchs, eager for income, made all males over six don woolen caps on Sunday, and had every corpse buried in a woolen shroud.

German-born Hans Holbein the Younger, court painter of Henry VIII, enhanced the grim Hansa Steelyard with his murals. His portraits immortalized London Hansards like Georg Gisze (opposite), limned as he opens mail from his brother, the bishop of Danzig. Oriental carpet and carnations brighten a desk crowded with merchant's implements: inkstand, quills, scissors, coin box, signet ring, pestle-shaped seal, and a "self-going horologium"—a cylindrical clock.

Edward III its king. Weavers in Ypres fled to England, helping to launch that country's own cloth industry. Bruges, center of all Flemish trade and weaving, fought to keep its woolen ties with the island kingdom.

German merchants signed their first treaty with Bruges in 1252 and gradually gained a primacy reflected by the city's lion-and-crown coat of arms; it bears the Hanseatic colors of red and silver. But the Hansa could never conquer Bruges, for it catered to traders from all Christendom.

The city's harbor lay at the mouth of the Zwyn, a narrow river that bore barges and lighters ten miles upstream to the market quays. Canals spread the goods through the heart of the city. Sacks of wool went to merchants' trade-houses on porters' backs, for carts could not navigate the narrow, twisting streets.

Famed for its amenities, Bruges fascinated visitors from other medieval cities. Travelers told of the "officer of mud," charged with keeping the streets clean and plucking the grass from between the paving stones. Men with lead clubs solved another medieval urban problem: stray dogs. Arsonists, a familiar bane, were put to death, as were those who even uttered their poetic threat: "I will send the red cock flying over your house!" To discourage firetrap housing, the city paid one-third the cost of tile roofing.

And the air smelled of wine! The 14th-century traveler who reported this also exulted over the courtesy of Bruges merchants, whose standard soft-sell line was:

"I have such a variety of goods that I can serve you well and cheaply." The variety dazzled traders, who saw gold-threaded tapestries, fruits from Damascus, furs from Russia —and live lions, parrots, bears, and monkeys.

No other city on earth in 1430 could have given Philip the Good, Duke of Burgundy and lord of Flanders, a more splendid setting for his marriage to Isabella of Portugal. Bruges's fountains ran with wine. Banners fluttered from housetops and draped over the streets. Mystery plays were staged at corner after corner. Gold and silver flashed in the long procession that wound through the city. At night, as the celebrants feasted, men at sea gasped at the glow of lamps in the spires of Bruges.

Twenty-one knights escorted the meat-servers to the tables. Jesters, acrobats, dancers, and actors regaled the guests. While a juggler performed before the raised head table, an enormous pastry was carried into the room. From it emerged a blue-fleeced sheep with gilded horns.

By day Bruges's great square blazed with the pageantry of a tournament. Trumpets blared and drums thundered.

"Ghent...sovereign city of Flanders...in the number of its houses"

Jean Froissart's 14th-century accolade seems fitting today to quayside strollers along the River Lys. Nourished by three rivers and an army of skilled artisans, Ghent grew to greatness weaving Flemish cloth that robed much of Christendom. Here Hansa traders met stiff competition from local merchants who, allied with entrenched guilds, vied with the count of Flanders for control of the city. Like piled profits, buildings rose by the Lys in a spectrum of styles dating back to the grim, Romanesque grain warehouse of the 13th century (center).

WALTER MEAYERS EDWARDS, NATIONAL GEOGRAPHIC STAFF

Knights galloped past their admiring ladies. Mock battles churned dust that could not shroud the gleaming armor, the silver trappings of magnificent steeds.

In this medieval splendor, Philip proclaimed the Order of the Golden Fleece, dedicated to the preservation of chivalry and the church. Knighthood seemed destined to last forever. But what Philip had reigned over, what the sailors had seen, was the last great glow of Bruges.

Even as Bruges hailed the golden fleece that day, silt was choking the River Zwyn. By the end of the 15th century Bruges would barely have a path to the sea. The city would die, but not as so many others have died—gutted, burned . . . bombed. Deserted for Antwerp by traders, Bruges would simply go to sleep, like an enchanted town of a medieval tale. And men some day would rediscover her.

M EN WOULD COME to see what Philip had not seen: the first brush strokes of a new age. He had marshaled knights to hold the world he knew. But he harbored in his court a painter who would lead men's eyes out of the Middle Ages. "Jan van Eyck was present," the artist painted on one work. Present to record reality in an age of awe, he made a mirror of art. And in it glinted the Renaissance.

His genius appears as the sacristan reverently unfolds the panels of his masterpiece, the "Adoration of the Mystic Lamb," in St. Bavo's Cathedral in Ghent. I stood enthralled before it, gazing on medieval faces proclaiming that men have flesh and blood to clothe their souls. They adore the Lamb, but some look away, beckoned by the horizon. I

AS RICH AS LIFE *in France and Flanders, a 15th-century tapestry (right) idealizes winemaking with glowing finery and flowers underfoot. Nobles draped beds and stark castle walls with gems of an art that thrives today (below). Even children wove by sun or candle on works as long as 30 yards. Flanders, whose looms fed Hansa warehouses, led the art; Arras, today part of France, gave its name to fine tapestries. In* Hamlet, *Shakespeare hid an eavesdropper behind one.*

DETAIL FROM "THE VINTAGE," C. 1490; CLUNY MUSEUM, PARIS. OPPOSITE: WEAVER OF AUBUSSON, FRANCE; WALTER MEAYERS EDWARDS, NATIONAL GEOGRAPHIC STAFF

knew the technical explanation for the painting's lustrous enchantment: Van Eyck's perfection of oil, rather than egg white, as a medium; his translucent layers of color. But there is in the works of Van Eyck and his Flemish followers the deeper medium of awakening minds, the illumination of new thoughts.

In Bruges, I walked as though through a museum, past shimmering canals, down serene streets, into cloistered courts. Behind the walls of St. John's Hospital, in a once-stark 13th-century sickroom, I found works of Hans Memling, another Flemish master of the new realism. Again, the glow of dawning lit the painting. What, I thought, had the Hansa merchants seen when they looked on these paintings? Did any of them wonder, sense the change? More likely, I decided, their minds were filled with worry about the silting up of the Zwyn.

When they began moving out of Bruges and Antwerp, they were little different from the Hansards who had founded the league three centuries before. Eyes on goods, ears cocked for bids, they did not sense the winds of change. In their Baltic stronghold of Riga, the weathercock on a church steeple is still painted black on one side, gold on the other. Wind from the sea showed Riga a cock of gold, for trade rode on that wind. And gold was all the Hansa looked for.

While the Hansards worked at building profits, in the 15th century other men were building nations. Poland fought for and won the realm that Hansards and

From a Flemish master came "the fairest work ...in all Christendom"

Hailed since its creation by Jan van Eyck in 1432, the "Adoration of the Lamb" still kindles awe in the cathedral of St. Bavo in Ghent. In its great central panel the Virgin, God, and John the Baptist sit above angels, prophets, and apostles revering the Divine Lamb. Napoleon, thieves, dealers, and the disruption of World War II caused repeated dismantling of the altarpiece. Except for one never recovered, its 24 oak panels unfold today as the artist assembled them for his client, a Ghent merchant who bought immortality; a panel portrays him.

Van Eyck also served the duke of Burgundy, as did Rogier van der Weyden, whose delicate brush graces the portrait opposite. Nobles and burghers, spending fortunes on art, made Flanders a gallery mirroring chivalry's golden sunset — and a new dawn.

WALTER MEAYERS EDWARDS, NATIONAL GEOGRAPHIC STAFF. OPPOSITE: "PORTRAIT OF A LADY," C. 1455; THE NATIONAL GALLERY, LONDON

Teutonic Knights had ruled. Ivan the Great marched out of Moscow, conquered Novgorod, shut down the kontor, and expelled the Hansa. Christian II closed Denmark to the Hansards. Even the herring deserted the league. The fish, possibly because of a subtle drop in the Baltic's salinity, now spawned in the North Sea. Blessed by this new fishing boon, the Dutch found the wealth to build a trading fleet that challenged the weakening Hansa in its key port of Danzig.

England, bled by the Hundred Years' War and torn by the Wars of the Roses, could not yet challenge the Hansa. But as hardy nationhood grew on the isle, Englishmen began keeping a new ledger for future accounting with the Hansards. The entries included a Hansa atrocity: Ninety-six English fishermen were captured off Bergen, bound hand and foot, and thrown into the sea.

Not until the end of the 15th century could England strike back. Henry VII forbade the export of wool by German merchants. And, as England's own cloth industry began to flourish, so did her shipwrights. Bigger, better ships than the Hansa ever knew sailed from the ports of England. In a search for new markets, she discovered a New-found Land. All Europe now was pivoting westward, toward the New World and its new riches.

THE OLD HANSA had ventured eastward; England's new merchant adventurers sailed westward. Schooled by generations of German merchants, they had learned the ways of international trade. English companies—Hudson's Bay, Plymouth, Massachusetts Bay—could find ancestors among kontors. Another empire would flourish on trade, but its wealth would serve a nation, not a brotherhood.

In 1526, knights led by Sir Thomas More broke into the Steelyard and arrested five German merchants in a raid for forbidden Lutheran books. A Hansa official wrote to Germany, complaining that the Steelyard had "come under great and heavy pressure." It got heavier. Queen Elizabeth sicced her faithful sea dog Sir Francis Drake on the Hansa; he seized 60 of their ships en route to Spain. Then, in 1598, Elizabeth seized the Steelyard and evicted the Hansards.

"We left," a merchant reported, "and the gate was shut behind us, and we might nohow stay the night." Three years later, the secretary of the queen's proud Merchant Adventurers assessed the condition of the Hanseatic cities: "Most of their teeth have fallen out; the rest sit but loosely in their heads."

In that unfathomable moment when the medieval world began to disappear, so did that strangely medieval league, too stiff to bend, too old to grow. Historians do not agree on what caused the ultimate downfall of the Hanseatic League. For my own answer, I recall a poignant moment in Bruges.

I heard in the great belfry of Bruges words that others once may have spoken in Europe's medieval twilight. The bell keeper was telling me that he would soon retire from a craft that his father and his grandfather had followed. I asked what he would do. He said he would go elsewhere to tune bells. I asked where. He looked out over Bruges and echoed other seekers of new worlds:

"I will go," he said, "to America."

BRIGHT AS A PAGEANT *that sets the night in Bruges ablaze, the Middle Ages brought Western man from the rubble of Rome to the glories of soaring cathedrals, vibrant cities, blossoming commerce, and a faith that binds men still.*
A millennium that began in darkness and pulsed with the deeds of warriors, merchants, churchmen, and princes closed in a brilliance that would illumine all the ages to come.

LION OF FLANDERS ADORNS THE BELFRY IN THE HEART OF BRUGES AS THE CITY PRESENTS THE PLAY OF THE HOLY BLOOD, HONORING A RELIC HER CRUSADERS WON; LUIS MARDEN, NATIONAL GEOGRAPHIC STAFF

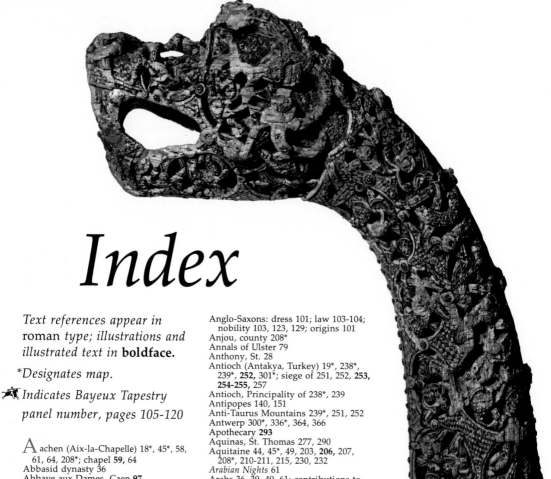

Index

Text references appear in
roman *type; illustrations and
illustrated text in* **boldface.**

*Designates map.

🐎*Indicates Bayeux Tapestry
panel number, pages 105-120*

A

Aachen (Aix-la-Chapelle) 18*, 45*, 58,
61, 64, 208*; chapel **59, 64**
Abbasid dynasty 36
Abbaye aux Dames, Caen **97**
Abbaye aux Hommes, Caen **97**
Abelard, Peter 140, 149, 277, 280, 289-290
Accursius, law professor 277
Acre 201, 222, 224, 226, 227-228, 232,
238*, 239*, 301*; Gothic hall **233**
Adhemar of Monteil, bishop of Le Puy
240, 248, 258, 263, 268
"Adoration of the Mystic Lamb"
(Van Eyck) 364, **366**
Adrianople 18*, 22
Africa 16, 18*, 25, 35, 82, 300-301*
Agincourt, France 324*; battle of 322
Agricola, Georgius 354
Agriculture **10-11**, 52, **53, 54, 56-57, 96,**
104, **134-135, 190,** 193, **260**
Aiguebelle, monastery, France **134-135,
141-148**
Aigues Mortes, France **232,** 238*, 300*
Alaric 22, 25
Albertus Magnus 277
Alchemy 295; laboratory **294**
Alcuin of York 62, 64, 67
Alen, measurement 79
Alexander III, pope **208**
Alexandria, Egypt 19*, 82, 300*, 304
Alexius Comnenus, Byzantine emperor
240, 241, 242, 245, 246
Alfonso VIII, of Castile **208,** 209
Alfred the Great, of England 82, 102
Alice, princess 222
All Saints' Day 320
Althing 80
Amber 331, 332, 347; amber bear **85**
Ambrose, St., bishop of Milan 27, 28
America 76*, 368; discovery 68, 76;
Viking colony **82**
Anacletus II, antipope 140
Andrew, St. 254, 256
Anesthesia: sleep sponge 292
Angevin Empire 208*, 209, 210
Anglo-Saxon Chronicle 67, 100, 101,
125, 126
Anglo-Saxons: dress 101; law 103-104;
nobility 103, 123, 129; origins 101
Anjou, county 208*
Annals of Ulster 79
Anthony, St. 28
Antioch (Antakya, Turkey) 19*, 238*,
239*, **252,** 301*; siege of 251, 252, **253,
254-255,** 257
Antioch, Principality of 238*, 239
Antipopes 140, 151
Anti-Taurus Mountains 239*, 251, 252
Antwerp 300*, 336*, 364, 366
Apothecary **293**
Aquinas, St. Thomas 277, 290
Aquitaine 44, 45*, 49, 203, **206,** 207,
208*, 210-211, 215, 230, 232
Arabian Nights 61
Arabs 36, 39, 49, 61; contributions to
Western culture 8, 36, 39, 62, 292;
empire 36; *see also* Moors
Archers 121, 264, **266-267, 322-323,**
🐎 **20, 23**
Archiginnasio, Bologna University
282-283
Architecture: Byzantine **30, 34,** 35, **59;**
Gothic **160-171,** 190, 193, **351;**
Romanesque 160, **178,** 211, **362-363**
Arian heresy 32
Arms and armor 7, 9, **202-203, 212-213,
229;** *see also* Bayeux Tapestry
Arnold of Brescia 149
Art: bronzes **42, 200, 302;** carvings **30,
69, 304;** frescoes **152-153, 284;** illumi-
nations **2-3, 10-11, 53-55, 134, 138, 210-
211, 218-219, 220, 223, 230-232, 241,
286-287, 288, 305, 309-314, 316-317,
322-323, 326, 328, 345;** mosaics **32-33;**
paintings **152-153, 350, 354, 360, 364,
366, 367;** sculpture **19, 48-49, 76, 169-
170, 184, 195, 206, 272-273;** tapestries
364-365; Bayeux **105-120**
Arthur, legendary king 101, **230-231**
Asia Minor 19*, 238-239*; Hunnic inva-
sion 23; Turkish invasion 36, 242, 243
Assisi, Italy **154-155, 157,** 208*
Astrolabe 337
Attila the Hun 19, 21, 23, 24, 25
Augustine, St., bishop of Hippo 27
Aurelian, Roman emperor 23
Austrasia 45*
Auvergne, region, France **4, 179-182,** 237
Avars 45*, 52
Avicenna 292
Avignon 308; papal palace **150-151**

B

Babylonian Captivity" 151
Bacon, Roger 277, 295
Bagpipes, Galician **192,** 196, 198
Baldwin of Boulogne 239, 242, 251

The Ballad of Dead Ladies (Villon) 288
Banking 8, 183
Barbarian invasions: Roman Empire
18-27, 18-19*
Barbary Coast 301, 304
Barber **310**
Bartholomew, Peter **253,** 254, 258
Basil, St., of Caesarea 30
Basilica and Convent of St. Francis,
Assisi **154**
Basilica of St. Mary of the Angels, Assisi
156; Porziuncola **155**
Basques 45*, **49,** 51
Battle, England **122;** Battle Abbey 121
Bavaria 45*, 49, 318
Bayeux, France 94, 99*, 104
Bayeux Tapestry 9, **92-93,** 94-95, 99,
101-120
Becket, Thomas à 168; canonized **208,**
209, 215; slain **208, 209**
Bede, the Venerable 102
Benedict of Nursia, St. 30, 134, **138,**
140; Rule of 135, 138, 142, 146
Benedictine Order 137, 138, 139
Beowulf 102, 286
Berengaria, princess of Navarre 222, 229
Bergen, Norway 77*, **330-331,** 332, **333,**
335, **336*,** 352
Bernard of Clairvaux, St. **131-140, 149-
152,** 239; letters 137, 139, 140, 149;
quoted 134, 135, 137, 139, 140, 146,
151; teachings 140
Bernardone, Giovanni Francesco *see*
Francis of Assisi
Bertran de Born 203

Bertran de Gourdon 230
Black Death *see* Plague
Black Prince 322
Black Sea 14, 19*, 77*, 88, 209*, 238-239*,
300-301*; trade 303
Blondel, troubadour 229
Boats and ships 241, 250, 301, ![] 2, 9,
11, 12-14; merchant (cog) 340, 341;
Viking 66-67, 72, 76-77, 79, 80-81, 84
Boccaccio, Giovanni 288, 289
Bohemond of Taranto 242, 245, 246, 254,
258
Bologna 341; university 277, 279, 282-283
Boniface, St., missionary 44-45, 52, 56
Bordeaux, France 175*, 208*, 300*, 308,
324*; vineyards 206, 207
Bourges, France 175*, 299, 300*, 301, 303,
308, 309, 311, 324*; mint 303
Breadmaking 73
Bremen 332, 336*, 338, 340-341, 346, 359;
Ratskeller 340; town hall 341
British Isles: Viking raids 67, 68, 76*,
78-79, 80, 82, 84
Brittany 45*, 99*, 208*, 210
Bruges, Belgium 300*, 312, 336*, 345,
362-364, 366, 368, 369; goldsmith 313
Burgos, Spain 175*, 190; cathedral 175*,
190, 193; gate 191
Burgundy 18, 44, 45*, 131-133, 208*, 324*
Burials 317; Viking customs 72, 76, 77,
80, 90
Byzantine Empire 30-35, 36, 209*, 238-
239*, 242, 270; Arab invasion 36; arts
35; court etiquette 35; emperor, divin-
ity of 30; language 35
Byzantium 14, 15, 77*, 84

Caen, France 99*; abbeys 97; ducal
palace 94-95
Calais, France 324*
Calixtus II, pope 175
Calixtus III, pope 320
Cambridge 208*; Cambridge University
279
Canon of Medicine (Avicenna) 292
Canterbury, England 18*, 102, 104, 127*,
175*, 208*; cathedral 168, 175*, 209
Canterbury Tales (Chaucer) 287; illumina-
tion 286
"Canticle of the Sun" (St. Francis of
Assisi) 158
Canute, of England 84, 90, 102-103
Capetians 160, 205, 207, 209
Carcassonne, France 306-307, 324*
Carolingian empire 45*, 48-52, 57-58
Carolingian minuscule 63, 64
Cassiodorus 29
Castile, region, Spain 189, 190, 193;
kingdom of 208*
Castles 104, 127*, 207; Cat Castle 46;
Château Gaillard 204-205, 230;
Crusader 238-239*, 256-258; Die Pfalz
348; Marksburg 214-217
Cathedrals 158-171; Burgos 190, 193;
Canterbury 168; Chartres 168, 171;
Cologne 351; León 193; Le Puy 177;
Notre Dame, Paris 160-170, construc-
tion of 160, 162-164; Santiago de
Compostela 172-173, 174, 176, 195,
195-197, 198, 199
Cattle 96, 180-181, 198, 275
Cavalry 104, 121, 221, ![] 19-23
Chanson de Roland (Song of Roland) 48,
49, 51, 203, 286
Charlemagne, emperor of the West
42-65, 371; campaigns 48-49, 50-52,
186; coronation 43, 58; court life 58,
61; empire 44, 45*; estates 57; family
61; monogram 63; palace 58
Charles VII, of France 299, 300, 303, 308,
320, 324-325, 328; coronation 326
Charles Martel 39, 44, 52
Charles the Great *see* Charlemagne
Charles the Simple, Frankish king 82
Chartres, cathedral 168, 171, 175*
Château Gaillard, France 7, 204-205,
208*, 230, 232
Chaucer, Geoffrey 286, 287
Chess 374-375
Childeric III, Merovingian king 44

China 35, 303
Chinon, France 207, 208*, 215, 217, 324*,
325
Chivalry 7, 8, 153, 202, 226, 231
Chrétien de Troyes 230, 231
Christian II, of Denmark 368
Christianity 13, 27, 28; growth 44-45,
51-52, 75, 79, 80, 88, 89, 252; heresies
28, 32, 56, 140, 149; state religion 13, 28
Church, Roman Catholic 35; conversion
to 44; ecclesiastical organization 28;
role in medieval society 160; *see also*
Monasticism; Papacy
Cid, the 174, 190
Cismontane University, Bologna 279
Cistercians 131, 135, 142, 153; monastic
life 137, 141-148
City of God (St. Augustine) 27
Clairvaux, France 137, 150, 208*;
monastery: founding 137, 139, 140
Clement V, pope 151
Clement VI, pope: coronation 151
Clocks 314-315, 360
Clonmacnoise, monastery, Ireland:
Viking raid 78-79
Clothing 218-219; academic garb 274,
295; Anglo-Saxons 101; Byzantine 35;
Huns 23
Clovis, baptism of 44
Cluny, France 208*; monastery 135, 137,
139
Codex Aureus 65
Codex Calixtinus 175, 181; quoted 174,
183, 184, 187, 189, 190, 192, 195, 196
Codex Manesse 220, 223
Codex Ragyndrudis 45
Coeur, Jacques 298-320; fleet 299, 304,
320; mansion 308, 309, 311; motto 311;
trade empire 300-301*
Coeur, Pierre 301
Cogs, ships 336, 340-341
Coinage 298; silver penny 94
Cologne, Germany 45*, 58, 208*, 237,
238*, 300*, 332, 336*, 350, 352-353;
cathedral 351
Commerce 300-301*; Hanseatic trade
arteries 336-337*
Common law 104, 126
Comneni, Byzantine rulers 209,
222, 240, 241, 242, 245, 246
Confessions (St. Augustine) 27
Conrad III, of Germany 149, 239
Constantine, emperor 12-16, 28
Constantinople 19*, 23, 30-32, 35,
90, 300*, 238*, 241, 300*, 303;
founding of 13-14, 14-15; Nika
Revolt 31, 32, 35; sacked 239
Coopers: coat of arms 313
Copernicus 295
Copper 337; mining 308, 354
Courts: manor court 54
"Courts of Love" 206, 207, 210-211
Cracow 209*, 300*; University of:
laboratory 294
Craft guilds *see* Guilds
Crafts: glass, stained 168-169; Viking
79, 85
Craftsmen 168, 310-313, 314, 352;
masons 164, 170
Crécy 324*; battle of 213, 322-323
Crossbows 9, 7, 212, 228, 232
Crusades 8, 200-271; routes 238-239*;
First Crusade 234-271; battle sites 238-
239*; battles: Antioch 251, 252, 254-
255, Dorylaeum 238, 246, Jerusalem

234-235, 239, 259-261, 263-264, 266-
267, 268, Nicaea 238, 244, 245, 246;
call to 236-237; leaders 242, 258, 263,
268; supplies 250-251, 252, 254, 261;
Second Crusade 239; Third 149, 165,
239, 346; Fourth 239, 303; Fifth 156,
239; Sixth 239; Seventh 239; Eighth
239; Children's Crusade 239; Peoples'
Crusade 239, 240, 243
Crusaders 236, 237, 242; castles 238-239*,
256-258; graves 259; hardships 249, 254

Dacia (Rumania) 18*, 19, 23
Daimbert of Pisa 268
Damascus, Syria 19*, 201, 239*, 301*,
303-304
Dancing 218, 295; dances 189, 196
Danes 45*, 52, 61, 68, 76, 80, 82, 84, 102;
England 103, 124, Danegeld 84, 129,
Danelaw 84, 102; Hansa conflict 336,
338, 347, 349
Danishmend dynasty 238*, 245, 246
Danzig (Gdansk, Poland) 337*, 346-347,
358, 368; Great Crane 344-345
Dante Alighieri 284, 285, 289
Danzig (Gdansk, Poland) 337*, 346-347,
358, 368; Great Crane 344-345
Days: name origins 102
The Decameron (Boccaccio) 288
Decline and Fall of the Roman Empire
(Gibbon) 23
Decretum (Gratian) 290
Deities: Germanic 19, 102; Oriental 28
Díaz de Vivar, Rodrigo *see* Cid
Dies Irae, poem 285
Diocletian, Roman emperor 14, 16
Divine Comedy (Dante) 285
Domesday (Doomsday) Book 125, 126,
129, 221; Exon report 127; survey 125,
128-129
Donjons 215
Dublin, Ireland 76*; Viking town 79
Durendal, Roland's sword 51
Dürnstein, castle 209*, 215, 229
Dyes 304-305; dyers 313

FURY AND FAITH *from days full
of both shine in medieval art.
Scenes of strife crowd a ninth-
century dragon (opposite)
in Oslo's Viking Ship Hall.*

*Christ and saints adorn a silver
and copper-gilt chalice (right)
given to an abbey about the year 780
by Duke Tassilo of Bavaria, foe of
Charlemagne. The Stiftsbibliothek
in Kremsmünster preserves the relic.*

Easterlings 349-350
Ecumenical Council, first: Nicaea 245
Edessa 238*, 239
Education 61, 62, 64, 133; see also Universities
Edward the Confessor, of England 90, 99, 100, 103, ⚔ 1, 9-10; rule 103
Edward III, of England 322, 356, 357, 358, 361, 362
Egypt 16, 19*, 28, 201, 238*; Arab conquest 36; Sultan of 301, 303, 304, 308
Einhard 49, 50-51, 52, 58, 61
Eleanor of Aquitaine 206, 207, 210, 211, 217, 222, 229, 232; carving of 206; character 206, 207, 215; children 206, 210; "Courts of Love" 207; death 232; marriages 206, 207, 210
Elizabeth I, of England 368
Ell, measure 353
Ellesmere manuscript: illumination 286
England 76*, 93-94, 99-100, 101-104, 121-129, 175*, 208*, 238*, 336*; castles 127*; Danelaw 102, 103-104; Hansa ports 356-359; invasions 101, 102, Norman 99*, Viking 80, 82, 84, 100; Norman influences 94, 97; taxes 100, 129; trade companies 368; wool trade 314, 332, 358, 359, 361, 368
English language 129; Norman influence 94
Entertainers 94-95
Ericson, Leif 82
Ethelred the Unready, of England 84
Eustace of Boulogne ⚔ 23
Excalibur, King Arthur's sword 231
Excommunication 28, 209, 239

Fairs 180-181, 304, 305, 312, 314
Falcons 218, 220, 221
Fatimid dynasty: Egypt 259
Fauvel, horse 222, 228, 232
Fealty, concept of 19
Festivals; St. James 172-173, 174, 194, 195, 196, 198; San Fermin 186-187; Viking 75, 91
Feudalism 8, 64, 104, 231; development of 16, 19, 52, structure 16, 19, 52, 54, 56-57; decline 271; France 97; Norman England 94, 97, 123-124
Fishing 16-17, 242, 261, 331, 332-333
Flanders 208*, 316, 332, 336*, 358, 361-366
Flemish painters 364, 366; works of 298, 360, 366, 367, 377
Florence, Italy 300*, 316; cathedral fresco 284
Fontevrault, France 208*; abbey 232
Foods 54, 57, 95, 218, 332, 341
Fortifications 104, 124; towns 104; see also Carcassonne; Castles; Visby
France 76-77*, 99*, 176-183, 184, 208*, 238*; cathedrals 160; commercial growth 299-320; Hundred Years' War 320-329; Moorish invasion 36; Pilgrim routes 175*; Viking raids 68, 80, 82
Francis of Assisi, St. 131-132, 152-158; death 158; early life 153; preaching 154, 156; travels 156
Frankfurt, Germany 45*, 341
Frankish kingdom: alliance with church 44, 48; counties 57; government 57-58
Franks 18*, 43, 44, 48, 61; Holy Land 224
Frederick Barbarossa, Holy Roman Emperor 64, 239, 279, 357; chandelier 59; death 201; invades Lombardy 208, 209; takes Cross 217
Frederick II, Holy Roman Emperor 221, 239
Frisia 45*, 52
Froissart, Jean 363; "Chronicles": illuminations 316-317, 322-323
Fulcher of Chartres: quoted 245, 248, 251, 252, 254, 257
Fulda, Germany 45*; monastery 45
Fulford, England: battle of 100
Fur trade 349
Furriers 310

Galahad 231
Gambesons 212, 213
Games 74, 85, 374-375
Gamla Uppsala, Sweden 75; burial mounds 72, 76
Gargoyles 170
Gaul 18*, 22, 24; Roman rule 44
Gdańsk (Danzig), Poland 346-347
Geismar, Austrasia 45*, 52
Genoa, Italy 300*, 303, 320
Germanic tribes 18-19*; warrior 19
Germany 77*, 208-209*, 238*, 336*, 337, 353; castles 214-217, 348
Gesta Francorum 243, 245, 246, 249, 252, 254, 259, 263, 264, 267, 268
Ghent, Flanders 336*, 362-363; cathedral 364
Gibbon, Edward: quoted 23
Gislebertus, sculptor: carvings 136-137
Glassblowers 312
Glazier 168
Godfrey of Bouillon 242, 245, 264
Godwin of Wessex, earl 99, 103
Gokstad ship 77
Gold mining 354
Golden Horn, Constantinople 13, 16-17, 240-241
Goldsmiths 313
Goslar, Germany 336*, 352-353, 354
Gothic architecture 160-171, 190, 193, 233, 351
Goths 23, 32; migrations 18-19*, 23
Gotland, island 18*, 74, 77*, 337*, 346, 347, 349
Granada, Spain 18*, 36, 186, 208*, 209
Greece 18*; Visigoths ravage 22
Greek fire 264, 266-267
Gregory of Nyssa, St. 28
Gregory the Great, St., pope 62
Gregory VII, St., pope 151
Guilds 8; craft and trade 312-314, 316-317, coats of arms 313, festivals 304, mystery plays 319-320; merchant see Hanseatic League; student guilds 279, 282-283
Guinevere 231

Hadrian, Roman emperor 235, 263
Hagia Sophia, Istanbul 30, 34, 35, 241
Halley's Comet 100, ⚔ 11
Hamburg, Germany 77*, 332, 336*, 338, 341, 344, 347, 359; harbor 342-343
Hanseatic League 8, 331-369; apprenticeship 335; decline 366-368; government of 335; history 335-336; kontors 335, 361; member cities 336-337*; power 332; secrecy 333, 335; trade arteries 336-337*
Harald Hardraada, of Norway 89-90, 99, 100, ⚔ 15; invasion route 99*
Harold Godwinson, earl of Wessex 90, 99*, 100, 101, 121, ⚔ 1-7, 15, 17, 19; coronation 100, 102, ⚔ 11; death 121, 122, ⚔ 24; troop movement 99*
Hastings, England 99*, 100, 121, 127*, ⚔ 15; battle of 92-93, 94, 101, 104, 121, 122-123, ⚔ 19-24
Hauberks 202, 212, 229, ⚔ 7
Hedeby, Denmark 77*, 84
Heidelberg, Germany 296-297; university jail 297
Helmets 202-203, 212-213, 225, ⚔ 7
Heloise 280, 289
Henry VI, Holy Roman Emperor 229
Henry I, of England 126, 140
Henry II, of England 126, 206, 207, 209, 210, 211, 215, 217, 222, 231, 357; carving 206; death 217; marriage 206, 210; rule 206, 211
Henry V, of England 322
Henry VI, of England 165, 300, 322
Henry VII, of England 368
Henry I, of France 96, 97, 242
Heralds 6, 222
Heresies 28, 32, 56, 140, 149
Herjulfsson, Bjarni 68, 82
Hermits 28, 248
Hippodrome, Constantinople 30, 31
Holbein, Hans the Younger: painting by 360

People and events that left their mark during the Middle Ages are listed here in chronological order. Most dates are known; others reflect scholarly consensus.

A.D.	Daily Life
300	Courts observe Sunday as day of rest c. 320 Gladiatorial combats prohibited in the East c. 325 Pneumatic organs common in Spanish churches c. 450
500	Stirrups introduced from the East c. 700 Saxons lead rebirth of mining for metals c. 740
800	Manorialism and feudalism become firmly established as Carolingian empire breaks up c. 860 Horseshoes permit horses to travel farther and faster c. 900 Horsecollar increases horsepower fourfold c. 900
1000	Motte-and-bailey castles rise in Normandy c. 1000 Study of medicine renewed, at Salerno c. 1050 Study of Roman law revived, at Bologna c. 1100 Crusades stimulate money economy c. 1150 Windmills appear in Europe c. 1180 Ships steered by rudder on sternpost c. 1180
1200	Labor-saving wheelbarrow aids workmen c. 1200 Hamburg and Lübeck form trade treaty, seed of Hanseatic League 1241 Paper manufactured at Fabriano, Italy c. 1270 Marco Polo travels to Far East c. 1271 Eyeglasses made in northern Italy c. 1285 Genoese ships, seeking sea route round Africa, disappear 1291 Development of mechanical clock c. 1300 Small cannon is invented c. 1320 Bubonic plague, the Black Death, reaches peak 1348-1350
1450	Johann Gutenburg, using movable type, prints the Bible at Mainz 1456

A Time Chart of Medieval History

Politics and Military	Church	Art, Literature, Philosophy
Emperor Constantine founds Constantinople 324 Emperor Theodosius divides empire into East and West 395 Visigoths sack Rome 410 Clovis crowned king of Salian Franks 481	Council of Nicaea formulates Nicene Creed 325 St. Ambrose imposes penance on Emperor Theodosius I for massacre at Thessalonica 390	St. Jerome completes Vulgate, standard Latin translation of Bible c. 400 St. Augustine of Hippo writes *City of God* 413-426
Justinian codifies Roman law 528-529 Merovingian king Dagobert dies; "major domus," chief palace official, takes over rule of Frankish realm 639 Moslems invade Spain and crush last Visigothic king 711 Charles Martel, major domus, turns back Moslems near Tours 732 Election of Pepin I King of the Franks establishes Carolingian line 751 Lombards take Ravenna 751 Charlemagne subdues Lombards 774	St. Benedict founds monastery at Monte Cassino c. 529 Pope Gregory I makes peace with Lombards and becomes temporal as well as spiritual ruler of Rome 590-604; sends Augustine as missionary to England 596 St. Boniface begins missionary work among the Germans 716	Byzantine mosaics composed at Ravenna c. 540 Justinian builds Hagia Sophia at Constantinople 532-537 Cassiodorus founds monasteries devoted to copying manuscripts of classical era c. 540 *Beowulf*, Anglo-Saxon epic poem, written c. 725 Venerable Bede completes *Ecclesiastical History of the English People* 731
Pope Leo III crowns Charlemagne emperor of the West at Rome 800 Treaty of Verdun partitions Charlemagne's empire, leads to creation of France and Germany; Viking invasions ravage Europe 843 Alfred the Great elected king of Wessex 871 Varangians take over Kiev 882 Charles the Simple cedes Normandy to Norse leader Rollo 911 Otto the Great, crowned emperor in Rome, unites Germany and Italy 962 Hugh Capet, elected king of France, establishes Capetian dynasty 987	Council of Constantinople ends iconoclasm—begun in 726 by Emperor Leo III—and restores veneration of images 843 St. Berno founds monastery of Cluny in Burgundy 910 Emperor Otto and Pope John XII split over supremacy 963	Charlemagne establishes schools throughout his empire c. 800 Death of Einhard, biographer of Charlemagne 840 Compilation of Anglo-Saxon Chronicle begins under Alfred the Great c. 890
William of Normandy invades England, wins Battle of Hastings 1066 Second Lateran Council forbids use of crossbows against Christians 1139 Thomas à Becket, Archbishop of Canterbury, murdered by knights of King Henry II 1170 Richard the Lionheart embarks on Third Crusade 1189	Hungary and Scandinavia embrace Christianity c. 1000 Complete rupture splits church into Orthodox (East) and Catholic (West) 1054 Pope Urban II preaches First Crusade 1095 St. Robert of Molesme founds Cistercian Order at Cîteaux 1098 First Lateran Council forbids clerics to marry 1123	Abbot Suger remodels Romanesque St. Denis into first Gothic church c. 1130 William IX, duke of Aquitaine, is first known troubadour 1086-1126 *Song of Roland* written c. 1100 Scholars begin teaching at Oxford c. 1125 Gothic art and architecture embodied in Notre Dame 1163 Chrétien de Troyes popularizes Arthurian legend in poems c. 1170
Constantinople sacked by Fourth Crusaders 1204 Pope Innocent III excommunicates England's King John for persecuting the church 1209 King John signs Magna Carta 1215 Simon de Montfort calls English parliament of lay and spiritual lords, knights, burgesses 1265 Philip IV calls first Estates-General at Paris 1302 England's Edward III claims French crown, precipitates Hundred Years' War 1337 English bowmen down French at Crécy 1346 Black Prince leads English to victory at Poitiers 1356 England's Henry V triumphs at Agincourt 1415 Joan of Arc burned at Rouen 1431 French take Bordeaux, ending Hundred Years' War 1453 Constantinople falls to Turks 1453	Order of St. Francis formed 1209 St. Dominic organizes Dominican Order 1215 Fourth Lateran Council reaffirms church dogma 1215 Pope Gregory IX begins Inquisition for trial of Albigensian heretics in southern France 1233 Gregory IX codifies canon law 1234 John Wycliffe attempts to reform the church c. 1375 Great Schism begins; two popes contend for power 1378 John Hus burned for heresy 1415 Council of Constance ends Great Schism 1414-1418	Cambridge University founded 1209 *Romance of the Rose*, popular French poem, begun c. 1237 Roger Bacon writes *Opus Majus* c. 1268 St. Thomas Aquinas writes *Summa Theologica* 1267-1273 Giotto paints celebrated frescoes in Padua's Arena Chapel c. 1305 Dante completes *Divine Comedy* c. 1321 Petrarch writes epic *Africa* 1342 Boccaccio writes *The Decameron* 1348-1353 Translation of Bible into English completed 1382 Chaucer begins *Canterbury Tales* c. 1387 Jan van Eyck completes altarpiece painting in Ghent 1432

Holy Grail 231
Holy Land *see* Crusades
Holy Roman Empire 27, 43, 64, 208-209*, 238*, 353
Holy Sepulcher, Church of the, Jerusalem 268, **269, 270**
Honorius, Roman emperor 25
Housecarls 103, 104, 122
Houses 54, **55**, 308, **309**, 311; Cappadocia **248-249**; Germany **353**; Norway **333**
Hundred Years' War 183; 299-300, 317, **320-329**, 356, 358, 361, 368; hardships caused by 300-301
Huns 18-19*, **20-21**, 22, 23; clothing 23; leader *see* Attila; migrations 22, 23

Iceland 68, 76*, 80; language 80
Innocent II, pope 140
Innocent III, pope 151, 152, 153, 156
Iona, island, Scotland 79, 102
Ireland 18*, 76*, 208*; Christianity 79; Viking raids 68, **78-79**, 90
Irminsul, sacred symbol 52
Iron 337; mining 354, 356
Islam 15, **36-41**
Istanbul, Turkey **16-17**, 30, **240-241**
Italy 18*, 24, 35, 303, 314
Ivanhoe (Scott) 229

James, St. 174-176; grave 196; legend 177; shrine *see* Santiago de Compostela; statues 174, **197**
Jerome, St., quoted 23, 27
Jerusalem 19*, 36, 201, 215, 229, 238*, 239*, 259, **270-271**; gates **262**, 264; Old City **263**, 270-271; siege of **234-235**, 239, 259-261, 263-264, **266-267**, 268
Jerusalem, Kingdom of 201, 238*, 239, 260
Jesters **288**, **304**
Jewelry 332; Viking **84-85**
Jews 220-221; Crusaders' victims 237, 240, 264, 268
Jihad, holy war 224
Joan of Arc 303, **320-329**; birthplace 322, **324-325**; death 328-329; travels **324**
John XXIII, pope 174
John (Lackland), of England 205, 206, 209, 210, 215, 229, 232
Jongleurs 207

Jousts 8; Joust of the Saracen: Arezzo 6, 224-227; spectator **211**
Jury system 8; precursors 104, 129
Justinian, Byzantine emperor 29, 30, **31**, 32, 35; law code 35, 277; mosaic **32**

Kiev, Russia 77*, **88-89**, 300*
Knarr, ship 84
Knights 7, **103**, 104, 121, **123**, **128**, 364; investiture 202, 231; knightly ideals 202, 231, 271; obligations 203; tourneys **223-225**, 227; training 228
Knights Hospitalers of St. John 232, 239; castle **256-257**
Knights of the Round Table **230-231**
Knights Templars 140, 239; castle 193
Kontors, Hansa communes 335
Koran 38
Krak de Chevaliers, Syria 239*, **256-257**

Ladby ship: replica **80**
Lancelot 231
La Pucelle *see* Joan of Arc
Las Navas de Tolosa, Spain, battle 209
Latin Quarter, Paris 280, 283
La Trappe, monastery, France 142
Law 58; common 104, 126; customary 103; maritime 300, 341; Roman 35, 277, 279; Saxon 103-104; town 311
Lead mining 308, 354, 356
Leipzig 279, 336*
Lendit Fair 305
Leo I, pope 24
Leo III, pope 43, 44
Leo the Mathematician 36, 39
Leopold of Austria, duke 215, 229
Lepers 317
Levant 16, 218, 239; European trade 301, 303-305
Lindisfarne, island 67, **76***, 77, 79, 102
Literature 285-288; poetry 207; sagas 74, 75, 80
Lombardy 18*, 45*, 48, 49, 208*, 209
London 76*, 99*, 208*, 300*, 312, 332, 336*, **356-357**, 359; Bridge 84; the City 124, 361; mayor 317; population 316; Tower of **124-125**
Longbow 213, **322-323**
Lorraine, duchy 208*

Lorraine, duke of 325
Louis VII, of France 140, 149, 206, 207, 215, 239
Louis IX, St., of France 177, 178, **232**, 239
Lübeck, Germany 312, 332, 336*, 336-337, 338, 346, 349; gate **339;** model **338;** seal **334**
Luttrell Psalter: illuminations **10-11**

Magdalen college, Oxford 274-275
Magna Carta 206
Malcolm, of Scotland 126
Mail **202-203**, 212, 8
Mangonels **266-267**
Manorialism: manor life **53-55**; rise of 16, 52, 54, 57
Manuel Butumites 246
Maps: Angevin Empire 238*; Barbarian invasion 18-19*; Charlemagne's empire 45*; Crusader routes 238-239*; Hansa trade arteries 336-337*; Joan of Arc's travels 324*; the Lionheart's world 208-209*; Mediterranean commerce 300-301*; Norman Conquest 99*; Pilgrim paths to Compostela 174-175*; Roman Empire 18-19*; Viking voyages 76-77*; William the Conqueror's castles 127*
Marco Polo 303, 317
Maritime law 341; Rolls of Oléron 300
Markets **180-181**, 198, **263**, **310-311**, 314, 331, 332, 340
Marriage: feudal 207; Viking 73
Marseilles, France 208*, 221, 229, 238*, 300*, 312, 320
Marshal, William 211, 217, 222
Mary, cult of 137
Masons 164, 170
Mathematicians 36, 39
Maurice de Sully, bishop 165
Mead 74, 75
Mecca, Saudi Arabia **40-41**, 301*
Medicine **292-293**, 304, 305
Merchants **299-320**, **330-368**
Merlin 231
Merovingian dynasty 44
Merovingian script **63**
Michael, St. **324**
Military service 52, 56, 203; Norman England 123
Miller's guild: coat of arms **313**

*T*hus chastised, an 11th-century bishop checkmated his frowning cardinal: unlike "sinful" dice, he retorted, chess was "a most honorable exercise for Christians." But clerics still censured such games; oaths of losers, they warned, help populate hell.

Persia's ancient pastime enthralled medieval Europe as nobles matched wits over richly wrought chessmen. Love might win all when couples dallied over a board (right). Pieces mirrored the players' world as king, queen, castle, knight, bishop warred across a map of squares; warriors often honed strategy on the board before a battle. At times tempers flared: Canute slew an opponent for scattering their game in rage.

For variety young bloods wrestled, tossed quoits, played backgammon, blindman's buff, and tennis without racquet or net, batting the ball back and forth with open hands. Al fresco billiards was played on the ground by hitting wooden balls with a hooked stick. And Norse swimmers vied at nearly drowning one another.

"Was it right...to sport away thy evenings amidst the vanity of chess?"

Attendants hold hawk and wreath as lord and lady vie on 14th-century French mirror case of ivory; The Louvre, Paris

Ivory king rides a lion, 14th century; National Museum, Copenhagen

Mining 193, 352, 353, **354-355**
Mints 303, 308
Miracle plays 319-320
Modred 231
Mohammed, prophet 36, 39, 264
Monasteries: Celtic 101-102, Ireland
  78-79; see also individual names
Monasticism **131-158;** daily life **141-148,**
  314; origins 28, 29, 30; Orthodox 30;
  reform 135; role of 133, 158
Mont St. Michel, France **98,** 99*, 99-100,
  324*, 🐎 6
Monte Cassino, Italy: monastery 30,
  138-139
Moors 190, 208*; effigies of **186-187,** 195,
  196; expulsion from Spain 174, 186,
  196, 209; invasion of France 36, 44;
  origin 36
More, Sir Thomas 368
Moslems **36-41, 234-271**
Mosques **30, 40-41, 240**
Musical instruments 218, **219;** bagpipes
  192, 196, 198

Navarre, kingdom 184, 187, 189, 208*
Newfoundland 76*, 368; Viking
  colony **82**
Nicaea, Turkey 209*, 238*, 243, siege of
  244, 245, 246; walls **245**
Nicene Creed 245
Nicholas, St. 295
Nicholas V, pope 320
Nika Revolt, Constantinople 31, 32, 35
Norman Conquest 93-94, 99*, **99-123**
Normandy, duchy 7, 82, **96,** 97, 205,
  208*, 209, 299
Normandy, dukes of see Robert I;
  Robert II; William the Conqueror
Norsemen see Vikings
Norwegians 68, 76, 79, 84, **332**
Notre Dame, cathedral, Paris **160-170;**
  cathedral school 283; construction
  162-164; sculpture **170;** stained
  glass **168-169**
Novgorod, Russia 77*, 84, 89, 90, 337*,
  349-350, 352; court 89, 90

Odin, god 72
Odoacer, barbarian general 25
Olaf I, of Norway 90
Old Uppsala, Sweden 75, 76; church 72
Order of the Golden Fleece 364
Orléans, France 45*, 175*, 208*, 322,
  324*, **327;** siege of **326**
Oseberg ship 76-77, **81**

Ostrogoths 18-19*, 25, 29, 35
Otto the Great 353
Otto III, Holy Roman Emperor 64
Oxcart **190**
Oxford University 273, **274-275,
  278;** riots 273-274

Padua University 279; anatomy
  amphitheater **291**
Palestine 28, 201, 222-229; Arab
  conquest 36
Papacy 100, 303; conflicts with East 35;
  rise of prestige 28, 36; schisms 140,
  151; supremacy of 28; temporal powers
  28, 35, 58, 151
Paris, France 45*, 76*, 82, 99*, 175*, 208*,
  300*, 300, 312, 324*; population 314,
  316; university **279-281,** 283, 289
Patrick, St. 79
Paul, St. 28
Paul VI, pope: quoted 165
Paul the Deacon 61
Peasants **10-11,** 16, **53-55,** 103, 104
Peddlers **304**
Peoples' Crusade 237, 240, 243, 245
Pepin the Short 44-45, 48
Peter, St. 28, 252
Peter Lombard 290
Peter the Hermit 237, 240, 243
Pevensey, England 99*, 100, 🐎 14-15;
  castle 127*; mint: coin **94**
Philip II (Augustus), of France 7, 201,
  205, 209, 212, 215, 217, 222, 229, 230,
  232, 283; castles 205
Philip IV, of France 165
Philip the Good, duke of Burgundy
  363, 364, 366, **377**
Picaud, Aymery 181, 184, 186, 189, 190,
  193, 194, 195, 198
Piers the Plowman 287
Pilgrimages 8; Compostela **174-199,**
  guidebook 175, routes 174-175*; goals
  176; hazards 174, 184, 187, 195; Mecca
  40-41
Plague 24, 288, **317**
Plantagenets 205, 232
Plows: ox-drawn **11;** wheeled **53, 286-287**
Poetry 74, 75, 80, 207, 285-288
Poland 209*, 337*, 346, 366
"Portrait of a Lady" (Van der Weyden)
  367
Prague, Czechoslovakia: town clock **315;**
  university 279, 295
Primogeniture 221
Priscus, historian **21;** quoted 19
Procopius: quoted 32, 35

Rabelais 289
Ragnarok (Last Day) 90
Rammelsberg, mine 352, 353-354, **355**
Raubritter (robber knights) 346-347
Ravenna, Italy 18*, 25, 29, 32
Raymond of Aguilers **255,** 257; quoted
  236, 246, 248, 251, 256, 258, 260, 263,
  264, 266, 268
Raymond of Poitiers 207
Raymond of Toulouse 242, 245, 246, 258,
  264
Reims, France 44, 45*, 175*, **321,** 324
Religions: Norse 72, 75, 80; paganism
  52; see also Christianity; Islam
Rhine, river 18*, 19, 22, 45*, **46-47,**
  77*, 208*, 332, **348-349, 351,** 353
Richard the Lionheart, of England 7,
  200-231, 239; birth 203, 210; corona-
  tion 220; Crusades 201, 215, 217, 220,
  222, 227; death 232; disputed lands
  215; imprisonment 215, 229; legends
  229, 232; ransom 229
Riots: students 273-274, **279;** workers
  316-317
Robert I, duke of Normandy 95-96
Robert II (Curthose), duke of Normandy
  97, 124, 242, 245
Robert Guiscard of Sicily 221
Robert of Flanders 261
Robert of Mortain 96, 🐎 16
Robin Hood 230
Roger Guiscard, of Sicily 221
Roger II, of Sicily 221
Roger of Hoveden 221
Roger of Salerno 292
Roland, count 49, 51, 184, 186, **341**
Rollo 82, 97
Roman Empire **15-27,** 94; aristocracy
  15, 16; barbarian invasions 18-19*;
  Christianity 13, 27-28; city life 15; de-
  cline 18; Eastern: rise of 14, 15; Western:
  emperors 25; Justinian's reconquest of
  29, 32, 35; see also Byzantine Empire
Rome, Italy 18*, 45*, 208*, 238*, 300*;
  catacombs **26;** Forum **24-25, 27;**
  pilgrimages to 176; population 35;
  sack of **24-25**
Roncesvalles Pass 45*, 48, 49, **185,** 186;
  battle **48-49**
Rouen, France 76*, 99*, 126, 175*, 208*,
  230, 232, 299, 308, 324*, **328-329,**
  🐎 4, 5
Rug making **242**
Rule of St. Benedict 30, 135, 138, 140
Rus 84
Russia 238*, 332, 337*, 349-350; Christianity 88, 89; Vikings 84, **86-87,** 88

*Danish queen rides a horse
of walrus bone, 13th century;
National Museum, Copenhagen*

*Twelfth-century English bishop sits a throne of
ivory; Metropolitan Museum of Art, New York*

*Ivory knight, probably English, c. 1370;
Metropolitan Museum of Art, New York*

*German castle, carved
from bone in the
11th century;
Staatliche Museen, Berlin*

S agas 74, 80
St. André Cathedral, Bordeaux 207
St. Bavo's Cathedral, Ghent 364, **366**
St. Damian, Church of, Assisi 153, 154,
  156, 158; garden **155**
St. Denis, France 45*, 139
St. Étienne, cathedral, Bourges 301
St. Foy, church, Conques **178-179,**
  181; relics 178, 179, 181
St. Francis, Basilica and Convent of,
  Assisi **154**
"St. Francis Preaches to the Birds"
  (school of Giotto) **152**
"St. Francis Renounces the World"
  (school of Giotto) **153**
St. Hillaire, Poitiers 211
St. James, Feast of **172-173,** 174, **194,**
  195, 196, 198
St. John, chapel, Tower of London 124
St. Julien le Pauvre, church, Paris 283,
  289
St. Lazarus Church, Autun: carvings
  136-137
St. Margaret Lothbury, church, London
  361
St. Marie, chapel, Rocamadour 182
St. Mark's Basilica, Venice **302**
St. Martin's Church, Oxford 273
St. Mary of the Angels, Basilica of,
  Assisi **156;** Porziuncola **155**
St. Mary's Church, Oxford 273
St. Mary's Church, Visby 347
St. Peter's Basilica, Rome 43
St. Peter, church, Antioch **253,** 256
St. Peter's Church, Assisi 154
St. Peter's church, Novgorod 349-350
St. Scholastica's day riot: Oxford
  273-274
St. Séverin, church, Paris **280-281**
St. Simeon, Syria 239*, **250-251,** 254
St. Sophia Cathedral, Kiev **88,** 90
St. Sophia Cathedral, Novgorod 350
St. Valéry, Normandy 99*, ⚔ 2, 12, 13
Sainte Chapelle, church, Paris 178
Saladin 7, 224, 226, 227, 228, 229, 260;
  captures Jerusalem 201, 215;
  reconquers Jerusalem 239
Salerno 209*; medical school 221, 277,
  292
Salt 56, 308, 332, 336
Salvian, priest: quoted 15
San Salvador, monastery, Spain 186
San Vitale, church, Ravenna **32-33,** 58
Santa Maria della Porziuncola, Assisi
  154, **155,** 156, 158
Santiago de Compostela, Spain 8, **172-**
  173, 174*, 193, **194-195;** cathedral 172-
  173, 174*, 176, **195, 196-197,** 198, **199;**
  markets 198
Santo Domingo de la Calzada, Spain
  175*, 188, 189, 190; cathedral **188,** 190
Saracens 36, 51, 201, 224, 228, 261, 264,
  268; leader see Saladin; slaughter at
  Acre 227, 228
Saxons 18, 49, 50-52, 101-102; beliefs
  101; embrace Christianity 101-102
Scandinavia 72, 76, 77*, 84
Scholars 39, 61-62, 64; see also
  Universities
Schools 61-62, 63
Scot, Michael 292
Scotland 76*, 79, 127, 208
Scutage 203
Scyllacium: monastery **29**
Secret History (Procopius) 32
Seine, river 18*, 45*, 76-77*, 80, **160-161,**
  204-205, 208*, 324*, **328-329**
Seljuk Turks 36, 209*, 238*, 240, 243; capi-
  tal 245; Byzantine territory seized by
  242; empire 243; sultan 245, 246
Sentences (Peter Lombard) 290
Serfs 52, **53-55,** 56
Sheep raising: England 358, **358-359**
Sheriff (shire reeve) 103
Ship burials 72, 77, 80, 90
Sic et Non (Abelard) 290
Silk industry: Byzantine Empire 35
Silver mining 352, 353-354, 356
Simeon Stylites, St. 28

Slavery 16, **74,** 84, **87,** 90, 103
Slavs 45*, 52
Sorbonne: founding 279
Spain 18*, 45*, 76*, **184-199;** Arab invad-
  ers 49; Moors 36, 193, expulsion 174,
  186, 196, 209; patron saint 174; pilgrim
  routes 174-175*; Vandals 25, 35
Spices 218, 304
Spurs **229**
Squires 228, 231
Stained glass **168-169, 182,** 193, **301**
Stamford Bridge 99*; battle of 100, 121
Steelyard, London 357, 359, 361, 368
Stephen of Cloyes 239
Stilicho, Roman general 25
Stirrups 7, 104
Students 39, 61-62, 64, 279, 283
Suger, abbot 139, 168
Suleiman the Magnificent 263
Surgical instruments **292**
Sweden 68, 72, 76, 77*, 84, 208-209*,
  336-337
Swords **86;** broadswords **202-203, 229**
Syria: Arab conquest 28, 36, 239*

T acitus 18-19, 68
Taillebourg, battle of 211
Tailors **310;** guild arms **313**
Tancred of Lecce 221-222
Tancred of Sicily 251, 260, 261
Tax censuses 221 see also Domesday
  Book
Teutonic Knights 209, 345, 346
Thanes 103, 123
Theodora, Byzantine empress 30, **31;**
  mosaic **33**
Theodoric the Great 29
Theodosius, Roman emperor 22, 28
Theodulf, scholar 61, 64
Theophilus, Byzantine emperor 39
Thor, deity 19, 72; symbol 79
Threshing 193
Thunor (Thor), deity 19, 52
Tolls 305, 318; decrees against 308
Toulouse, France 208*, 290, 324*
Tournaments **6,** 207, **223,** 225, 230, 232;
  Joust of the Saracen **224-227**
Tours, France 208*, 215, 221, 308, 324*
Tower of London **124-125**
Towns: class struggles 316-317; councils
  312; daily life 318; entertainment 319-
  320; government 316, 336; growth of 8,
  308, 311-312; late Roman Empire 16;
  sanitation problems 318, 362;
  university conflicts 273-274, 279
Trade 8; Byzantine Empire 16; fostered
  by Crusades 218, 232, 241, 270-271;
  hazards of 303, 304, 305, 332; Hundred Years' War 301; Moslems 36, 39;
  papal strictures on 301, 303; Roman
  Empire 16, 19; trade routes 300-301*,
  336-337*; see also Hanseatic League
Trials: Saxon England 104
Troubadours 153, 203, 207, 224, 229, 231
Turks 236, 240, 242, 243, 248

U ltramontane University, Bologna 279
Universals, philosophy of 140, 149
Universities 8, **272-297;** curriculum 277;
  rise of 275-276
University life **276-277,** 290, 295; academic dress 274, 295; colleges 279;
  degrees 279, 295; freshman hazing
  290; graduate privileges 279; lectures
  272-273, 276, 282, 283, 295; masters'
  guild 283, 295; professors, position of
  279, 282; riots 273-274, **279;** student
  guilds 279; tutorials 275
Urban II, pope **236,** 237, 240, 268

V alens, Roman emperor 22
Valentinian III, emperor 16, 18, 28
Valhalla 75, 90
Valkyries 75, **90;** silver image **85**
Van Eyck, Jan 364, 366
Vandals 18*, 19, 22, 25, 27, 32, 35;
  migrations 18-19*, 22, 25; North Africa
  25, 35; Spain 25
Varangian Guard 88

Vassals 16, 52, 56, 316
Venice 18*, 45*, 208*, 238*, 239, 300*,
  302-303, 316, 337
Vikings **66-90,** 97, 100; arts and crafts
  69, 79, 81, 85, 370; burials 72, 80
  90, mounds 72, 76, 77*; colonies 68,
  82; discoveries 68; gods 72, 75, 90;
  houses 70; livelihood 70, 72; marriage
  73; pastimes **74-75;** poetry 74, 75, 80;
  routes 76-77*; royalty **75;** settlements
  72-73, 79, 80; ships **66-67,** 68, **72,** 76-77,
  80-81, 84; trading centers 77*, 84, **86-**
  87; weapons 68; women, status of 73
Villon, François 285, 288, 289
Vinland 76*; Viking colony **82**
Viollet-le-Duc 165
Visby, Gotland 337*, **346,** 347, 349
Visigoths 18-19*, 22, **24-25,** 35, 44
Vladimir, St., prince of Kiev 88, **89**

W ales: castles 127*
Wars: bans on 203; feudal 202, 203, 237;
  see also Crusades, Hundred Years' War
Wars of the Roses 368
Waterwheels 354, **355**
Weapons 102, 104, 122, **202-203, 212-213,**
  216, 224, **228, 229;** siege machines 202,
  261, 264, **266-267;** swords 68, 209
Weavers **242**
Wergeld 103
Westminster, England 125; abbey 100,
  121, ⚔ **10;** palace 220, ⚔ **9-10**
Wheat **10-11, 190,** 193, 345
Whittington, Dick 317
William the Conqueror 90, **92-129,** ⚔ 1,
  4-6, 8-9, 12-13, 16-18, 23; armies 100;
  birth 95-96; castles 127*, ⚔ **10;** cav-
  alry 104; claims to England 99, 100;
  coronation 121; courts 125; death 126;
  enemies 124; fleet 100, **101,** 121, ⚔
  12-14; marriage 96, 97
William II (Rufus), of England 126
William II, of Sicily 221
William IX, duke of Aquitaine 207
William of Malmesbury 101; quoted
  135, 137, 142
William of Poitiers 93, 97, 100, 121,
  ⚔ 3, 5, 19, 21, 24
Winemaking **364-365**
Witan, council 103
Woden, deity 19
Women, status of 8, 73, 207, 211
Wool trade 308, 314, 332, 358, 359, 361,
  362, 368
Writing **62-63;** Carolingian minuscule
  63, 64

Y aroslav the Wise, prince of Kiev 88-89,
  90; daughters 89, 90
York, England 76*, 123, **126,** 336*; battles
  at 99*, 100; castles 127*
Yorkshire revolt 123, 126
Ypres, Flanders 336*, 362

Z ero, concept of 39
Zwyn, river 362, 364

Composition by National Geographic's
Phototypographic Division
Color separations by Beck Engraving
Company, Philadelphia, Pa., Graphic
Color Plate, Inc., Stamford, Conn.,
The Lanman Company, Alexandria, Va.,
Progressive Color Corporation,
Rockville, Md., Stevenson Photo Color
Company, Cincinnati, Ohio, and R. R.
Donnelley & Sons Co., Chicago, Ill.
Printed and bound by Kingsport
Press, Kingsport, Tenn. Paper by
Westvaco Corporation, New York.

Endsheets crafted by E. N. Crain,
Master Bookbinder, Colonial
Williamsburg Foundation

Acknowledgments
and Reference Guide

THE EDITORS are grateful to many individuals for valuable information and advice and especially wish to thank the librarians, town officials, and curators of museums in this country and abroad—from Paris, Visby, and Novgorod to Prague, Palermo, and Istanbul—who were so helpful to our authors, photographers, and artists; and the following scholars and historians: Kenneth John Conant, Harvard University; Kemp Malone, Johns Hopkins University; Walter F. Starkie, University of California; Vsevolod Slessarev, University of Cincinnati; John G. Allee and Avery Andrews, George Washington University; Régine Pernoud, National Archives, Paris; Arne Emil Christensen, Museum of Antiquities, Oslo. We are also indebted to the monks of Holy Cross Abbey, Berryville, Va.; Richard E. Ford, John Woodman Higgins Armory, Worcester, Mass.; and to William Childress, Jeanne A. Davis, and Ferdinand Monjo, who helped write picture captions.

We studied many contemporary chronicles, among them the Early Lives of Charlemagne by Einhard and the Monk of St. Gall; the Anglo-Saxon Chronicle, and Procopius's Secret History. The Codex Calixtinus, The Letters of St. Bernard of Clairvaux, The Rule of St. Benedict, and English Historical Documents edited by David C. Douglas and George W. Greenaway, were well-thumbed sources.

To relive the Crusades we read eye-witness accounts in August C. Krey's The First Crusade, John Hampden's Crusader King, and the Chronicles of Jean Froissart, among others. Books of general scope frequently consulted were Medieval History by Norman F. Cantor, An Introduction to Medieval Europe by James Westfall Thompson and Edgar Nathaniel Johnson, The Shorter Cambridge Medieval History by C. W. Previté-Orton, and The Age of Faith by Will Durant. We gained enlightenment from shorter works including The Making of Europe and Medieval Essays by Christopher Dawson, The Birth of the Middle Ages, 395-814 by H. St.L. B. Moss, The Making of the Middle Ages by R. W. Southern, Medieval Europe: A Short History by C.

A BOOK FOR BURGUNDY: Duke Philip the Good receives the "Chronique de Hainault" in this 15th-century miniature in the Bibliothèque Royale, Brussels

Warren Hollister, French Chivalry by Sidney Painter, and Mediaeval Feudalism by Carl Stephenson.

Personalities of the time have inspired well-documented biographies: William the Conqueror by David C. Douglas, Charlemagne by Richard Winston, St. Benedict and His Monks by Theodore Maynard, St. Bernard of Clairvaux by Watkin Williams, St. Francis of Assisi by T. S. R. Boase, Richard Coeur de Lion by Philip Henderson, Eleanor of Aquitaine and the Four Kings by Amy Kelly, Saint Joan of Arc by V. Sackville-West, and Jacques Coeur by Albert Boardman Kerr. Other stimulating accounts: Medieval People by Eileen Power, Carolingian Portraits by Eleanor Shipley Duckett, Six Medieval Men and Women by H. S. Bennett, and The Plantagenets by John Harvey.

Books helpful in specific areas were The Myth of Rome's Fall by Richard Mansfield Haywood, Constantine and the Conversion of Europe by A. H. M. Jones, The Invasion of Europe by the Barbarians by J. B. Bury, The End of the Ancient World and the Beginnings of the Middle Ages by Ferdinand Lot, Constantinople in the Age of Justinian by Glanville Downey, Mohammed and Charlemagne by Henri Pirenne, History of the Byzantine Empire by A. A. Vasiliev, and Thought and Letters in Western Europe by M. L. W. Laistner.

We also consulted Feudal Society by Marc Bloch, The Medieval Papacy by Geoffrey Barraclough, The Carolingian Empire by Heinrich Fichtenau, A History of the Vikings by Gwyn Jones, The Viking by Tre Tryckare, The Bayeux Tapestry and Anglo-Saxon England by Sir Frank Stenton, The Making of England: 55 B.C.-1399 by C. Warren Hollister, The Normans in European History and The Renaissance of the 12th Century by Charles Homer Haskins, Medieval Sicily by Denis Mack Smith, and The Waning of the Middle Ages by J. Huizinga.

We traveled with Vera and Hellmut Hell on The Great Pilgrimage of the Middle Ages and with Walter F. Starkie on The Road to Santiago. Other guides were A History of the Crusades edited by Kenneth M. Setton and A History of the Crusades by Sir Steven Runciman. We traced the growth of towns and commerce in Medieval Cities by Henri Pirenne, The Hansa by E. Gee Nash, and The Hansa Towns by Helen Zimmern.

Glimpses into the life of the times were afforded by Life and Work in Medieval Europe by P. Boissonnade, Everyday Life in the Viking Age by Jacqueline Simpson, Life On a Mediaeval Barony by William Stearns Davis, How They Lived by W. O. Hassall, France in the Middle Ages by Paul Lacroix, and Daily Living in the Twelfth Century by Urban T. Holmes.

We traced the growth of universities in Charles Homer Haskins's The Rise of Universities, in Hastings Rashdall's The Universities of Europe in the Middle Ages, and in Lynn Thorndike's University Records and Life in the Middle Ages. Other specialized volumes include A Fifteenth Century Cookry Boke by John L. Anderson, A History of the Art of War in the Middle Ages by Charles Oman, Medieval and Early Modern Science by A. C. Crombie, and Medieval Technology and Social Change by Lynn White, Jr. For art and architecture we turned to André Grabar's The Golden Age of Justinian, Kenneth John Conant's Carolingian and Romanesque Architecture 800 to 1200, Emile Mâle's The Gothic Image, Henry Adams's Mont Saint Michel and Chartres, and Allan Temko's Notre-Dame of Paris.

Preparing special maps we consulted William R. Shepherd's Historical Atlas and Karl von Spruner's and Th. Menke's Hand-Atlas. Michelin, Nagel, Blue, and Hachette guides detailed sites visited by our authors.

National Geographic Society staff members in many departments contributed to this book. See listing on the following page. The lands where medieval civilization flowered are portrayed in many issues of National Geographic. Consult the National Geographic Index.